MYSTICAL UNION IN JUDAISM, CHRISTIANITY, AND ISLAM

MYSTICAL UNION IN JUDAISM, CHRISTIANITY, AND ISLAM

An Ecumenical Dialogue

Edited by
Moshe Idel and Bernard McGinn

Continuum · New York

1999

The Continuum Publishing Company
370 Lexington Avenue
New York, NY 10017

Printed in the United States of America

Library of Congress Cataloging in Publication Data

Mystical union and monotheistic faith.
    Mystical union in Judaism, Christianity, and Islam / edited
by Moshe Idel and Bernard McGinn.
        p.   cm.
    Originally published: Mystical union and monotheistic faith.
New York : Macmillan, c1989.
    Includes bibliographical references and index.
    ISBN 0-8264-0882-6   (pbk.)
    1. Mysticism — Comparative studies.   I. Idel, Moshe,
1947–   . II. McGinn, Bernard, 1937–   . III. Title.
BL625.M88   1996
291.4'22 — dc20   96-21215
                                                          CIP

Contents

Preface   vii

Contributors   xi

Introduction

Louis Dupré, *"Unio mystica:* The State and the
Experience"   3

Studies

Moshe Idel, "Universalization and Integration:
Two Conceptions of Mystical Union in
Jewish Mysticism"   27

Bernard McGinn, "Love, Knowledge and *Unio
mystica* in the Western Christian Tradition"   59

Michael Sells, "Bewildered Tongue: The
Semantics of Mystical Union in Islam"   87

Daniel Merkur, "Unitive Experiences and the
State of Trance"   125

Comments

Moshe Idel   157
Michael Sells   163
Daniel Merkur   175
Bernard McGinn   185

Notes   195
Name Index   243
Subject Index   247

Preface

In early 1985, as a part of the celebrations for its one-hundreth anniversary, the Jewish Theological Seminary in New York hosted a series of discussions on kabbalah based on Moshe Idel's manuscript, later published under the title *Kabbalah: New Perspectives* (New Haven, 1988). As one of the invited participants, I was especially taken with the evidence that Professor Idel had amassed questioning the common assumption that there is little, if any, talk of mystical union among the Jewish mystics. In 1984 I had written a brief paper on medieval Christian ideas of mystical union trying to show that the usual typologies did not do justice to the complex dynamics portrayed in the texts. The mutual enrichment we found in sharing our parallel lines of research was the stimulation for this book.

The notion of mystical union with God, of being one with the divine, has seemed scandalous to some thinkers in the three monotheistic faiths of Judaism, Christianity, and Islam. How can any individual human claim union with God without compromising divine transcendence and elevating the creature beyond its proper status? Are not claims to union inherently blasphemous?

Mystics who spoke of their union with God have come under suspicion in all three religious traditions, sometimes, at least in Christianity and Islam, to the extent of condemnation and execution. Nevertheless, in all three religions the tradition of *unio mystica* is deep and long. Many of the spiritual giants of these three faiths have seen the attainment of mystical union as the heart of their beliefs and practices.

Despite its importance, mystical union has rarely been investigated in itself, apart from the wider study of mysticism, and even more rarely from the aspect of comparative studies, especially those based upon broad and expert knowledge of the inner life of the three related monotheistic faiths. Professor Idel and I were convinced that the only way to come to grips with this central phenomenon in Western mysticism was through a collection of individual essays that would fully respect the distinctive character of each tradition's understanding of *unio mystica* while at the same time being open to an ecumenical discussion of the broader issues implied in union with a monotheistic God.

In achieving this goal, he agreed to work up some of the ideas present in his research on kabbalistic notions of mystical union into a more systematic and general piece surveying Jewish mysticism as a whole, while I developed my 1984 paper, expanding it both chronologically and substantively. For our third major essay, on union in Islamic mysticism, we approached Professor Michael Sells of Haverford College, an Islamicist and student of comparative religion and literature, who enthusiastically agreed to become part of our team. Professor Daniel Merkur of Syracuse University, a scholar of comparative religion with a strong background in psychoanalytic studies, had become known to Professor Idel during the time that he spent in Jerusalem as a Lady Davis Fellow. We agreed that the perspective Professor Merkur could bring to our enterprise would provide a valuable and thought-provoking complement to the more tradition-specific pieces. From the start we had also felt that the nature of the book, growing out of ecumenical discussion as it did, should reflect this ongoing conversation by including brief responses from each of the authors.

As the manuscript took shape, it was due to the inspiration of Paul Bernabeo, our editor at Macmillan, that the final component was added. Noting the diverse and at times technical discussion of the major essays, as well as the fact that they dealt with three different religious traditions, he suggested the need for a good introduction that could set the stage for the more detailed studies within. It was certainly no easy task to write such a synoptic piece, but fortunately we knew just the person—and we were more than pleased when Professor Louis Dupré agreed to undertake this difficult job. In effect, then, this volume consists of three essays devoted to mystical union in the three Abrahamic faiths, two theoretical essays surveying the issue of union from philosophical and psychoanalytic perspectives, and four brief responses to the ensemble.

Our model has been that of a conversation, an academic discussion in which we come to learn, not necessarily to agree. We are under no illusion that we have settled all the issues relating to the mystery of mystical union. Indeed, we hope that mystical union (if that is even the best term) will appear richer, more complex, more mysterious to the reader after finishing these essays than at the outset. Our task has been to begin a conversation that we hope will be continued not only by Jews, Christians, and Muslims but also by all those interested in that supreme possibility, union between God and the human person.

BERNARD McGINN

Contributors

Louis Dupré is the T. L. Riggs Professor of the Philosophy of Religion at Yale University and the author of many books on the philosophy of religion and on mysticism, such as *The Other Dimension* (1972), *Transcendent Selfhood* (1976), *The Deeper Life* (1981), *The Common Life* (1984), and an anthology of Christian mysticism, *Light from Light* (1988).

Moshe Idel is Professor of Kabbalah in the Hebrew University of Jerusalem and has written extensively in Hebrew. Two of his books currently available in English are *The Mystical Experience in Abraham Abulafia* (1988) and *Kabbalah: New Perspectives* (1988).

Bernard McGinn is Professor of Historical Theology and the History of Christianity at the Divinity School of the University of Chicago. He has written widely on medieval mysticism, including the translation of two volumes of Meister Eckhart's writings for the Classics of Western Spirituality series.

Daniel Merkur is Research Reader in Religion at the University of Toronto. His books on mysticism include *Gnosis: An Esoteric Tradition of Mystical Visions and Unions* (1993) and *The Ecstatic Imagination: Psychedelic Experiences and the Psychoanalysis of Self-Actualization* (1996).

Michael Sells is Assistant Professor of Islam and Comparative Religions at Haverford College. In addition to his writings on Islamic mysticism and on Plotinus, he has a book forthcoming on early Arabic poetry entitled *Desert Tracings*.

Introduction

Unio Mystica: The State and the Experience

LOUIS DUPRÉ

One of the most serious problems facing monotheistic faiths in an age of instant communication and global dialogue originates in the exclusive claims of truth they advance. Believers have attempted to cope with this in a number of ways. The oldest method consists, of course, in diluting doctrinal affirmations. Even a mildly symbolic interpretation may considerably weaken the mutual opposition. Others have tried to construe a *philosophia perennis* that, though not explicitly legitimated by the doctrines themselves, may nevertheless appear to be instituted by a philosophical reflection on them. The experiment here presented takes a different direction. Fully recognizing an irreducible diversity both in doctrinal expression and in symbolic experience, its authors have nevertheless succeeded in identifying a moment—the *unio mystica*—in which the three major monotheistic faiths converge.

To assess the significance of what they have essayed we must carefully separate it from a position that may seem to be implied in their own but is essentially different. Its most common form runs somewhat as follows. The mystical experience is everywhere identical; only the interpretation given to the experience depends upon the theological tradition within which the mystic receives it. Underlying this position is a rather simplistic assumption—possibly derived from eighteenth-century empiricist theories—that experience consists of an immediate mental content and is not the *function* that mediates the mind with reality. If one accepts the latter position, as we do, all experience becomes *interpreted* experience,

3

while all interpretation is mediated by experience. This implies that the religious tradition within which the mystical experience takes place is itself informed and shaped by experience. Nor does the presence of common features "override" the difference: the differences remain, and they remain essential.

The acceptance of those principles, however, does not force one religious tradition to regard parallel experiences in another as tentative, preparatory, or even perverse with respect to its own. Mystics themselves, speaking the doctrinal language within which they were raised, have not always sufficiently recognized this parallelism. Yet their descriptions, as the reader will see, clearly point in a direction in which analogy dominates conflict. Consciously or unconsciously they borrow freely from traditions other than their own. Thus Christian mystics consistently wrote and spoke in Neoplatonic language. Judaic spirituality borrowed much of its intellectual apparatus from Neoplatonic (occasionally through Christian writings) and Gnostic sources. Much of Islam's mysticism remains unintelligible without the impact of Aristotelian philosophy.

As we see it, the *unio mystica* existed in all three religions and was articulated in terms that were consistent with a specific tradition and yet displayed a clear affinity with those of others. In Christianity, where the term originated, the concept of *unio mystica* emerged at the end of a long and complex process. At the risk of oversimplifying it we may describe that process as a gradual restriction, a delimitation of the more general idea of a divine presence in the believer. In the Pauline as well as in the Johannine writings of the New Testament, life in Christ consists in a dynamic union with God. Depending on the (never exclusive) emphasis, this union is presented as being with Christ as with God's divine self-expression, or with God (the Father) in and through Christ. God's spirit seals the union and initiates an ever-growing participation in the intimacy of the divine life. The presence of the Holy Spirit endows the Christian with a "sense" of the divine that if properly developed enables the believer to "taste" (*sapere*) God and all that relates to him. Out of this "inner instinct," this mysterious resonance to a divine inhabitation, Christians developed various theologies of experienced grace.

The Greek Fathers of the first six centuries assumed some ability to experience God's Spirit as conveyed to all believers. Indeed, a few writers came close to equating mature faith itself with this direct experience.[1] Reactions followed. Did such a theology of experience not appropriate what had to remain transcendent and, by its very nature, beyond appropriation? The debate around this question continues to divide and even to separate Christians.

Other, more subtle issues, gave rise to further questions. Theologians, first in Alexandria, then in Cappadocia and much of the Greek world, and later in the Latin world, began to express the soul's progress toward union with God in Platonic and Neoplatonic language. The "erotic" philosophies of Plato and Plotinus appeared particularly apt to describe the "ascending" quality of the unifying process. But did the idea of *ecstatic* union of the mind with an unnameable and invisible One not unduly spiritualize a religion of which the central mystery was that God had become flesh? Did Christianity not require a less abstract, perhaps a humbler, approach to union? The biblical anthropology that Christianity had inherited certainly ruled out any theory of *spirit* that did not include the whole person. Does the idea of a mystical union as Platonic theologians had come to develop it not conflict with the very temper of the Christian faith? Is the so-called mystical theology more than a misguided attempt to attain an unmediated union in a religion that centered on the very concept of mediation? To interpret the *com-union* of even that most intimate encounter with God as *union*, one easily risked shifting the basis of what had started as a promise of redemption for sinners.

From the beginning these problems were perceived as serious, and the controversies surrounding them continue in our own day, even within the Catholic and Orthodox communities that traditionally have been more favorably disposed toward the idea of a mystical union.[2] In the face of these controversies the persistence and development of a mystical theology all the more demands an explanation. The core of that theology—the affirmation that in a most intimate way the Christian is united with God—belongs to the undeniable essence of Christian faith. Even those theologians of the Reformation who most strenuously resisted any pretenses on man's part of appropriating God's nature did not question the occurrence of *some* unification at the heart of the redemptive process. Moreover, the assumption of a Christian *experience* of God's presence in *all* devout believers persisted in the West well into the twelfth century and in the East much longer. This experience, though differentiated in degree, was held to be qualitatively identical for the mystic (a term that was not used as a noun until the sixteenth century!) and for the ordinary believer. Again and again spiritual theologians attempted to correct the Platonic excesses of what had become a common language. Thus, instead of a pure "spirit" unifying itself with an unknown One, the terminology gradually shifts toward spiritual "senses," toward love of God, and, increasingly from the thirteenth century onward, toward the humanity of Christ. Thus the union itself has come to include a mediation.

Strong opposition to the idea of mystical union did not emerge until theology had begun to separate the universal element of experience implicit in the original idea of grace from the privileged consciousness of union attained by few. Indeed the tendency, noticeable since the beginning of the modern age, to sever faith from experience altogether resulted in marginalizing mystical life into a highly exceptional and hence suspect position. That the mystical drive survived these constant suspicions in all three branches of the Christian faith raises the question of whether it is not an inherent feature of that faith itself.

Turning to Islam we find equally strong expressions in the face of even greater doctrinal resistance. Not surprisingly, the controversies raged with equal vehemence. The idea that the soul is capable of a certain intimacy with God appears in the Qur'an—not surprisingly, since some such aspiration belongs to the core of all religion. But the idea that it passes away into a divine reality could only have appeared blasphemous to the orthodox Muslim. How, then, could the Sufi idea of *fanā'*, the transition of human consciousness into the divine and its assumption of divine qualities, ever have gained entrance in the most austerely monotheistic faith? The appeals to, and interpretations of, the Qur'an by the Sufis appear as far-fetched to us as to some of their suspicious contemporaries. Nevertheless the Sufi mystics *did* find some support for their claims of orthodoxy in the primordial profession of God's oneness to which the mystic attempts to return by dying to this world. Thus the mystic "is as he was, when he was before he was."[3] This would lead some Sufi mystics to claims of total identification. Best remembered are those of al-Hallaj, who paid for them with martyrdom. But others are equally, if not more, radical, such as the ones ascribed to al-Bistami: "There is no God save I; so worship me", and "Moses desired to see God. I do not desire to see God— He desires to see me."[4]

The case of Judaism appears no less puzzling. Given the essentially dialectical relation between God and man presented in the Bible and the Talmud, the existence of a Jewish mysticism is in itself as remarkable a fact as the existence of a Muslim mysticism. Since the work of Gershom Scholem at least, the fact has been recognized. Scholem himself, however, denied the existence of an *unio mystica,* a state of identification with God. An essay included in this collection should convince the reader, we believe, that such a radical denial can no longer be maintained.

Here, then, we have three monotheistic faiths, each based upon a clear and insurmountable distinction between God and man, giving rise to movements that converge in their drives toward mystical union. Before considering the specific nature of such a union we should perhaps pause at a preliminary question provoked by this paradoxical state of affairs. Is religion itself, regardless of its particular structure, mystical in its very essence? The present text does not require us to enter this controversial area, so I will state without arguments a position I have developed elsewhere.[5] The mystical drive to live in the experienced presence of God (in whatever degree) belongs to the core of all religion. Without this living flame to warm its life, religion rapidly degenerates into moralism, ritualism, legalism, or pure speculation. Yet one cannot therefore deduce that mysticism *constitutes* the core of all religion. Such a mystical definition may apply to some religions (such as Vedantic Hinduism or at least some parts of it) but clearly not to most. The three monotheistic faiths here discussed contain other elements far different from that mystical drive. One cannot reduce them to it without seriously distorting the faiths themselves. All believers enjoy *some* experience of what they believe, but it would be patently absurd to call this enjoyment mystical in the specific sense the term has acquired in modern usage. Nevertheless, that experience stands in generic continuity with the intense, exceptional experience.

Related to the universality of the mystical drive is the question of whether all religions, which meet in this drive, are, at least in their mystical expression, identical? If different traditions share a state in which distinctions disappear, should we not conclude that in its highest form all mysticism is identical? What role do doctrinal differences still play when the mystic attains the state of union? To the extent that the state of union is held to consist of an ecstatic, intrinsically transient experience, the conclusion that mysticism is identical in all religions is indeed inescapable. William James has considerably contributed to the success of the "ecstatic" concept of the mystical by including transiency as one of his four primary characteristics of the mystical life. Yet that life never, or almost never, consists of a single experience but of a many-staged process that culminates in an *unio mystica.* To separate that final moment of union from the preceding stages is an abstraction. Likewise, to reduce the state of union to ecstatic occurrences (which, according to Saint Teresa, occur rarely during the state) is a gross simplification.

Thus far we have assumed that the following discussion centers on experience. But what do we know about experience? A study on mysticism is bound by the limits of expression and, if it deals with past mystics, by the limits of written expression. Preverbal experience lies beyond our field of access. We are never in a position to claim with absolute certainty that a person has actually been privileged with extraordinary experiences. Aside from the remote possibility of outright deception (usually ruled out by the context of an author's moral and religious life), we face the more serious problem that few mystical writings are straightforwardly confessional. This is particularly true in Judaism. But even Christianity possesses few mystical confessions before the twelfth century. Only the lyrical quality of many Sufi writings seem to place Muslim mysticism in a different position. Still, those confessional writings that exist tend to translate the original experience into the universal terminology of the current religious language. How faithfully does such an interpretation reflect the primary experience?

Language, especially language about the ineffable, never copies: it always creates. A perceptive reader of French mystics recently advanced the daring claim that in the modern-era language has become a substitute for experience.[6] According to him, spiritual men and women who were unwilling to accept the enormous spiritual loss brought on by their secularized culture attempted to compensate for the loss by creating a religious refuge for themselves in a highly refined and articulate mystical language. Thus language functions in a performative way, as a means for acquiring what it expresses. Without fully ascribing to this theory, we have to admit that mystics have always found at their disposal a ready-made spiritual language that has influenced their expression and, we presume, their experience. They rarely appeal to the kind of "extraordinary experience" with which we identify the term mystical and instead try to articulate an awareness of God's presence in the soul in an established language.

My purpose in raising these doubts is not to sever expression from experience but to reunite what a romantic expressionism tends to separate. If language *mediates* experience, each text possesses an intentionality of its own. It is to this intentionality, not to inaccessibly private experience, that we address ourselves. In doing so we fully assume that a unique spiritual text expresses a unique

manner of experiencing. But we escape involving ourselves in un-
solvable problems.

Meanwhile, unavoidable questions about experience as conveyed in the text confront us. Foremost is this fundamental question: Does the Christian term *unio mystica* refer to an *experience*
or to a *state of being* that lies beyond experience? In the latter case,
that state surpasses, of course, the kind of relationship to God that
the believer on the basis of his belonging to a particular community
of faith assumes to be present in all its members (e.g., Christians
in good standing assume that they are united with God through
grace; Jews through a divine covenant with the people of Israel).
Obviously, a less universal condition is at issue. A careful reading
of the texts seems to suggest that mystics claim a unitive state of
being. Still, entering this state causes fundamental changes of consciousness. How much these changes, or at least their expressions,
differ from one mystic to another will appear clearly enough in the
following discussions. Nevertheless, very real analogies emerge
through these differences.

An analysis of mystical descriptions also raises a question about
changes in consciousness. The descriptions suggest, directly or indirectly, that consciousness recedes at the peak moments of the
unitive state or at least comes to function in ways incompatible
with ordinary states of mind. For example, Teresa's description of
mystical marriage mentions an ecstasy "so complete that it seems
as though the soul no longer existed."[7] Does the mystic lose consciousness? He or she certainly appears to enter the ecstasy in full
awareness and, afterward, to remember it well enough to write
clearly about it. Hence the term *unconscious* seems inappropriate,
even though some reports refer to the unitive ecstasy as "beyond
consciousness." One of the essays in this collection suggests that
self-consciousness is temporarily lost while consciousness remains.
This distinction may be impossible to maintain consistently: how
could one be at all conscious without being in some way *self*-con-
scious? Nevertheless, the distinction usefully evokes the apparent
shift of the center of awareness from the self to a point beyond the
self. This change drastically transforms the field of consciousness
and also unifies it in a unique manner. In a classic essay on the
psychology of ecstasy, Joseph Maréchal refers to a "polarized unconsciousness," that is, a "*subconsciousness* not disintegrated but
gathered together and directed."[8]

Maréchal's statement would need to be qualified. How would
such an interpretation account for what the sixteenth-century

Spanish mystics call an intellectual vision, which they considered strictly unitive and which includes some sort of *comprehensive* intuition? Ignatius Loyola describes such a vision:

> Without having any vision he understood—knew—many matters both spiritual and pertaining to the faith and to the realm of letters, and that with such clearness that they seemed utterly new to him. There is no possibility of setting out in detail everything he then understood. The most that he can say is that he was given so great an enlightening of mind that, if one were to put it together, all the helps he has received from God—and all the things he has learned, they would not be the equal of what he received in a single illumination.[9]

More objective and impersonal descriptions of the unitive state display an even more articulated content. Thus in the Flemish and Rhineland schools a highly complex Trinitarian theology plays a dominant role. Teresa of Ávila also reports several Trinitarian visions, as does the seventeenth-century French Ursuline nun Marie of the Incarnation.

Rather than accepting the preceding solutions, I submit that we distinguish the general *state* of union, which implies a unified vision of reality, from those ecstatic experiences that occasionally accompany it but by no means constitute its essence. As mentioned earlier, the unitive state may include fewer ecstasies than the one preceding it. It seems that consciousness in the unitive state remains on a different level that transforms *all* experience. Teresa claims that the unitive state begins with an intellectual (i.e., non-imaginary) ecstatic vision.[10] In such visions, according to John of the Cross, God touches the *substance* of the soul; Teresa says these visions take place "in the center of the soul." These descriptions suggest that the mind enters a wholly new awareness of *being* that so exceeds familiar forms of *experiencing* that language must turn to such objective terms as *substance, center of the soul,* and *beyond consciousness.* The concept of *deification,* common to the three monotheistic faiths, indicates how far behind in the mystic's mind the ontological transformation has left ordinary modes of awareness.

How could the mind experience a reality that lies beyond its measure? Consciousness here merely appears to reverberate at the impact of an ontological reality that surpasses it. Still, we would misinterpret the mystic's meaning if we considered this reality as lying beyond or outside the mind. Where knower and known are substantially united, that union no longer allows any *distance* for subject-object oppositions such as those that determine ordinary epistemic processes. The mind functions here in the different mode of *being with* reality, not of *reflecting upon* it. This unique connaturality—born of identity—between the mind and what never could be its "object" has induced the few philosophers who have given these matters serious thought to distinguish it from all other forms of human cognition. Maréchal speaks of "an intellectual intuition"—a term that his Kantian epistemology rules out for any other mode of knowing. Jacques Maritain interprets the union as the only instance of the soul directly knowing its own "substance" (within the divine substance).[11] There lies, of course, a paradox in such references to exceptional *insight* when we compare them to other declarations that hold that *unio mystica* occurs beyond consciousness. Descriptions continue to oscillate between extraordinary awareness and loss of (ordinary) consciousness.

I see no other way of reconciling these two contrasting descriptions but by assuming that the center of the mind has turned from self-consciousness to God-consciousness. In the latter state, the mind becomes at once a center of presence and of absence. This interpretation seems to be confirmed by the mystic's need to empty the self from its own content before the final state of union. Julian of Norwich writes: "No soul is at rest until its will has despised as nothing *(naughted)* all things which are created. When it by its will has become nothing *(naught)* for love, to have Him who is everything, then is it able to receive spiritual rest."[12] The "naughting" of the self is the other side of unification. Thus Rabbi Naḥman of Braslav claims that a return to divine unity is not possible save by a complete annihilation of the self.[13] Obviously he is not referring to a single act but to a slow and presumably painful process of self-emptying.

Precisely at this point we must place that "dark night" that purifies the soul, beyond its own will and ability, of attachment to itself and, by a process of "progressive unification,"[14] prepares it for a state of union. No contemplative can attain the radical reversal of attachment—the total displacement of the original center of meaning and value demanded by such a state—without previously having simplified his or her moral attitude. The mystic cannot achieve this simplification actively. The attachment to the self must be burned out passively, as John of the Cross expresses so powerfully in the second book of *The Dark Night of the Soul.*

Assuming, then, that the *unio mystica* consists more of a state of being than of a transient experience, how do we define the union? In the highest "mansion," the seventh, of her *Inner Castle of the Soul*, Teresa refers to the union as "an abiding place for God and a second heaven." It commences with what she calls an intellectual vision, that is, an imageless intuition during which for a brief period all mental functions unite while receiving a comprehensive insight into the source and coherence of all reality. Although clearly not intellectual in any discursive, rational sense, such a vision possesses a distinctly cognitive quality, which John of the Cross calls a "knowledge of naked truth," that is, a "comprehending and seeing with the understanding the truths of God, whether of things that are, that have been or that will be."[15] This insight reflects a direct union with God that takes place "in the substance of the soul."[16] Teresa likewise refers to the union as occurring "in the deepest center of the soul, which must be where God himself dwells."[17] The final state of permanent union is characterized by an uninterrupted awareness of God's presence. Although that presence may not always be fully sensed, it remains the horizon against which all other phenomena appear.

> We might compare the soul to a person who is with others in a very bright room; and then suppose that the shutters are closed so that the people are all in darkness. The light by which they can be seen has been taken away, and until it comes back, we shall be unable to see them, yet we are nonetheless aware that they are there.[18]

The permanent quality of the union distinguishes this state of "spiritual marriage" from the so-called betrothal, in which the presence is still punctuated by periods of absence. A divided consciousness enables the mystic to take care of ordinary duties, even to suffer and to be disturbed on one level while preserving tranquillity on another. The "center of the soul" remains untouched by what preoccupies the mind's surface; no pain or unrest enters that inner sanctuary. "A king is living in his palace: many wars are waged in his kingdom and many other distressing things happen there, but he remains where he is despite them all."[19]

Such highly metaphorical language evokes more questions than it answers, yet it is by no means arbitrary or the result of theological indoctrination. The division between a deeper and a surface level of the mind runs through all of Western mysticism. The great Muslim mystic al-Hallaj speaks of the transformation of the carnal *nafs* (the animal soul) into the *rūḥ* (the spirit). Rabbi Eliah de Vidas distinguishes soul, spirit, and higher soul. In Christianity the distinction between two or, more commonly, three levels of the soul appears in the writings of several Greek Fathers, as well as in those of twelfth-century Cistercians and Victorines, thirteenth- and fourteenth-century Flemish mystics, sixteenth-century Spanish Carmelites, seventeenth-century French masters, eighteenth-century Quietists, and beyond. Richard of Saint Victor expressed the levels with surpassing precision.

> We must not understand a twofold substance by these two words (soul and spirit), but when we distinguish between the twin powers of the same essence, the higher is called spirit, the lower soul. In this distinction the soul and that which is animal remains below, but the spirit and that which is spiritual flies upward. That which is of the body and subject to corruption, perishes and as a dead body falls back into itself and below its nature. That which is subtle and purified ascends upward like a breath of air, rises above and transcends itself.[20]

The division of the mind postulated here enables the mystic to combine a contemplative life with one of active service. Yet by describing the two attitudes as juxtaposed, one risks missing their real nature. For one is not superimposed to the other: the two intimately collaborate and reinforce each other.

Among the outstanding qualities of the religious attitude we must certainly count its remarkable ability to *integrate* life, to achieve unity within the complexity of opposite tendencies. The mystical state, far from diminishing this unique ability to integrate, enhances the powers from a single dynamic source of concentration. It is precisely in this respect that a mysticizing philosophy differs from a genuine personal or communal mystical inspiration. The spiritual onesidedness of Neoplatonism is what disturbed Augustine, even though his speculative inclination disposed him to follow its philosophy. The theory of the "spiritual senses," developed by Origen in Eastern Christianity and by Gregory in Western, constituted a clear attempt to counteract the all-too-exclusive emphasis upon the spiritual part of mystical psychology.

The need for a *total* response to the divine call to union appears nowhere more clearly than in Islam. The erotic quality of many Sufi texts, far from jeopardizing the religious purity of their piety, presents a stunning witness of the comprehensive, affective and sensitive, involvement of the genuine mystic. Judaism rarely experienced the spiritualizing currents that occasionally affected Christian Neoplatonic theologies, and hence it felt no need to react against any spiritualism of pure contemplation. Its integrating tendency all the more openly takes the form of a holy worldliness. No degree of contemplation dispenses the Jewish mystic from the obligations of a life ethically committed to a task in this world. Generally speaking, for each of the three religions, the mystical union enhances a person's capacity to fulfill his or her given or assumed task. Evelyn Underhill perceived this well:

> It is the peculiarity of the unitive life that it is often lived, in its highest and most perfect form, in the world; and exhibits its works before the eyes of men. . . . The spirit of man having at last come to full consciousness of reality, completes the circle of Being, and returns to fertilize those levels of existence from which it sprang. Hence the enemies of mysticism . . . are here confronted very often by the disagreeable spectacle of the mystic as a pioneer of humanity, a sharply intuitive and painfully practical person: an artist, a discoverer, a religious or social reformer, a national hero, a "great active" among the saints.[21]

All genuine mysticism results in spiritual fecundity. Even a work as unworldly as *The Cloud of Unknowing* emphatically stresses this communicative move. Having come to partake in God's life, the contemplative also feels called to share in God's life-giving love.[22] The mystical marriage leads to spiritual parenthood. Mystics have never shied away from the paradox that the highest results in the humblest. While the third degree of love, according to Richard of Saint Victor, glorifies the soul in the likeness of God, in the fourth, supreme degree, the soul descends from the lonely peaks of contemplation to the lowly practice of charity. "He who ascends to this degree of charity is truly in the state of love that can say: 'I am made all things to all men that I might save all.'"[23] We know the wonders that this conversion to the humblest brought to such mystics as Francis of Assisi, Catherine of Siena, or Ignatius Loyola. Marie of the Incarnation, who spent the latter part of her life in Quebec, left a unique account of this need to transform contemplation into charitable action. In the 1654 *Relation* of her spiritual journey, she distinguishes thirteen stages of prayer, of which the spiritual marriage is only the seventh. This is a surprising assertion coming from one trained in the mystical classics. In traditional theory, the mystical ascent culminates in the spiritual marriage. Apparently Marie felt that the state of union, which she herself declares to have been permanent, remains incomplete if it does not fully incorporate the various active modes in which it finds its expression. Only through them does the state of union become fully real.

In the works of al-Hallaj and the great Hasidic rabbis we find a similar conversion toward others initiated by the unitive experience itself. For Hallaj, God is present in all his creatures, but he is found most intimately in man. The contemplative responds to this loving presence of God in creation with a love originating in God that returns creation to its source. The mystical union converts this created presence into an uncreated one.

> Thus in the very depth of this weak and divided humanity, in this heart which, having heard and recognized (God's voice), bows to the dust, a new divine intonation is born, which mounts to the lips, more "mine" than myself, which replies to Him: the ray received in the mirror has aroused a flame therein.[24]

In the kabbalah the mystic also sanctifies creation, though by a different, more cognitive activity. One passage by Rabbi Eliah de Vidas (quoted in Moshe Idel's essay) eloquently illustrates how the mystic takes all creatures with him when he enters the divine realm:

> All the worlds are bound together by the soul, spirit and higher soul of man, and this (i.e., the bond of the three spiritual powers of man) causes the illumination of all the worlds by the Emanator, the king of all kings—and then the worlds are bound to each other and so also the soul of man and his spirit and higher soul will illuminate and will be integrated on high and will suck an abundance of influx from the source of all blessings.[25]

In the idea of *tikkun* the later kabbalah of Isaac Luria proclaims a cosmic restoration through the unitive vision. The mystical life actively contributes toward the restitution of the primeval, divine order. It calls the lowest of the divine manifestations (sefirot), the *Shekhinah*, which has been expelled from the godly realm, back to the divine fullness. Reuniting the scattered divine forces, the mystic becomes the very lever of the universe, the source of the ascending energy that balances the descending divine powers.[26]

How central a role this cosmic return to the source plays appears in the astonishing declaration of the Hasidic rabbi Naḥman of Braslav that the world was created for the sake of Israel in order to allow it to return to its source, together with the entire cosmos.[27] The idea of cosmic integration in Jewish mysticism evokes comparison with similar ideas in the works of the Greek Fathers (e.g., in Maximus the Confessor) and continues to play a role in the writings of such modern contemplatives as Teilhard de Chardin. The worldliness of Jewish mysticism, which insists on the need to return to creation, contributed to the doubts later raised about the existence of a unitive experience. But some of those Christian mystics generally considered to have lived in the unitive state also led extremely active lives.

A purely negative theology would never result in such a commitment to creation. Yet unitive mysticism moves beyond a mere denial of the finite. To be sure, the mystic who enters the union finds the finite incommensurate with God's Being. But as he or she is admitted to *participate* in that Being, the mystic ceases to *compare* the finite with the infinite. Instead, he or she takes the finite on its own terms and asserts the divine meaning of the finite as it remains within God's own Being. Thus once it is allowed to shine in its own light, the divine manifestation reaches down to the smallest creature. The spiritual perception of the finite as part of God's own creative act made Ignatius Loyola conclude his *Spiritual Exercises* with an exhortation to consider "how God dwells in all creatures." Here begins a new way of seeing the finite, namely, as it exists within the infinite. Thus the *unio mystica* restores a divine meaning to the finite that the mystic ignored in the early stage of his or her spiritual ascent and that negative theology permanently ignores. The *unio mystica* overcomes God's otherness. In himself God is not opposed to anything, since he integrates all things in his divine Being. Transcendence, then, in the end ceases to consist in a negation of the finite and turns into its elevation. At that point God appears as the ultimate dimension of the finite, the inaccessible within the accessible.

All mystics who attain the divine union practice at least some mode of this reintegration of the created world with God. But few have consistently attempted to justify the return to the finite through a participation in God's own inner life. One who did so in a most powerful theological synthesis was Jan van Ruusbroec. For him the relations among the Persons of the Trinity form the basis of the mystic's view of the finite within the infinite. When God unites himself "without means" to the soul, he surpasses the intermediacy of created grace and virtue. In that encounter the soul loses itself in "a state of darkness in which all contemplatives blissfully lose their way and are never again able to find themselves in a creaturely way."[28] Yet in this blissful union the soul comes to share the dynamics of God's inner life, a life not only of rest and darkness but also of creative activity and light. The contemplative admitted to this union is permitted to see by the light in which God sees himself and to follow the outflowing movement of the Godhead. The contemplative participates in the eternal Word as it proceeds from the divine silence, containing all creation within itself. Union with God, then, means, for Ruusbroec, union with God's self-expression—the internal one of the Word as well as the external one of creation. Partaking in the divine rhythm of contraction and expansion (expressed in the doctrine of the Trinity), the state of union combines active charity with contemplative solitude. Sharing what Ruusbroec calls the "life-giving fruitfulness of the divine nature," the contemplative accompanies God's own move from hiddenness to manifestation within the identity of God's own life.[29]

Is all this more than speculative theology? If through its ontological dependence upon an eternal source, the soul does indeed reside in God throughout all eternity, then a union realized from the beginning, in even the least devout person, appears to require no mystical ascent at all—only intellectual speculation. Does not the "virtual" existence of the soul in God's eternal self-expression constitute the very heart of its ontological status, regardless of its subjective attitude? Nevertheless, descriptions in all three traditions stress the *particular* character of the *unio mystica* as well as its universal, ontological foundation. The union described by Teresa, Rumi, Rabiah, and Ignatius takes place not in the order of pure speculation but in that of *praxis*. It is in the practical order, then, that the answer to this objection lies. A persistent use of the language of love should alert us that far more than intellectual speculation is at stake. Even those speculative mystics who speak of a substantial union grounded in man's ontological nature (such as Ibn 'Arabi or Eckhart and some of the kabbalists) have recourse to the language of love and *praxis*.

Bernard McGinn draws a distinction between two different concepts of union: one refers to a *unitas spiritus* (moral or psychological in orientation), the other to a *unitas indistinctionis* (ontologically oriented). The former consists of an interpersonal relation of love; the latter of an ontological or substantial union. The distinction is undeniable and significant. Equally significant, however, is that those Christian and Muslim mystics who consider the union to be ontological or in some way substantial nevertheless express themselves in interpersonal terms, while some of the most articulate exponents of love mysticism (such as John of the Cross, Teresa, and Hadewijch of Brabant) do not shy away from a terminology proper to substantial union.

Underhill adopts a similar distinction between *spiritual marriage*, which refers to interpersonal communion, and *deification*, whereby the self becomes transformed in what she calls (somewhat inappropriately, it seems) an impersonal Absolute. Yet almost immediately she qualifies her description of the latter by adding:

> The personal and emotional aspect of man's relation with his Source is also needed if that which he means by "union with God" is to be even partially expressed. Hence, even the most "transcendental" mystic is constantly compelled to fall back on the language of love in the endeavor to express the content of the metaphysical raptures: and forced in the end to acknowledge that the perfect union of Lover and Beloved cannot be suggested in the precise and arid terms of religious philosophy.[30]

The statement proves true even in such an extreme case of substantial union as that of al-Hallaj. Love for him constitutes the essence of God's Being, as well as the human attitude that unites all creation with God and transforms it into him. In the Sufi tradition, love converts what otherwise might have remained theosophical speculation into deeply personal religion. The divine life that flows into the mystic derives from a personal encounter with God. Even substantial union maintains the language of personal love, as in these lyrical verses of the Persian mystic Rumi.

> With thy sweet soul, this soul of mine
> Hath mixed as water doth with wine.
> Who saw the wine and water part,
> Or me and Thee when we combine.
> Thou art become my greater self
> Small bounds no more can me confine.

This description of substantial union ends with an ardent profession of love:

> I rest a flute laid on Thy lips;
> A lute, I on thy breast recline.
> Breathe deep in me that I may sigh;
> Yet strike my strings and tears shall shine.[31]

The language of deification that Hallaj so daringly uses does not differ that much from the "naughting" demanded by humble love. Rumi defends the Bagdhad martyr's expression "I am God" as being inspired by humble love.

> This is what is signified by the words *Ana 'l-Haqq* "I am God." People imagine that it is a presumptuous claim, whereas it is really a presumptuous claim to say *Ana 'l 'abd* "I am the slave of God"; and *Ana 'l-Haqq* "I am God" is an expression of great humility. The man who says *Ana 'l 'abd,* "I am the slave of God," affirms two existences, his own and God's, but he that says *Ana 'l-Haqq,* "I am God," has made himself non-existent and has given himself up and "I am God," i.e., "I am naught, He is all": there is no being but God's.[32]

The kabbalistic writings also preserve the personal quality in substantial union. The development of the term *devekut* from a purely devotional to an ontological meaning continues to connect one with the other. Originally *devekut,* "cleaving to God," denotes the attitude presented in the *Pentateuch* as an ethico-religious ideal. This term of practical piety possesses no mystical implications. After acquiring a wealth of Aristotelian, Neoplatonic, and Gnostic determinations in medieval esoteric circles, *devekut* became the kabbalistic term for the mystical entrance into the divine sphere. Some very explicit pronouncements, such as this one by Rabbi Shneor Zalman, leave no doubt that it had come to refer to substantial union: "This is the true cleaving, as he becomes one substance with God in whom he was swallowed, without being separate so as to be a distinct entity at all."[33] Yet individual existence is not dissolved in this immersion.[34] The very persistence of an intrinsically dualistic term for expressing substantial union suggests the persistence of a devotional attitude.

In Christianity it was also the language of love and devotion that conveyed a personal quality to ontological union. Indeed, an equivalent of *devekut* led love mysticism toward the idea of such union. Saint Bernard, the first love mystic in the West, justifies much of his theory by the Vulgate version of *1 Corinthians* 6:17: "Qui autem adhaeret Deo unus spiritus est." Others would follow his interpretation.[35] John of the Cross in *The Living Flame of Love* attempts to explain the paradox of love paralleled to ontological identity.

> How can we say that this flame wounds the soul, when there is nothing in the soul to be wounded, since it is wholly consumed

by the fire of love? It is a marvellous thing: for, as love is never idle, but is continually in motion, it is ever throwing out sparks, like a flame, in every direction.—Wherefore these wounds, which are the playings of God, are the sparks of these tender touches of flame which touch the soul intermittently and proceed from the fire of love, which is not idle, but whose flames, says the stanza, strike and wound.[36]

Images similar to that of the flame that consumes yet never destroys may be found in Rabbi Zalman's analogy of the wick that nourishes the fire while at the same time it is consumed by it, and of the iron being heated or liquefied by fire in Bernard and Richard of Saint Victor.[37]

No one, to my knowledge, has traced the dialectic of union and communion more carefully than Ruusbroec. Outlining the progress of contemplative life in *The Spiritual Espousals*, he distinguishes various modes in which the soul attains its superessential unity with God ("with means," "without means") and thereby shows how the mystical life *develops* within the initially given, ontological unity of the soul with God. Rather than being a reflective awareness of what the soul is from the start, the union attained at the end never existed before. By its dynamic quality the mystical experience surpasses the mere awareness of an already present, ontological union. The process of loving devotion *realizes* what existed only as potential in the initial stage, thus creating a *new* ontological reality. This insight gives Ruusbroec's theology its uniquely dynamic and realistic quality. Without the contribution of contemplative love, the virtual inexistence of the human spirit in the divine Logos never exceeds the level of a philosophical assumption. Only the process of love makes the mystical union *real*. Without love the ontological assumption itself easily degenerates into the reified representation of a mind existing as a thing *within* the divine Logos. Ruusbroec identifies the unique nature of mind, which instead of being a mere segment of the real functions as a powerful lever of being. For him, the mystical life possesses an ontological quality that renders it constitutive of the real.

The mystic, then, emerges as *Homo religiosus* par excellence, that is, as one who recognizes that reality remains incomplete until it becomes reunited with its source. All the monotheistic religions aim at some union with God. But while to the ordinary believer this union remains mostly a spiritual or a moral ideal essential to the mind's perfection but not basically affecting the structure of the real, for the mystic it brings reality itself to completion and, as such, becomes the intrinsic *telos* of all being. To the question ever again emerging in Western thought—What is the specific being of mind?—the mystic answers: that dynamic power without which being cannot fully *be.* All mystics, explicitly or implicitly, have held some variation of Rabbi Naḥman's amazing assertion that God has created the world in order to enable Israel to return to the source. Without that return, the world itself would be left in an estranged state of being.

To the mystic the cosmic structure appears forever waiting for a completion that only the God-loving mind can convey. At the opposite end of the static metaphysics that dominates much of Western philosophy from Parmenides to Spinoza—according to which being *is* and becoming is not—the mystical mind views itself as derived from, and guided by, a higher power. This power destines it to be the link that unites what is only in part with what is wholly and unqualifiedly real. In the process of fulfilling this function, the mind moves from a level of mere consciousness to one in which consciousness coincides with being. All of Western mysticism, and much of what I know of Eastern, consists of a transition from a lower or more superficial level to a higher or deeper level in which mind turns into being. In the process of moving from one level to the other the mind achieves a synthesis that the mystic considers essential in a predestined cosmic order. Although aiming at supreme rest above commotion, the mystic knows himself to be occupied in conveying definitive meaning and value to a restless world.

Viewed in this light the question that provoked much discussion among theologians from the twelfth to the fourteenth century— whether the final station of the contemplative process, the *unio mystica,* is cognitive or affective in nature—loses much of its urgency. To call it cognitive *or* affective is to treat an essentially unified and unifying consciousness as a divided and oppositional one. Unless consciousness is both cognitive and affective, it misses the very wholeness characteristic of the final union. To *understand* the real as an object that reason places before the mind—rather than as a totality of which the mind constitutes an integral, dynamic part—conflicts with the very essence of the mystical experience. Likewise, a love that fails to recognize in itself the secret of the real may characterize a moral or sentimental attitude but not a mystical one. Of course, distinctions and emphases remain, even in the *unio mystica.* Differences between one mystic and another, between one school and another, and also within the same religious tradition continue to influence the very nature of the union. Never-theless, mystics constantly break through existing theological the-ories in order to stress the unity of love and cognition (this includes Christian mystics, for whom theories play a significant role). Gre-gory the Great's formula *amor ipse notitia* ("love itself is knowl-edge") provided Western contemplatives with a basis for affirming, again and again, that the highest love includes supreme knowledge. Gradually the emphasis will come to rest on love. In Bernard and William of Saint Thierry this process has become completed. We detect a similar favoring of love among Muslim mystics, even among those who daringly defend an ontological union. Purely cognitive mysticism, in which an intellectual process returns the soul to the native identity with its source, rarely occurs in mon-otheistic faiths. Even Ibn 'Arabi, the main representative of the Gnostic current in Islam, does not interrupt this tradition, as Mi-chael Sells's essay shows. Judaic mysticism displays Gnostic traits in some of its manifestations, and so does the Beguine movement among Christians in the Low Countries and Rhineland. But by and large Western mysticism before Jacob Boehme was rarely Gnostic or theosophical. One of the reasons, I suspect, is that the self-suf-ficient attitude of the Gnostic resists mystical surrender. This may explain Plotinus's surprising favoring of love over understanding as well as his aversion to Gnosticism despite its apparent similar-ities to his own philosophy.

Still, love inevitably implies duality. Why, then, did mystics who advocated an ontological union so often recur to the language of love? Should we not hold the *dynamic* quality, so essential to the mystical process, responsible for this persistence of an erotic terminology? While knowledge essentially consists in an awareness of *what is*, love must attain its goal slowly and often painfully. Hence even those mystics who presuppose the ontological presence of the soul in God, as all Neoplatonists do to some extent, regard mystical union as the result of a dynamic process for which the initial, ontological presence merely established the necessary con-dition. In choosing the language of love in spite of its inherent in-adequacy of expression, the mystic translates experience into the-ory. For the great majority, that experience undeniably consists of *a process*.

Yet a second factor—one that many have assumed but few have dared to express—appears to have influenced the priority of love. It is the idea that love changes God himself. Richard of Saint Victor, one of the first in the Christian tradition to mention this concept, boldly asserts that love "wounds" God.[38] We find other examples of this belief in the writings of many mystics. For example, Teresa of Ávila becomes unintelligible unless we assume that her divine Lover responds in accordance with the way her words affect him. The same holds true for Thérèse of Lisieux and Marie of the Incarnation. Angelus Silesius expresses the mutuality succinctly:

> There are but you and I, and when we two are not
> The heavens will collapse, God will no more be God.

> God shelters me as much as I do shelter Him,
> His Being I sustain, sustained I am therein.[39]

Among love mystics, only the Quietists (Molinos, Guyon, Fénelon) form a possible exception to this rule. For them the highest love consists in accepting God's immutability and in acquiring an attitude of total indifference toward one's own fate. It is precisely this position, however, that caused the movement no end of troubles with authorities suspicious of an ideal so contrary to human inclination.

Sufi love poetry, which may well have influenced Spanish Christian mystics of the sixteenth century, shows similar tendencies. Love is expressed as hardly conceivable without a mutuality of feelings, implying change on both sides. But for the most part Christian and Muslim mystics merely *assume* a divine change that no available theology allowed them to justify. Judaism is somewhat different. Here the dialogal model that determines the entire religion has also affected nearly all mystical expression. Since all relation to God is conceived in the form of an exchange, the need for a love mysticism is felt less acutely. Kabbalists assumed from the start that their attitude would have a direct impact upon the Godhead. The task of restoring the sphere of the divine sefirot rests, to a great extent, with the mystic.

In conclusion, the language of love and devotion, despite its inherent dualism, provided, at least for Muslims and Christians, a much-needed discourse for expressing the dynamic quality so essential to the mystical process. Yet to articulate the goal and final stages of this loving communion, many mystics introduced expressions of ontological union that are hardly compatible with the duality of love. At the same time, mystics who start from ontological union see themselves as being forced to use a language that can express the *growing* nature of that union. The language of love among humans is the most obvious, though not the only, candidate for that purpose.

Studies

Universalization and Integration: Two Conceptions of Mystical Union in Jewish Mysticism

MOSHE IDEL

The mystical experience, the most important source and trigger of mystical literature, is unfortunately beyond the direct reach of those who are interested in fathoming the nature of mysticism; according to this conception, the core of the mystical phenomenon is as inaccessible to the scholar as its literary expressions are easily accessible in his library. Experiences that were transformed into words are the raw material for learned analysis, which deals, consciously or not, only with literary creations. However, even if this attitude is correct, mystical literature is far from being a branch of literature conceived as belles lettres. The religious authority of mystical literature surpasses the authority profane literature enjoys, apparently because of the creative ambiguity of the greatest part of mystical literature: it expresses at the same time the most intimate experiences of the individual and the religious ideals of certain communities. As such, the literary expression of mystical experiences may provide important insights for the understanding of the individual, sometimes one who played an important role on the historical scene, and at the same time it provides for a better evaluation of the shared ideals that activated both the mystic and his surroundings.

The present study attempts to describe the history and significance of two recurring expressions for mystical experiences in Jewish mysticism: universalization and integration. Both are qualifications of the more common designation of the contact of the individual with the divine in Judaism, *devekut*, a term whose large mystical semantic field includes a variety of meanings, from imitating divine behavior to the total fusion with the divine.[1]

The basic assumption of the following discussion is the conviction, which I hope I have demonstrated in some of my previous studies, that Jewish mysticism includes extreme unitive expressions, comparable to the most extreme views to be found in non-Jewish mysticism. This assumption does not mean that the experiences themselves are comparable and that therefore a phenomenology of mystical experiences is to be preferred to one of mystical expressions. The analysis of the two expressions is to be understood as a modest contribution to the phenomenology of unitive language rather than a typology of the experiences.

Devekut and Becoming Universal

A recurring motif in the philosophical and kabbalistic discussions on *devekut* is the assertion that by the process of cleaving to a comprehensive object the soul of the mystic becomes comprehensive like that object. Sometimes the soul is united to the universal soul of the Neoplatonists, sometimes to God himself; however, in both instances the soul undergoes a significant transformation, testifying, according to the descriptions of the mystics or the philosophers, to the conversion of the individual into a universal entity. A survey of the development of this motif of becoming universal will complement the following treatment of the integration of the soul in the universal.

It seems that the first, and most important, discussions of *devekut* as connected to universalization in the Jewish tradition are to be found in Rabbi Abraham ibn 'Ezra's writings, in the middle of the twelfth century. He asserts that "when the part knows the All and cleaves to the All, it may create signs and wonders by the All."[2] According to the Ibn 'Ezra, "All" stands for God, who is described also as the origin of everything or, according to another possible understanding, as the origin of the universal soul.[3]

The transformation of the individual into a more comprehensive being is possible because the human soul originates from the universal, and therefore after her separation from the body she returns to the universal. Thus the cleaving of the soul is a return to her primordial state and, implicitly, a restoration of her primordial universality. Moses cleaved to the universal, according to one passage of this author, and he became universal according to another.[4] A major result of this recovery of universality is the acquisition of magical powers, which are exercised by means of identification with the universal soul that is ruling mundane affairs or by union with the Tetragrammaton that apparently stands for God. Therefore beginning with Ibn 'Ezra, medieval Jewish thought adopts as a major theme of *devekut* the conception of the transformation of the individual soul into a universal one or into God. This theme ran in a large series of philosophical texts, most of them having been recently analyzed in two articles dealing with the theory of miracles in this literature.[5]

Before entering the mystical cast of this view, it would be pertinent to adduce a text that was rather neglected by the scholars of Ibn 'Ezra's thought. I refer to a quotation in the name of the philosophers by Rabbi Shem Tov ibn Falaquera, a mid-thirteenth-century thinker and translator flourishing in Spain. In his *Commentary on The Guide of the Perplexed* he cites the following view:

> When the particular soul will receive the influx of the universal soul by the intermediacy of the spheres, she will elevate and ascend from the degree of "part" and will be called "All" and the part will not be separated from the All since[6] the part will receive the influx from the All insofar as it can emanate upon her. And if [the part] will see the influx and [nevertheless] will turn by itself to a different thing, it will be cut off from *devekut* to the essence of the All; its ways will become dimmed as happened to those who separated from the prophets of the Creator, blessed be He, who rebelled against His words.[7]

This text does not overtly assert the sequence of the universalization of the soul and *devekut;* however, it is obvious that the part will return to its previous state as the result of the separation of the two, which were previously united in a state of *devekut*. I assume that the two events happened in this order: the reception of the influx establishes a relationship between the individual and the universal understood as *devekut;* the universalization is the result of this link. The separation between the two is regarded as the state commonly referred to in mystical literature as the "dark night of the soul." If the quotation stems from some Muslim source, as I am inclined to assume, then it contains a significant parallel to

Ibn 'Ezra's conception of universalization by cleaving to God; furthermore Ibn 'Ezra also portrays the particular soul as "receiving a great power from the supernal power . . . and then she will cleave to the Illustrious Name."[8] Here, as in the anonymous passage, the reception of the power or influx from above is a precondition of cleaving. I would like to focus now upon the kabbalistic elaboration of this theme.

Important repercussions of universalization through cleaving are found in the ecstatic kabbalah and afterward in Hasidic mysticism. Abraham Abulafia describes the union of the human spiritual faculties with the Active Intellect in these terms:

> [They] will be united with it after many hard, strong and mighty exercises, until the particular and personal prophetic [faculty] will become universal, permanent and everlasting similar to the essence of its cause, and he and He become one entity.[9]

Following Ibn 'Ezra, Abulafia regards Moses as a person who turned universal, comprising in himself the entire people of Israel, each of its members being considered as a part in relation to him.[10] The motif of comprising in order to become universal recurs in another text of Abulafia that I will discuss later.

The nature of the exercises mentioned in the previous quotation is the Abulafian technique of combining letters of the Torah or letters that form the divine names. This becomes obvious from another discussion of universalization, found in Abulafia's work *Ozar 'Eden Ganuz*. He describes the seventh and highest method of interpreting the Torah, which is singularly based upon the combination of letters, thus:

> the secret of the real operation, which changes the nature of the parts of the creature by the virtue of the totality of speech, until your intellectual spirit will become universal after he was partial, and it will comprise in you all the general substances which are from your species, even more those forms that are inferior to your species[11] . . . and you shall apprehend with your senses and intellect true apprehensions. And those similar to you will possess an image and likeness.[12]

The totality of speech mentioned here is crucial for the proper understanding of the passage; it is the theory of letter combinations intended to change the nature of the creature. However, in Abulafian terminology, the real change, alluded to here, is not con-

nected to the external nature but to the inner one. Combining letters, the mystic changes his psychic constitution. According to this
text, the nature of the change is clear; the intellect expands, becoming more comprehensive and, at the same time, acquiring the
real human image, the intellect *in actu*. The expansion of the intellectual faculty is indicated in a conspicuous way when he mentions the integration into himself of the forms of the species, namely
the *intelligibilia*. However, the individual does not become absorbed
in the Active Intellect or in God but remains, according to this
quotation, a separate entity, distinguished from those similar to
him. In other words, the universalization as presented here does
not include a previous experience of *devekut*. It seems that Abulafia
envisioned the possibility of reaching a state of universalization
and perpetual eternity of the individual soul also without *devekut*,
as becomes clear in an additional passage of the same kabbalist:

> By the elevation of man he will become similar to one of the
> everlasting stars since he turns to be a [real] man; and he will
> stand forever becoming All since [only] All is standing.[13]

Apparently, the tension between the view of universalization
through *devekut* and that which assumes the possibility of turning
universal even without cleaving, and ultimately remaining an ev-
erlasting individual entity, can be partially solved by a third passage of Abulafia. In the same book he states that the ultimate purpose of man is

> to reach to the degree of the angels named *Ishim* and to cleave
> to them for the everlasting life, until the men will become the
> angels which are also separate [from matter] after they were man
> *in potentia* and angels *in actu*, but on a lower degree.[14]

Therefore the cleaving to the *Ishim* is tantamount to union to
a totality of angelized human intellects; however, the term *Ishim*,
which points in Maimonidean terminology to the Active Intellect,
has an ambiguous linguistic nature. Although it refers to an individual entity (the Active Intellect), it is also a plural form, its
literary meaning being "men."[15] This Maimonidean quandary enables Abulafia to present a complex theory of cleaving to the Active
Intellect, becoming universal and, at the same time, remaining an
individual. All this is the result of the double nature of *Ishim*. In
an unnamed treatise, Abulafia describes the separate entities denominated in the medieval terminology as separated intellects:

> . . . divine causes, the simplest of them being composed out of
> all the others and the most composite of them being the simplest
> one [i.e., the most spiritual].[16]

Therefore, according to Abulafia, simplicity of a certain entity is
a dialectical state; it implies separation from corporeality, but at
the same time such a simple being contains all the other separated
forms.

An important issue to be remarked upon in relation to Abulafia's concept of universalization is the fact that he envisions the
intellect rather than the soul as the expanding entity; in an untitled
fragment, he asserts that there are three categories of being.[17] The
first, namely the intellect, is partial and at the same time universal
and indivisible. The second kind of being is the soul, which, though
also indivisible, is nevertheless only a part, namely partial, and
never universal. The last category, the body, is not only partial but
also divisible. These categories refer to created reality. God, being
uncreated, is designated as the universal that is partial in no way
and is denominated as the universal of the universal *in extremis*.
This distinction does not allow a universalization of the soul as in
Ibn 'Ezra's Neoplatonically oriented system, but it focuses the main
interest on the expansion of the intellect as the major mystical organ. Another representative of the ecstatic kabbalah, Rabbi Isaac
of Acre, indicates that the final stage of the development of the soul
consists in the cleaving to *Eiyn Sof*, and then she will "become
total and universal, after she had been individual, due to her palace,
while she was yet imprisoned in it, and she will become Universal,
because of the nature of her real source."[18]

Under the cumulative influence of Ibn 'Ezra and the anonymous passage quoted by Falaquera and Abraham Abulafia, the unknown author of the treatise *Toldot Adam* states that we may infer
from the anonymous passage that whosoever "cleaves to the intellect and to the prophet (!), he will become universal . . . and by
this turning one's soul universal you will be able to change the
material issues from their natural course."[19] As with Abulafia, the
way of cleaving is a combination of medieval Aristotelian elements,
such as the emphasis upon the intellect as the organ of cleaving,
and the Neoplatonic trend, represented by the mentioning of the
universalization of the particular soul and her ability to perform
miraculous changes in the natural course of events.

Finally a Hasidic example will suffice to demonstrate the impact of the medieval material on the last mystical phase in Judaism.

In Rabbi Menaḥem Nahum of Chernobyl's *Meor 'Einayim* we find the following view:

> . . . to bring himself closer to the divine part which dwells in him closer to the root of all, to Him, blessed be He, and he becomes attached to the Divine Unity by the means of the union of the part to the All, which is *Eiyn Sof.* Consequently, the light of the holiness of *Eiyn Sof* shines in him, as the part cleaves to its root.[20]

All the previous examples testify to the extent of the influence of philosophical concepts and terminology on Jewish mysticism and the role played by the Neoplatonic conception of the basic affinity and even the continuity of the divine and the human spiritual powers. This is to be contrasted with the function of the emanational scheme in the elaboration of the theosophical system in kabbalah, where the intricacies and the subtleties of the sefirotic system, substantially influenced by Neoplatonic thought, can be regarded as a screen between man and the inmost facet of the divinity. In the ecstatic kabbalah, Neoplatonism contributes to the emergence of the terminology of the unitive descriptions.

Devekut as Entering God

The reigning view in modern scholarship insists that *devekut* as a mystical ideal does not include extreme forms regularly designated as *unio mystica.*[21] A detailed refutation of such an unqualified understanding of *devekut*, as formulated in Gershom Scholem's opus and in the works of his followers, was done elsewhere on both conceptual and textual grounds.[22] Here I should like to discuss additional examples of the understanding of *devekut* as involving some form of obliteration of the human personality by means of the experience of a self-inclusion of the mystic in the divine realm. Such a conception, shared as we shall show by important Hasidic figures, strengthens the need for a substantial modification of Scholem's thesis concerning the moderate nature of *devekut* in Jewish mysticism. At the beginning, the early kabbalistic material will be presented; afterward, some Hasidic passages will be adduced and analyzed. The authors, Rabbi Pinḥas of Koretz, Rabbi Menaḥem Mendel of Vitebsk, Rabbi Shneor Zalman of Lyady, and Rabbi Abraham of Kalinsk, are major figures of early Hasidism. The last three were good friends and disciples of the outstanding leader of post-Beshtian Hasidism, Rabbi Dov Baer of Mezhrich, known as the Great Maggid. The fact that the following discussions corroborate the possibility that *devekut* also comprises an extreme aspect points to the conclusion that the master has to be interpreted in the light of the concepts of his two leading disciples. Moreover, the occurrence of similar views in Rabbi Menaḥem Mendel's work and in that of Rabbi Pinḥas apparently indicates, together with the evidence adduced from the kabbalistic sources, that the Great Maggid was not the first source of the extreme understanding of *devekut*.

Before entering the kabbalistic elaborations on the subject of the integration of the human in the divine, let me recall two earlier instances of usages of the verb *KLL*, which, though occurring in puzzling passages, might have been understood as referring to the mystical relation with the divine or, at least, might have facilitated the reception of this mystical notion. According to *Genesis Rabba*,[23] the Aramaic rendering of the verse "The righteous shall crown themselves in me" (Psalm 142: 8) is "Itkalelun bi zaddikaya." This phrase may be understood as a slightly different version of the original meaning of the verse, the form *Itkalelun* being derived from *Kalil*, namely "adornment." However, another reading, less plausible and perhaps even impossible, suggests that the Aramaic verb points to the integration of the righteous in the person who prays to God. Another prekabbalistic text, a *piyyut* to be read in the *musaf* service of Yom Kippur,[24] says, "The offspring [of Jacob] are comprised in Your name." What exactly is intended in this verse is far from clear, but the occurrence of the notion of the inclusion of Israel in a divine element is conspicuous. Moreover, these passages occur in well-known texts, so that these usages of the verb *KLL* were accessible to every average Jew.

The theme which will be examined in the following pages is the integration of the human in the divine as a phase that represents the peak of preceding mystical stages: *devekut* and self-annihilation. Before surveying the history of this theme in medieval Jewish mysticism, however, it is important to discuss briefly another ancient view that may point to a Jewish precedent: a well-known designation of God in Tannaitic literature as *Makom*, or "the place," thereby referring to Divinity as the place of the world. In a peculiar instance, we learn that God as place is the place of the refuge of man, a statement that is rather obscure. Philo asserts:

> God himself is called place from the fact that he contains all, but
> is contained by nothing whatever, and that he is a place of refuge

for all, and because he is his own space, having occupied himself and being contained in himself alone.[25]

The spatial description of God, in close vicinity to the idea of entering the divine place, constitutes an interesting parallel to the eighteenth-century interpretation of Rabbi Pinḥas of Koretz.

The concept of integration is expressed in a peculiar term, *hitkalelut*, whose history I will briefly survey. The term's root, *KLL*, regularly refers to the notion of universal, comprehensive or general. Its mystical significance, seems to be mainly connected to the integration of some elements into a more comprehensive entity or to the fact that this entitity comprises a plurality of components. Thus, for example, Adam was portrayed in the Midrash as comprising all creation in his body; according to Geronese kabbalistic sources, man comprises all the sefirotic realm in his structure. Later kabbalistic terminology employs this root to express the integration of various divine attributes in each other. So, for example, one sefirah can be integrated in another. However, it should be pointed out that according to the kabbalists, this process of integration does not abolish the individuality of the integrated sefirah.

According to two Catalan kabbalists, Rabbi 'Ezra and Rabbi 'Azriel of Gerona: "The diadem is a simile of the soul that enters and cleaves and is crowned around by the bright light."[26] The significance of this passage is obvious enough: the human soul, like the diadem or the last sefirah, Malkhut, ascends to a higher level, that of the sefirah of Binah, the root of souls according to this kabbalistic school, and is adorned there with the eschatological garment of light.[27] For our discussion it is important to stress the occurrence of the entering into the sefirotic realm as part of the *devekut* process. However, the mystical or, more precisely, the ecstatic aspect of the experience is not so clear, since the focus of the context is on the eschatological fate of the soul rather than her mystical experience.[28]

The link between *devekut* and the integration of the soul in the divine realm occurs in an early kabbalistic passage that describes the experience of an ancient mystic:

"Ben Azzai[29] looked and died." He gazed at the radiance of the *Shekhinah*, like a man with weak eyes who gazes into the full light of the sun, and his eyes are dimmed, and at times he becomes blinded, because of the intensity of the light which overwhelms him. Thus it happened to Ben Azzai: the light overwhelmed him, and he gazed at it because of his great desire to cleave to it and to enjoy it without interruption, and after he cleaved to it he did not wish to be separated from the sweet radiance, and he remained immersed and hidden within it. And his soul was crowned and adorned by that very radiance and brightness to which no man may cling and afterwards live, as it is said: "for no man shall see Me and live."[30] But Ben Azzai only gazed at it a little while, and then his soul departed and remained (there), and was hidden away in the place of its cleaving, which is a most precious light. And this death was the death of the pious whose souls are separated from all concerns of the lowly world and whose souls cleave to the ways of the supernal world.[31]

What is of interest for us in this remarkable passage is the description of a mystical state that may follow the state of *devekut*. The human soul may remain immersed in the divine light,[32] her state being portrayed as "hidden within it" or, as a medieval author would put it, "treasured or stored in the divine light," apparently pointing to the penetration of the soul in the inner part of the light rather than adhering to its external facet. The description of the soul as "crowned" and "adorned" by the divine light presupposes again the entering of the soul of the mystic into the radiant realm of divinity and her lasting stay there after her transformation. Therefore, already at the very beginning of kabbalah as a historical phenomenon, the image of entering the divine realm after the experience of *devekut* is obvious enough. It should be noted that this immersion of the soul of the mystic does not assume a state of total fusion with the light but a certain kind of apotheosis whose main feature is the acquisition of the divine aura that surrounds his soul. The anonymous author does not mention, and I assume that he even does not imply, an experience of *unio mystica* involving a complete absorption of the soul into the divine essence. Conspicuously absent is any hint at the transcendence of plurality after entering the supernal light.

According to an anonymous kabbalistic text,[33] the prophetic experience is produced by the encounter, as the revelation of one's own form,[34] with that "which is comprised in the *Shekhinah*, and when the *Shekhinah* reveals to him he sees his form as if he looks in a mirror." Therefore, according to this passage, the human form, or *eidos*, exists already in the supernal divine manifestation designated as *Shekhinah*. Although the archetypal form is included in the *Shekhinah*, its individual existence seems to be safeguarded. In other words, the highest aspect of the human person is part of the divine, and revelation is the encounter with this aspect. No doubt we witness here a kabbalistic version of the encounter with the alter ego as a high spiritual experience. The emphasis on the *eidos* and its role in the revelatory process renders *devekut* unnecessary as a meaningful experience. The assumption that the divine structure is so comprehensive renders superfluous the return of the soul to divinity in order to achieve perfect divine structure or harmony. These two examples deal with the *devekut* experience as a matter of the individual; his mystical achievement has no significant impact upon the supernal structures.

Although belonging to another type of mysticism than that of the earlier-mentioned kabbalists, Rabbi Abraham Abulafia, the central figure of the ecstatic kabbalah, interprets in his peculiar way a theosophical perception of the integration of the spiritual element in man into the divine. In an important epistle describing his system, he asserts:

> It is known that all the inner forces and the hidden souls in man are differentiated in the bodies. It is, however, in the nature of all of them that when their knots are untied they return to their origin, which is one without duality and which comprises multiplicity, until the *Eiyn Sof*; and when it is loosed, it reaches till above, so that when he mentions the name of God he ascends and sits on the head of the supreme Crown, and the thought draws from there a three-fold blessing.[35]

According to this text, God comprises a certain multiplicity, so that the ascending spiritual forces experience no loss in the divine realm. The ultimate attainment is even presented in a mythical image as the sitting on the supreme Crown (*Keter 'Eliyon*), an overt reference to the highest sefirah. The use of this image is premeditated: Abulafia's intention is to reinterpret the mythical integration of the soul already in existence in the theosophical kabbalah (as the preceding discussions have shown) so as to indicate the reunion of the dispersed intellectual powers with their origin. His basic conception of the nature of mystical union, as analyzed earlier, advocates the possibility of a total transformation of the intellect in a universal entity, a theory substantially different from the integration version of mysticism.

A combination of these two kabbalistic ideals in connection with the matter of integration is found in a work of Rabbi Moses Cordovero, a leading kabbalist in sixteenth-century Safed. Although he obviously belongs to the Spanish theurgico-theosophical kabbalistic tradition, Cordovero was open to the oriental version of ecstatic kabbalah to the extent that he could regard Abulafia's kabbalah as superior to the Zoharic kabbalah. According to Cordovero, the ultimate goal of the divine service is to cleave to the simple divinity.[36] The following passage is an illuminating demonstration of the merger of the two kabbalistic trends and the evaluation of the role of *devekut* and integration in his axiology:

> This is our *bonum*, that we shall attain this unification,[37] and to illuminate in the light of the Torah, to be integrated light into light up to the level of *Binah* and *Ḥokhmah*, since we may not cleave but until there because *devekut* on the higher level is possible only in an intermittent manner[38] . . . all the other *boni* being not (genuine) *boni* at all, but a certain apprehension, and that *devekut* is the main *bonum*, all the other *boni* being but a preparation to this *bonum*.[39]

This kabbalist explicitly presents cleaving and integration as the highest states in the kabbalistic modus vivendi beyond the preparatory acts of unification of the lower sefirot. Man's acquisition of the stage of illumination, union, and integration into the sefirah of *Ḥokhmah* is a constant state, and his intermittent cleaving to the sefirah of *Keter* is a substantial expression of the paramount importance of *devekut* even when the theosophical system remains the basic theological framework of the mystic. Pertinent to the understanding of the new role *devekut* will play in subsequent stages of Jewish mysticism is the emphasis here on the location of *devekut* above theurgical operations. Although Lurianic kabbalah rejected this hierarchization of these ideals, Hasidism will return to the stand that Cordovero expressed in the previous passage.

Meanwhile, Cordovero's disciples cultivated and propagated the ideal of *devekut* and produced a great literary corpus designated in scholarly terminology as the Safedian Mussar literature.[40] So, for example, Rabbi Eliah de Vidas refers to the above text of his master and writes about the way of cleaving to God:

> All the worlds are bound together by the soul, spirit and higher soul of man, and this [i.e., the bond of the three spiritual powers of man] causes the illumination of all the worlds by the Emanator, the King of all kings . . . and then the worlds are bound to each other and are comprised in each other and so also the soul of man and his spirit and higher soul will illuminate and will be integrated on high and will suck an abundance of influx from the source of all the blessings.[41]

Again, the integration of the human spiritual faculties is presented as an interpretation of the meaning of *devekut*. Although this *devekut* is preceded by a theurgical event—the integration of the worlds into each other—the final human achievement is the human integration on high, something that may be facilitated by establishing a harmonious relationship between the worlds.

A crucial development in the understanding of the role of the integration of the soul is found in the Lurianic kabbalah. According to Isaac Luria, the goal of the study of Torah, the most important Jewish ideal is "to restore and complete the (supernal) Tree and the supernal *Anthropos* by the restoration of their souls [i.e., the souls of Israel], and they return [so as] to be integrated in Him."[42]

This conception of the kabbalistic ideal of *tikkun* (i.e., restoration) recurs in the Lurianic corpus, but apparently only in this instance is the notion of *tikkun* and integration of the souls expressed in connection with the idea of *devekut* and restoration. Consequently, the improvement of the soul, her cleaving to the divine hypostasis, and even her integration in this superstructure, are intended to accomplish the restoration of the divine perfection and harmony, whereas the achievement of the individual is judged only from this perspective. *Devekut* and the integrating return basically have theurgical significance; their mystical implications remain beyond the speculation of the classical part of the Lurianic literary corpus. Moreover, the integration of the soul is part of the perfection of a complex theosophical structure, the tree, or the *Anthropos*, which consists, according to kabbalistic theology, of a very detailed construction. Therefore, the return of the soul cannot be understood as a total union with a supernal unified entity and her absorption in it but rather as the completion of the divinity by the ascent of a dispersed part of it to its proper place.[43]

Interestingly, the supreme ideal in this text is the restoration of the Godhead, which is the major beneficiary of the return of the soul to her proper place. The mystic, however, is instrumental to this purpose; for the theosophical kabbalist, the essential matter is the perfection of the supernal structures much more than his own mystical union with the divine. In other words, the soul's integration is more a divine need than an individual drive. The major difference between Lurianic kabbalah and Hasidic mysticism is precisely this attenuation of theosophy that enables the mystic to focus his interest on his own mystical experience at the expense of the elaboration on the supernal structure. In passing, it is pertinent to remark that this understanding of the purpose of *devekut* and integration is congenial to the theurgico-theosophical understanding of the unitive experience. For example, Rabbi Joseph Alashkar, an Andalusian kabbalist writing in Tlemsen in 1528, states, "We were commanded by God to eat the *Mazzah* in order to cleave to the Pure Power and to add power to It."[44] The theurgical ideal, indicated by the necessity to add power on high, is presented here as the ultimate goal of cleaving. The Lurianic interpretation of cleaving and integration as a divine need is therefore only one version of the basic tendency of the Spanish kabbalah to emphasize the instrumental role of the unitive experience by giving priority to the theurgical activity. According to Rabbi Pinḥas of Koretz, man ought to cleave to God during the whole year. This cleaving is understood as the imperative "to go into God, Blessed be He" or, as he put it originally in Yiddish, "Muz sich arein gein in Ha-Shem Itbarakh."[45] Immediately afterward, he describes God as surrounding man and as the place.[46] Thus the entering, which is part of the *devekut*, can easily be understood as a process of self-inclusion of the mystic in the all-comprehensive divine nature.

In his *Sefer Peri HaArez*,[47] Rabbi Menaḥem Mendel of Vitebsk mentions the stupefaction of the mystic who apprehends that the source of the influx that he receives is God himself, whereas he is its recipient. Mendel continues:

> The nature of all recipients is that they are stupefied and this is the matter of their annihilation,[48] since they self-annihilate themselves and they become comprised[49] in the sources of (their) influx, and therefore this *tremendum* is [tantamount to] the complete *devekut*, since he [namely, the mystic] is comprised in *Eiyn Sof*, Blessed be He.

The self-annihilation is the result of the attainment of the total *devekut*,[50] and it is tantamount to extinction of the individuality of the mystic. Again, according to the same master: "The man who possesses the *tremendum* of the High . . . is comprised in Him. Blessed be He, out of the annihilation of his whole individuality and his whole vitality."[51]

Prime facie the affinity of "awe," which I have translated as *tremendum*,[52] and *devekut* is bizarre. The feeling of awe seems to constitute an obstacle in the quest of total union because of the distance it creates between the two entities involved in the experience of union. However, at least for such experts of mysticism as J. Récéjac and R. Otto, it is precisely this feeling of initial *tremen-*

dum that may ultimately generate the experience of union. As Ré-céjac ingenuously puts it: "Mysticism begins through fear, through the perception of a universal and invincible dominion; later it becomes a desire for union with that which rules in such a way."[53]

As we have seen, R. Menaḥem Mendel indicates that the recipient's overpowering by his awareness of the majesty of the source triggers the process that culminates in the mystical union. The understanding of the end of the mystical quest as complete annihilation may also contribute to a feeling of anxiety rooted in the recipient's awareness of extinction as the possible result. This correlation between self-integration as the end of the *devekut* experience and the fear of God is reminiscent of Rabbi Pinḥas of Koretz's connection of *devekut* and fear in another passage.[54] No definitive answer to the problem of who is the ultimate source of this nexus between *devekut*, fear of God, and self-integration is yet available. It is possible that the three concepts were already related to each other earlier.

Let us return to the same passage of Rabbi Menaḥem Mendel. In an exegetical tour de force, he maintains that God possesses only treasures of *tremendum*[55] since "after the *tremendum*, nothing remained, because if he is here everything is here, since he is the beginning of everything and the aim of everything by his self-integration into Him, blessed be He, and [then] what does remain [at all]?"[56] This statement concerning the treasures of the *tremendum* refers to the remnant of individuality: It disappeared, leaving only vestiges of the *tremendum*. Concentrating exclusively on the feeling of awe, the mystic is changed into an entity formed of awe, which alone survives the experience of self-integration. This is the reason God possesses solely these treasures.

Notwithstanding his apparent extinction, the mystic, in precisely the same context, is portrayed as omnipotent, since he "is comprised in Him, blessed be His name, and in his hand is [i.e., he is able to do] everything." This is an interesting paradox indeed: by the extinction of one's personality in the divine ocean, one achieves the status of an archmagician, probably because of the utmost identification of the person to the omnipotent divinity.

Rabbi Shneor Zalman of Lyady, an outstanding acquaintance of Rabbi Menaḥem Mendel, contributed some important discussions on *devekut* as self-integration in the divine realm. As interesting as his formulations are, their main importance lies not so much in the daring nature of his expressions as in the fact that they became part of the doctrine of the major faction of Hasidism.

By being included in exoteric writings, Zalman's formulations penetrated wider circles than the documents of kabbalah—all this without the slightest protest concerning this issue. This point is worth emphasizing from the perspective of comparative mysticism. With the major exception of Hindu and Buddhist mysticism, authoritative theologians were highly suspicious of extreme formulations of feelings of extinction in entering the divine realm. Sometimes these extreme mystics had to pay with their lives for their spiritual achievements. The case of Rabbi Shneor Zalman is an important exception. The self-integration is presented as an ideal or, as we shall see, a natural inclination of the Jewish soul; moreover, in a short period of time, it turned into a most significant kind of theology, judging on a statistical basis alone. This development is of paramount importance for a better understanding of the mystical potentiality inherent in the Jewish religion. Contrary to Scholem's well-known thesis regarding the absence of extreme unitive expressions in Jewish mysticism, the texts of some Jewish mystics indicate that it is incontestable that the extreme formulations of *unio mystica* are not only possible in Judaism but also function as an integral part of the most widespread form of Jewish mysticism, the mystical theology of Ḥabad, whose founder was none other than Rabbi Shneor Zalman of Lyady. The assumption that Jewish mystics avoided extreme formulations out of fear of the criticism of the theologians[57] may hold in the case of some medieval authors, but it seems to be incorrect as a generalization on Jewish mysticism in its entirety. Let us now turn to Rabbi Shneor Zalman's discussions on *hitkalelut* and *devekut*.

In his commentary on the *Siddur*, he asserts that the existence of souls "is annihilated and they are comprised in the aspect of Nought in the source wherefrom they were extracted at the beginning . . . exactly as in the parable of the extinction of the wick in the fire that lies just beside it."[58] Elaborating on the above parable, the author explains that the more the wick is consumed in the fire, the more the flame of the fire prevails in it and enters the inmost part of the wick. God as the consuming fire is the major metaphor in this parable. Following biblical and kabbalistic motifs,[59] the soul is here conceived as consumed by the divine flame that is apparently envisioned as surrounding it, just as the fire surrounds the wick. In accordance with the parable, the wick nourishes the flame while it is at the same time consumed by it. Such a conception of the interpenetration of the human and the divine illuminates another passage of the same author where he uses the following example to explain the nature of *hitkalelut:*

> When man cleaves to God, it is very delightful for Him, and very savorous for Him, so much so that He will swallow it into His heart, etc., as the corporeal throat swallows. And this is the true cleaving, as he becomes one substance with God in whom he was swallowed, without being separate [from God] to be considered as a distinct entity at all. That is the meaning [of the verse] "and you shall cleave to Him"—(to cleave), literally.[60]

Again, the penetration of the human into the divine realm is portrayed as a profound metamorphosis that makes the soul an inseparable element in the bosom of divinity. Just as the consuming organism is strengthened by food, so also the fire is nourished by the wick. Moreover, the meaning of the term *hitkalelut* implies an interpenetration of the two elements involved in the process as well as the emergence of a different entity combining the previously separate components of the synthesis. According to a detailed discussion in *Likkutei Amarim,*[61] the study of Torah and of the Jewish canon in general leads to comprehension, namely, the inclusion of the contents of this body of literature in the mind of the student. In the virtue of the well-known Aristotelian epistemological thesis on the identification of the knower and the known, the student identifies himself with the studied matters, which are envisioned as identical with God. In precisely the same context, the author dwells also on the mystical repercussions of the enactment of the contents that someone studies—the aural aspect of the study, as well as the performing of the commandments, wrap the student with a cloth of divine light. Therefore a double movement takes place between man and God. The divine is absorbed by the intellect of the student of the Law, whereas a divine garment wraps him. The interpenetration of the two realms is posited in a clear fashion. In the context of this passage, the author uses the image of food to exemplify the comprehension of the Torah, which is presented in classical Jewish texts as the food of the soul.

Immediately after the last parable, the author refers to the relationship between a master and his disciple to exemplify the relationship between the human and the divine. Although the course of this discussion is irrelevant for our point, it is striking to find the same metaphor occurring in a previously cited passage of Rabbi Menaḥem Mendel of Vitebsk dealing with *hitkalelut*.[62] Rabbi Shneor

Zalman puts the relationship between the recipient and the donor in categories of annihilation and *hitkalelut*, precisely as his friend did. Whereas the preceding text refers to the integration of the spiritual element into divinity, another discussion by Rabbi Shneor apparently goes beyond this point. In his *Commentary* on the *Zohar*, he implies the elevation of the corporeal powers that are generated by the food:

> When someone prays with intention *(kawwanah)* and deep dedication the verse "and you shall love, etc.," of the prayer of *Shema'*, then even the corporeal power which originates in the material food is transformed and swallowed and comprised in this deep dedication, since in this enthusiasm there are surely powers of the body and material food. Thus even the power of the material food is comprised in the Godhead by the deep dedication.[63]

Hence the process of inclusion or of entering the divine realm involves not only the human soul but also those elements that are metamorphosed in human spiritual forces out of the material world. The human organism is considered to be not only the material substratum of the soul but also part of a mechanism that enables the elevation of the material to the domain of the divine; through enthusiastic and dedicated prayer, man is able to serve as a transforming channel that offers to the divine the opportunity to absorb or swallow the spiritual and spiritualized elements into him.

The above discussion serves as appropriate background for a proper understanding of a passage occurring in the classic text of the Ḥabad literature, Rabbi Shneor Zalman's *Likkutei Amarim:*

> . . . the soul [of Israel] is comparable to the light of the candle that moves always upwards by its nature, since the light of the fire tends by its nature to separate from the wick and to cleave to its source above, to the universal element of fire which is under the sphere of the moon. . . . In spite of the fact that thereby it will be extinguished and it will not shine below at all and also above in its source, [and] its light will be annihilated, nevertheless this is its natural desire. So is the human [spiritual] soul, and the aspects of the spirit and [lower] soul. It wants and desires by its nature to separate from its body and to leave it and to cleave to its source and origin, in God, the Life of Lives, blessed be He, in spite of the fact that it will become nothing and nil and will be completely annihilated there, nothing remaining of it, neither out of its essence or out of its initial substance.[64]

The image of the returning fire as the symbol of the desire of the soul to join its primary status is not a novel one;[65] however, what is peculiarly interesting in Rabbi Shneor Zalman's use of it is his overemphasis on the "suicidal" facet of this natural inclination—the return of the lower flame is tantamount to its extinction. Consequently, the mystical quest involves ostensibly escapist aspects; entering God is identical to leaving the world in a very extreme way.

Another interesting description of the last mystical stage as an integrative experience is found in the writings of Rabbi Naḥman of Braslav, a leading Hasidic figure at the beginning of the nineteenth century and, like Rabbi Shneor Zalman, the head of a Hasidic movement that lasted until our time. Again, as in the case of the Ḥabad texts, the following passages are extracted from the basic and exoteric texts of a relatively large mystical movement. According to Rabbi Naḥman:

> When one finally is integrated in *Eiyn Sof*, his Torah is the Torah of God Himself, and his prayer is the Prayer of God Himself. . . . We thus find that there exists a Torah of God and a prayer of God. When a person merits to be integrated in *Eiyn Sof*, his Torah and prayer are those of God Himself.[66]

A more detailed description of the acquisition of this high state is found in another teaching of the same master:

> The main purpose of the creation of the world was for the sake of Israel, [namely] so that they will perform His will and will return and cleave to their root, namely, so that they will return and integrate in Him, blessed be He, who is the Necessary Being. And for this everything was created. Consequently, inasmuch as Israel are performing the will of the High and are integrated in their root . . . thereby the entire world is integrated. . . . However, in order to merit to be integrated in the root, namely, to return and be integrated in the unity of God, blessed be He, who is the Necessary Being, you do not merit it save by the annihilation by which someone completely annihilates himself until he becomes integrated in His unity, blessed be He. And it is impossible to attain annihilation but by the means of seclusion.[67]

The conception of integration in these quotations is clear enough; it is but a synonym for cleaving. Notwithstanding the unitive connotations of these descriptions, the fusion with the Nec-

essary Being is not total. The entire world is assumed to undergo
the same process together with the souls of the people of Israel.
Therefore, even when the ultimate mystical integration is attained,
it is portrayed as triggering the cosmic return to the source, preventing an extreme interpretation of the experience of the obliteration of the self as the appanage of the mystic alone. Instead, he
may be considered as pioneering the process that the entire world
will undergo. According to Rabbi Naḥman, the self-annihilation is
intended to purify the mystic of his egocentrism so that he may
better participate in the suffering of the other: "He self-annihilates
and does not care for himself at all; he feels the anguish of Israel,
his friend, and by this annihilation he is integrated in the Nought."[68]
Therefore, the annihilation is far from being an escapist endeavor.
It enables someone to partake the fate of the other.

In another pertinent discussion, Rabbi Naḥman combines integrative expressions with universalizing ones:

> Eternal life belongs only to God, who lives forever. But he who
> is integrated in his root, in God, also has eternal life. Since he
> is integrated in the One and is one with God, he lives eternally
> just as God does. And there is no perfection but the perfection
> of God, apart from Him everything being deficient; but whoever
> is integrated in Him acquires perfection. The basis of this inte-
> gration in God is knowing Him, as the sage said,[69] "If I knew
> Him I would be Him." The core of the man is his mind. Where a
> man's mind is, there is the whole man. He who knows, and attains
> to a divine understanding, is really there [in God]. The greater
> his knowing, the more he is integrated in his root, in God."[70]

According to this text, the vehicle of the integrative process is
not the mystic's participation in the suffering of others (a purely
emotional state) but his broadening of the intellect or mind, which
allows him to assimilate the divine knowledge. However, in spite
of the divine attributes acquired during the integration, the process
of assimilation cannot be completed, since the meaning of the dictum regarding knowing God is part of a negative theology that
rejects the possibility of knowing God in a perfect way. It is note-
worthy that the integration is attained by the universalization of
the mind, though the object of this knowledge is not completely
clear. I doubt if Rabbi Naḥman refers to the philosophical sort of
understanding of the Forms, or Ideas, in the world; more likely, he
intends progress in knowing God.[71]

Rabbi Naḥman's views on integration are similar to those of

the Great Maggid and his circle. In both systems, union through *devekut* and integration are given the highest religious value. The differences between the two approaches are negligible, thus strengthening Green's critique of Weiss's typology of Hasidic mysticism.[72] (Weiss unilaterally limits the religious phenomenon of Rabbi Naḥman's thought to a religiosity of faith, versus the mysticism of contemplation and union of the school of the Great Maggid.)[73] Rabbi Naḥman's view is also very similar to Cordovero's. Both describe the elevation of the worlds in connection with the integration of the soul of the mystic.

A distinctive conception of union and *hitkalelut* is found in the writings of Komarno Hasidism. These nineteenth-century Hasidic masters worked up a synthesis between Hasidic mysticism and Lurianic Kabbalah that far exceeded the regular use of Lurianic motifs in the classical Hasidic types of thought. Consequently, in this mystical system, the soul's integration into the divine realm is only partial, given the necessity to maintain a certain aspect of individuality as the core of the theurgical activity so important in Lurianism and in the thought of the Komarno school. In the early nineteenth century, Rabbi Alexander Safrin of Komarno described Rabbi Akiva's martyrdom in a paradoxical fashion:

> Would he desire to strengthen the love and awe in his heart, and to cause his soul to cleave to his root, [in order to] cause the integration of the light of his higher soul in *Eiyn Sof*, blessed be He, his higher soul would certainly depart from him and ascend upwards . . . and would he do so, the sufferings would separate from him; but, out of his will and desire to perform the commandment,[74] . . . he maintained his soul with him so as to endure the sufferings. . . . He intended [mystical intention] during the recitation of the [prayer of] "Hear Israel," in order to unite his higher soul, namely to elevate his higher soul in the secret [i.e., in the realm] of the holiness of God, [an act that is tantamount to] the annihilation of his light in the light of *Eiyn Sof* . . . but it is known out of the words of our master, the holy Ar'i [namely, Isaac Luria] . . . that whoever sacrifices himself to die unifies the [sefirot of] *Tiferet* and *Malkhut* and whoever sacrifices himself for the sake of the holiness of God, unifies the [sefirot of] *Hokhmah* and *Binah*[75] but does not become a chariot in a perfect way unless he sacrifices himself for the sake of the Torah and commandments and for the sake of the holiness [of God] as R. Akiva actually did. . . . And his desire was to perform the act of sacrifice so as to become a perfect chariot for God, namely to elevate his soul into the holiness of God.[76]

The hierarchy of religious values is conspicuous in this discussion. Following the Lurianic way of thought and action, Rabbi Alexander gives importance to the theurgical impact of the symbolic self-sacrifice during the prayer. Greater than the self-sacrifice, however, is the mystical self-integration into God, which is preceded by an experience of *devekut*. Rabbi Alexander's approach recalls Cordovero's stand as expressed in *Shi'ur Komah* (analyzed earlier). Indeed, Rabbi Alexander presents the Cordoverian ideal of integration, which transcends the theurgical ideal, as extremely difficult to attain since only an actual sacrifice may enable someone to surpass his theurgical activity in favor of a more mystical achievement. The Safedian kabbalist did not require such an extreme act, but even in one of the most important strongholds of nineteenth-century Lurianism, Cordovero's theoretical scale of values is preferred here, at least de jure, to Luria's.

In his *Netiv Miẓvotekha*, Rabbi Isaac Jehudah Safrin of Komarno, the most important figure of Komarno Hasidism as well as the son of Rabbi Alexander, describes the capacity of Israel to annihilate in a complete way:

> Just like the Nought . . . and they stir all the worlds to return to the aspects of the Nought, and [then] the unification is attained, since all the aspects of unification and intercourse are an ascent to the aspect of *Eiyn Sof*. And [then] the worlds would be annihilated and would completely return to the Nought, to the aspect of *Eiyn Sof*. There, however, in this annihilation, is comprised also Israel, the holy nation, which necessarily has a body and a vessel and being and an ego that is necessary to the worship. This is the reason they [Israel] draw all the worlds so as they would not be completely annihilated.[77]

This understanding of the unique nature of Israel has the prerogative of preventing the attainment of the ultimate absorption of the world in the bosom of the Infinite because of the necessity of worship. Total annihilation would achieve the sublime mystical goal of complete union at the expense of the obliteration of the theurgical operation that needs the personality of the worshiper. As a Lurianic kabbalist and a halakhist, Rabbi Isaac recognized that the transcendence of the commandments in the name of a unitive ideal is highly problematic. He attempted to avoid it by assuming that the ritualistic essence of Israel is an obstacle in the way of an escapist mysticism. Although the difference between Rabbi Isaac and his father seems to be conspicuous, it is so only

in principle. Rabbi Alexander did not prescribe an actual self-sacrifice as a necessary ideal; therefore, like his son, he maintained
the Lurianic theurgical activity as a daily requirement for the kabbalist.

As seen above, the individual soul was integrated into the all-
comprehensive divine or quasi-divine realms. However, all the evidence is rather theoretical: none of the previously discussed texts
overtly confesses a personal experience of absorption as the result
of *devekut.* I shall now discuss two passages stemming from the
ecstatic kabbalah, where the experience of the universal enters a
more comprehensive realm. According to the anonymous kabbalist
who wrote *Sefer ha-Zeruf:*

> . . . when the sphere of the intellect is turned about by the Active
> Intellect, and man begins to enter it and ascends in the sphere
> which revolves upon itself, as the image of the ladder, and at the
> time of ascent his thoughts will be indeed transformed and all
> the images will change before him and nothing at all that he
> previously had will be left in his hands. Therefore, apart from
> the change in his nature and his formation he is as one who is
> translated from the power of sensation to the power of the in-
> tellect, and as one who is translated from the tellurian process
> to the process of burning fire. Finally, all the visions will change,
> and the imaginative apprehensions will be confused since in truth
> this sphere purifies and tests.[78]

The entering of the intellectual, according to this kabbalist, is
tantamount to the profound transformation of human nature into
an intellectual entity, being moved and transformed by the Active
Intellect. Interestingly, the images of entering, like those of ascending and being translated, apparently indicate a certain physical
phenomenon or experience that the mystic underwent. This change,
however, is not the mystic's final achievement; after death he may
reach the *Causa Causarum*, provided that he previously attained
the transformation into an intellectual being in the manner described.[79]

Another ecstatic kabbalist, Rabbi Isaac of Acre, testifies that
during a certain ecstatic experience, he was completely sure that
he had contact with the hand of Metatron, the main angelic mentor
of Jewish mystics: "The hand which I have seized and kissed was
for sure his hand. And I envisioned myself in the secret of the Universal that encompasses me just like the sphere encompasses the
globe of the earth."[80] According to the text, the contact with the

angel represents Rabbi Isaac's vision of himself as being encompassed by the Universal, which resembles the encompassing sphere of the world. The terminology used to refer to the comprehensive entity points to the highest realm in the divine world, the *Eiyn Sof*, which is portrayed in another passage as "encompassing everything."[81] Therefore, contact with the hand of the angel symbolizes the integration of the mystic in the *Eiyn Sof*.

Compare this illuminating description with another text of the same kabbalist from the same book:

> Now you, my son, strive to contemplate the supernal light since
> I have certainly introduced you into "the sea of the ocean" which
> encompasses the [whole] world. But be careful and guard your
> soul from gazing . . . lest you sink; and effort shall be [made] to
> contemplate but [at the same time] to escape from sinking. . . .
> Let your soul contemplate the divine light and certainly cleave
> to it, as long as she dwells in her palace [i.e., body].[82]

Here, *devekut* is a stage that precedes the more mystically advanced state of sinking in the divine ocean, which Rabbi Isaac describes in "comprehensive" imagery. Although he warns against suicidal mystical attempts, the context of Rabbi Isaac's text implies the positive value of entering the ocean. He attributes only to Moses the request to die an ecstatic death, something denied to him because of Israel's need of his leadership.

The view of an encounter with the divine as an entry into an encompassing entity corroborates the objective or theoretical descriptions that abound in the kabbalistic and Hasidic texts. Although it would be dangerous to extrapolate the possible experiential content of all the other discussions on *hitkalelut* from the previous two passages indicating the *experience* of penetration and contact with the divine, we may assume that similar experiences of penetrations were undergone by some of the authors previously mentioned.

Comparative Dimensions

Having briefly surveyed the two different types of relationship between the human and the divine, let us now focus on the theological backgrounds against which they developed. The universalization of the soul or of the intellect appears in philosophically oriented writings under the influence of the speculations of Rabbi Abraham ibn 'Ezra. *Mutatis mutandis,* only when the reigning theology is philosophical, defining God as totally spiritual and "simple" (namely not as a system of divine powers, as the sefirot are), does the mystic describe his assimilation to God, or to another supernal being, in terms of universalization. The human spiritual faculties cannot penetrate a realm in which the dimensions of differentiation and hierarchy are irrelevant. By purifying one's soul, or actualizing one's intellect, the mystic escapes the domain of limitation and multiplicity and becomes similar to the upper spiritual world.

On the other hand, the integration version of contact with the divine flourishes in the theosophical systems of thought. In these systems the dynamics of the various divine manifestations are crucial, and human beings may influence the processes on high by their acts below and by their participation through integration. Based upon an architectonics that can be compared only with the Gnostic systems, the kabbalistic theosophy implies the possibility of adding to the divine powers not only by the influx descending from above, namely from the Infinite, but also by the integration of human energy when it is directed correctly through the performance of the commandments with kabbalistic intention, or *kavvanah.* This ascent of energy is necessary, according to some important kabbalistic texts, to the well-being of the divine world. Therefore, the possibility of the integration of the soul is part of a larger scheme of the inclusion of powers and energy in the divine realm.

Another reason for the differences between the theologies that constitute the background for the universalization versus the integration types of union is the former's attitude to theurgy. This concept is seen as pointing to the capacity of human acts—in the case of the Jewish mystics, the commandments—to affect the divine realm. The medieval philosophical theologies, whether Neoplatonic or Aristotelian, assume a conception of the divine world in which no inner processes that are significantly dependent on human deeds take place. Although these two versions of theology allow an ongoing flow of divine essence outward or downward in the widespread concept of creation of the world by emanation, this dynamic must not be confused with the kabbalistic discussions of the intradivine dynamic, which is related to the processes taking place in the lower world. On this ground, the universalization of the soul or of the intellect is a process that metamorphoses the human but has no vital impact on the divine; universalization is a purely anthropocentric type of mysticism. Integration, on the other hand, combines the mystical achievement of the individual with a certain transformation of the divine. By entering the complicated sefirotic realm, the mystic contributes something to it, just as he does beforehand through the observance of the commandments. Integration is therefore part of a dynamic theosophy, just as universalization is meaningful only in the more static philosophical theologies.

These differences in the theologies are reflected also in the anthropology, in which the universalization process is at the same time a process of objectification. Becoming universal, and thus being able to influence the universe, is the effect of the absorption of the forms in the world and expands the spiritual capacity of man. His individuality is obliterated; even his personality is an obstacle to universalization and to his becoming a receptor and repository of the *intelligibilia*. In integralist mysticism we also find, and in a more articulated form, that self-annihilation is a precondition to integration. I assume that this brand of mysticism's annihilative process is related to the obliteration of the ego-centered psychic process in which the higher soul is liberated. The Jewish mystics considered the higher soul to be the core of man, the spark hidden in the person, which alone will experience the integration. In other words, the return of the divine core to its source, or its integration, is the return of God to himself or, as we have already seen, the restoration of the divine *Anthropos*.

An interesting paradox seems to emerge when we compare the ultimate fate of the human spiritual faculties in mystical experiences with the universalization and integration descriptions. In the process of becoming universal, the human soul (which originally stems from the universal soul and therefore preexists its mundane existence) returns to the source and fuses with it. When the universalization is related to the intellect, the philosophical and mystical texts assume that the actualization of the intellect is also its emergence from its potential phase. Unlike the Platonic view of the soul, the Aristotelian understanding of the intellect only rarely assumes its preexistence. Nevertheless, as recognized long ago by the critiques of the Aristotelian theory of survival of the intellect, the actualization, or objectification, of the human faculty renders it as close to the supernal intellects as possible and obliterates the individual features of any particular intellect. The repersonalization of the intellect occurs because it loses its higher status under the influence of corporeal functions.

On the other side, the preexistent souls, or the cores of the souls that are integrated in the divine realm, are only rarely thought of as disappearing into the divine realm because of the obliteration of their uniqueness. Although the souls are divine from the very beginning, their return to their source, even their integration into it, fails to totally bridge the remaining gap between the souls and the realm. The texts assume that preexistence involves the existence of a *principium individuatorum*, and the return to the origin does not take place at the expense of this principle. In other words, without the presumption of a preexistent principle, it is hard to maintain the individual survival of either the soul or the intellect after its objectivization, whereas the presupposition of the divine nature of the soul, coupled with the assumption that a certain enduring core is present in the human psyche, ensures the survival of individuality even after an integration experience. Another way to express this difference is connected to the need of a certain amount of individuality for the purpose of divine service, and thus a polarity of the agent versus the action. The philosophical epistemologies, on the other hand, tend to reduce the importance of action in general, limiting the meaningful relationship to that of the knower and the knowing process and thereby substantially reducing the polarity to such an extent that in the perfect act of knowledge, which is from the mystical perspective a unitive experience, the distinction between the agent and the action is obliterated.

At this final phase of our discussion let me address a crucial part of the problems posed by the movement of the *devekut* ideal to the center of the mystical life in Judaism. The restructuring of the classical spiritual configuration of Jewish life by the emphasis on cleaving to God could generate antinomian tendencies, or at least frictions, between the halakhocentric version of Judaism and its mystical interpretations. However, this potentiality did not explode in a significant way as far as the subject of *devekut* is concerned. To the extent antinomianism stems from kabbalistic sources, it is connected to those components of kabbalistic thought that come to the fore as messianic impulses become dominant.

What is there in the overemphasis on *devekut* that might have exploded as antinomianism? First is that the direct contact with divinity could be, and indeed had been, regarded as higher than the halakhic imperative, which is focused on performance of the commandments. The transcendence of the regular human state of consciousness could easily be understood as the surpassing of the common religious life in order to sustain religious life on a higher level. As far as I know, no Jewish mystic formulated this possibility, or danger, on the basis of the superiority of *devekut* to the other forms of religious life. The commandments were considered obsolete in the various Sabbatian ideologies because of the assumption of entry into another aeon, the messianic one, when the religious requirements would be different from those in the premessianic time.[83] Nowhere is *devekut* a significant reason for the transgressions cultivated by the followers of Sabbatai Sevi.

On the contrary, *devekut* is presented as a conservative value, as we can learn, for example, by reading Rabbi Mordekhai of Nadworna. Explaining the sense of the verse "and thou shall cleave to Him," this late nineteenth-century Ukrainian Hasidic master asserts that the imperative of cleaving is the single positive commandment in the entire Torah; it is this imperative that "maintains any Jew," or, as Rabbi Mordekhai put it in Yiddish: "In dus stelt dem ganzen Id oif di fis."[84] Indeed, this far-reaching evaluation of *devekut* as the most important single commandment does not define the specific content of the concept, leaving it open to an extreme mystical interpretation as well as a much more moderate one. Taking into account the traditions concerning the long periods of time the members of this Hasidic family spend in a state of *ecstasis*,[85] a rather extreme interpretation would seem more congenial, but no conclusive solution can be proposed. From the literary and sociological context it is obvious that even such a strong understanding of the centrality of *devekut* does not imply any antinomian connotations.

Devekut has played a conservative role in kabbalah and Hasidism for two main reasons. First, most of the masters of kabbalah were the product of high rabbinic culture; for them, kabbalah was not an alternative to their earlier modus vivendi, nor was it a new modus operandi. For authors such as Naḥmanides, Rabbi Shelomo ben Abraham ibn Adret, Rabbi Joseph Karo, or the Gaon of Vilna, the kabbalah's real contribution was its raising the awareness of the Jew to the ultimate goal of the Jewish *regimen vitae*. Far from being conceived of as antagonistic or alternative to the halakho-centric way of life, kabbalah was regarded as the culmination of a life of studies. It enabled the advanced rabbinic student to understand the mystical raison d'être or his daily religious life. Therefore *devekut*, which was part of the kabbalistic ideals, could not be separated and cultivated in a vacuum; it had to be integrated in the already absorbed axiological structure. Even as the highest mystical value, *devekut* was not severed from the spiritual configuration that constituted their frame of mind. In other words, most of the theosophical kabbalists regarded the attainment of a state of *devekut* not as a mystical value per se but as the culmination of their observance of the commandments, an achievement far from contrary to halakhic performance. Furthermore, a significant number of the famous kabbalists and Hasidic mystics were also leaders of communities with all the responsibilities involved in being the religious and spiritual guides of a flock.

On the other hand, the ecstatic kabbalah proposed mystical techniques that are essentially anomean, that is to say, they do not use the commandments as an avenue to attain mystical union but combinations of letters and recitations of the divine names, together with breathing devices of incantational practices.[86] To a certain extent, this brand of kabbalah was indifferent, though not antagonistic to, the regular Jewish way of life as a mystical vehicle. Thus it found a way to accommodate the Jewish ritual without undermining its relevance for the common believer. Since the ideal of *devekut* was reserved to the few, it could, and indeed was, absorbed even by later theosophical kabbalists. Cordovero did this by envisioning this layer of kabbalistic practices as the crown of the studies of kabbalah, not as an alternative to the classical theosophical texts.[87]

It is more complicated to explain the rarity of the escapist potentialities inherent in the practice of unitive experiences. Abraham Abulafia, the first ideologue of extreme types of union, regarded the immersion in the state of *devekut* as the summum bonum, but, strangely enough, he was the most active of the thirteenth-century kabbalists, considering himself a prophet destined to enlighten not only his coreligionists but also the Christians. His self-consciousness as a public messiah demonstrates that immersion in an escapist type of contemplation was congruent with intense public activities. Also, according to Rabbi Isaac Jehudah Safrin of Komarno, presented earlier, the total annihilation of the spiritual core is not advisable precisely because of the necessity of worship.[88]

The reluctance of the Jewish mystics to escape this world in a final absorptive union with the Godhead has, in my view, nothing to do with the nature of the unitive experience. The fact that the mystics indicate, implicitly or explicitly, that man must return to this world and to continue functioning in society or in the framework of religious regulations does not imply that their experiences did not consist, in their eyes, in a complete, though temporary, union with God. The issue of the temporality of mystical experience must be emphasized, given the widespread opinion among various modern scholars writing on Jewish mysticism that the Hasidic masters, glorifying the extreme state of *devekut*, could conflict with the requirements of the halakhah. With rare exceptions, extreme mystical experiences are short events, notwithstanding their possible lasting effect. There are no problems about the submission of the Hasidic masters to the halakhic regulations when they come back from their excursions into the divine. At most, intense mystical experience may paralyze the mystic for a short while, but this state is no more than an intermezzo between the periods of awareness that precede and follow the experience. The same is true of the overemphasis on the passivity of the Hasidic masters; it can be considered a pause between their regular activities, and even during such pauses there is evidence of the ongoing performance of the commandments.[89]

We may cast some of the previous remarks in psychological terms as used by Erich Neumann. In Jewish mysticism the escapist tendency is totally negligible, though there are still expressions of inner experiences in bold unitive terms. In Neumann's categories, kabbalistic and Hasidic mysticism avoid that type of experience characterized as uroboric mysticism. Entering or reentering God was not presented by the Jewish mystics as a fusion that mounts to a total dissolution of the personality, from which there is no return, nor has this experience the terrible aspects of the absorption in the Great Mother. Notwithstanding the expansion of the human soul or intellect and the contact or union with a supernal being, the center, or the core, of the ego is never totally obliterated; on the contrary, it sometimes becomes omnipotent and capable of dominating nature much more than before the mystical experience. Hence, the mystic does not sever his relationship to the world, but he changes the situation from one of being dominated by nature to one of dominating it. Thus, we may characterize Jewish mysticism as a "world-transforming mysticism" (to use again Neumann's phrase), even in those cases when extreme unifying expressions are to be found, including the consummation imagery of the Ḥabad school. No mention of the dissolution of the mystical core of the personality is to be found. It is pertinent to quote Neumann's description of transformative mysticism for more than one reason:

> Normally the ego, transformed by the experience of the numinous, returns to the sphere of human life, and its transformation includes a broadening of consciousness . . . whenever the ego returns

to the sphere of human life, transformed by the mystical experience, we may speak of an immanent world-transforming mysticism.[90]

The congeniality of Neumann's description to Jewish mysticism is not a matter of coincidence.[91] The author, writing in Israel, draws most of the examples illustrating his appreciation of world-transforming mysticism from Jewish mystical sources, most of them Hasidic.[92] To what extent this concept of mysticism is central to other types of mysticism occurring in other religions is a matter to be examined by experts. Here it is enough to note that Neumann's distinction between absorptive and nonabsorptive types of mysticism, the first considered to be much more positive or "high" than the other, reflects an axiology already in existence in the Jewish understanding of mysticism.

Love, Knowledge and Unio Mystica in the Western Christian Tradition

BERNARD McGINN

May they all be one. Father may they be one in us, as you are in me and I am in you. (Jn. 17:21)

All ideals of Christian perfection, and mysticism is certainly one of these, are forms of response to the presence of God, a presence that is not open, evident, or easily accessible but one that is always in some way mysterious or hidden. When that hidden presence becomes the subject of some form of "immediate" experience,[1] we can begin to speak of mysticism in the proper sense of the term. The responses of the human subject to the divine presence have been discussed theologically in a variety of ways and according to many different models and paradigms, such as contemplation or vision of God, rapture or ecstasy, deification, living in Christ, the birth of the Word in the soul, radical obedience to the will of God, and especially union with God. All of these responses, which have rarely been mutually exclusive, can be called mystical in that they are ways of expressing the experience of divine presence. The mys-

A shorter version of this essay was published under the same title in *Church History* 57 (1987): 7–24. I would like to thank Richard Kieckhefer, Robert E. Lerner, Kent Emery, and Ellen Babinsky for attentive reading and helpful suggestions. Given the extensive nature of the apparatus, some texts will be cited according to the most available modern English version where this also includes a reference to the best edition of the original text.

ticism of union is just one of the species of a wider and more diverse genus or group.

Nevertheless, *unio mystica* has played a key role in the history of Christian mysticism and in reflection on its meaning. The classic schools of mystical authors in the Western Church from the twelfth through the sixteenth century used the language of union with God as the favored way of characterizing the goal of their beliefs and practices. The ways in which they understood union, however, were both varied and complex.

A good deal of the complexity in Christian understandings of *unio mystica* arises from the relation of union to the spiritual powers of the conscious subject, that is, to the faculties of intellect and will. The mystics spent much time analyzing the respective roles of love and knowledge in the path to mystical union, as well as the ways in which affection and intellect may or may not be present within union itself, both the union attainable in this life and the perfect union to be enjoyed in the life to come. To understand something of the richness of Western Christian concepts of union with God, it is necessary, however cursorily, to follow the interactions between changing notions of union and the ways in which love and knowledge relate to these both as *means* and as *end*.

There are, then, at least four related issues implied by our title. First, what understandings of union with God were found in Western Christian mystics between the twelfth and the sixteenth century? Second, what roles were assigned to love and knowledge in the process leading to union? Third, in what sense may love and/ or knowledge be said to be present within the experience or state of union attainable in this life? Fourth, in what sense is love and/ or knowledge present in the union to be enjoyed in heaven? Our concentration will be on the first three issues, though obviously the influence of the fourth area, the conception of heavenly bliss, cannot be excluded. While not all the mystics of this period have left us analyses of the whole range of issues involved, a broad picture can be presented on the basis of an investigation of some major mystical authors from this golden age of Western Christian mysticism.

The complex interaction of these four themes had a long history prior to the twelfth century. In the Christian Scriptures, a number of Johannine texts (e.g., *Jn.* 17:21) present the goal of the new life offered in Jesus as a form of union with God. Other Johannine passages stress that because God is love it is only through loving him that we become as he is (e.g., *1 Jn.* 4:1–19). In his famous hymn to love in *1 Corinthians* 13, Paul emphasized that all spiritual gifts, including knowledge (*gnosis*—v. 8), will come to an end; love *(agape)* alone will remain. But verse 12 of the same passage promises some kind of knowing in heaven: "The knowledge that I now have is imperfect; but then I shall know as fully as I am known." There was ample material in Scripture to fuel subsequent speculation on the nature of union and its relation to love and knowledge.

The rich heritage of Greek religious and philosophical thought about the relation of the soul to the Highest God, or First Principle, also contributed much, directly and indirectly, to Christian reflection on love, knowledge, and mystical union. Although Plato defined the goal of the true lover of wisdom mostly in terms of contemplation *(theoria)* rather than union, his analyses of the roles of both knowing and loving in the ascent to the vision of the Good anticipate much that is later found in Christian mystical theory.[2] A Neoaristotelian tradition of rational mysticism emphasizing the gradual perfecting of the human intellect until it attains union with God the Self-Thinking Thought was an important development of late antiquity, though one that was to be more influential in Judaism and Islam than in Christianity.[3] Of major significance for Christian mysticism was the thought of the greatest Greek mystic, Plotinus (204–70 C.E.), who made union *(henosis)* understood as merging or essential identity central to his teaching.[4] Plotinus absorbed the Neoaristotelian notion of intellectual union with Pure Thought and Being *(nous)*;[5] but, since *nous* itself as the second hypostasis is dependent on the primal hypostasis or the One *(to hen)*, the ultimate goal of the mystic is the return to absolute union with the One through the power of love *(eros)*, or "loving intellect" *(nous eron)*.[6] Although love is superior to intellect in Plotinus's mystical theory, love is not without a form of knowing.

A full history of Christian ideas of mystical union is too extensive for any single essay. The analysis that follows will focus on Latin Christianity between the twelfth and the sixteenth century, a period that saw some of the richest and most influential thinking in this area.

The Entrance of Union Language into Western Mysticism

Before the twelfth century in the West, union was not the basic category for the description of the experience of the presence of God in this life. Augustine, despite his dependence upon Plotinus, knows nothing of union.[7] This may well hint at a polemic reaction of the Christian mystic to the pagan one. The African doctor speaks of "*touching* Eternal Wisdom," or "*beholding* Eternal Wisdom," or "*cleaving* to [divine] unity" in this life[8] but not of union itself. Augustine does, however, stress the mutuality of both love and knowledge in the perfected soul of the "spiritual person" (*1 Cor.* 2:15): "Because he is above all things when he is with God, he judges all things. He is with God when he understands with perfect purity and loves with total charity what he understands."[9]

The other major sources of early Latin mysticism are also chary of using the language of union. Cassian, like his master Evagrius Ponticus, is greatly interested in the forms of contemplation leading to pure prayer,[10] but unlike Evagrius he does not dwell on union with God. Gregory the Great, the third master of traditional Latin mysticism, also disregards it.[11]

In the twelfth century analysis of the nature of union with God and the role of love and knowledge in achieving it became widespread. The reasons for this shift are not fully evident, but some factors can be mentioned. Greek patristic sources that became popular in the twelfth century, most notably the *De mystica theologia* of the Pseudo-Dionysius, as well as some texts of Maximus the Confessor, make use of the notion of union as the goal of the ascent to God;[12] but the turn toward desire to be one with God cannot be reduced merely to an issue of reading old texts, however weighty the apostolic authority of Dionysius was. The explosion of systematic expositions of mystical theology at the time, as well as the appearance of personal descriptions of rapture and union, bear witness to a broad new interest in the mystical life found especially, but by no means exclusively, among the new orders of Cistercians and Victorines. In the dynamic mediation between text and context in the history of Christian mysticism, we cannot afford to neglect either side.

Bernard of Clairvaux, the central figure among the Cistercians, is the best starting point, not only because of the explicit attention he gave to the question, but also because his fame and sanctity gave him a canonical status among later mystics and mystical theologians. In his *De diligendo Deo*, probably written in the 1130s, the abbot presents his famous four degrees of the ascent of charity and discusses the union with God that is the goal of this journey. Bernard's doctrine is basically Pauline, with a strong dependence on *1 Corinthians* 6:17—"Who cleaves to the Lord is one spirit with him" ("Qui autem adhaeret Domino, unus spiritus est").[13] The three metaphors that Bernard uses to express the union—the drop of water in a vat of wine, the iron heated in the fire, and the air transformed into sunshine (all in use in philosophical and theological discussion for more than a millennium before Bernard wrote)[14]— suggest some form of fusion of substance between man and God. But this is exactly what the abbot is anxious to avoid, since he insists that "the [human] substance remains, but in another form."[15] Taking this text together with other Bernardine discussions of union with God, especially in *Sermo in Cantica* 71,[16] we can characterize the abbot's notion of union with God as primarily an affective, operational union of willing and loving, an *unitas spiritus*, not an ontological union of essence or substance. It is tempting to think that the detail of the abbot's discussions of union imply that he thought that some had or were likely to have incorrect ideas on the issue.

The *Sermones in Cantica* insist that the only power by which humans can deal reciprocally with God is love and that marital love is the highest form, the love that best expresses union.[17] This insistence, joined with Bernard's well-known itineraries of the ascent of love,[18] have been the grounds for the description of the abbot's system as one of affective mysticism. We must not forget, though, that for Bernard the ascent to union, as well as union itself, involves our powers of knowing too. Bernard does not tell us much about how love and knowledge are actually related in whatever momentary attainment of *unitas spiritus* is possible in this life; but he does insist, along with Gregory the Great, that "love itself is a form of knowing" ("amor ipse notitia est") to show that the powers of the intellect as well as those of the will are fulfilled in the marital embrace.[19] His teaching here shows fidelity to both Gregory and Augustine.

Bernard's contemporary and friend, William of Saint-Thierry, shares and deepens his approach. William discusses union with God in some detail, using the Pauline *unus spiritus* formula from a Trinitarian perspective that identifies this union with the activity of the third divine Person.[20] Like Bernard, William insists that there is no transmutation into the divine nature,[21] and he finds in the marital imagery of the *Song of Songs*, specifically in the embrace of lover and beloved (*Song* 2:6), which he identifies with the Holy Spirit, a fitting image for this union.[22] William also stresses the role of love in the process of ascent. As Odo Brooke showed, he sketches out a twofold path to union, an intellectual ascent (*credo ut intelligam*) and an affective ascent (*credo ut experiar*) that he attempts to fuse in his concept of the *ratio fidei*.[23] William loves to cite the Gregorian dictum in the form "amor ipse intellectus est."[24] For Jean Déchanet and others, the equation of *amor* with a form of knowledge is a crucial element in William's mystical thought.[25] It should be noted that *intellectus*, not *ratio*, is the word he uses, thus indicating a higher, intuitive awareness beyond conceptual knowing. Déchanet takes issue with Étienne Gilson, who claimed that William was really speaking metaphorically when he said that love was a form of knowing.[26] Déchanet also denies the view of Pierre Rousselot, who thought that the ecstatic love of mystical theologians like William led to a confused identity of knowledge and appetite.[27]

What William teaches might be best described as an *intelligentia amoris*, neither confused identity nor mere metaphor but a mutual interpenetration of love and knowledge on a higher level.[28] In explaining the relation of the two operations in his *Expositio* on the *Song of Songs*, William says: "In the contemplation of God where love is chiefly operative, reason *passes into love* and *is transformed* into a certain spiritual and divine *understanding* which transcends and *absorbs* all reason."[29] This text is a lapidary formulation of what we can call the transformative or subsuming pattern of the intellect-love relation in the path to union—that is, love is higher than knowing, but the height of love attained in the *unio mystica* includes a transformed knowing. Although both the context and the content have important differences that should not be neglected, the parallel with Plotinus's *nous eron* is striking.

Other Cistercians, such as Isaac of Stella in his *Epistola de Anima*, present a similar, if less evolved, picture. Love and knowledge are described as the two feet by which the soul journeys towards its encounter with God.[30] The four stages of the advance of love accompany the five of the advance of knowledge, though the abbot is more interested in the intellectual path.[31] Gilbert of Hoyland, the continuator of Bernard's sermons on the *Song of Songs*, also has valuable remarks on the relation between love and union.[32]

The Victorines share the same approach. Hugh of Saint Victor is traditional in his concentration upon *contemplatio* and his general avoidance of speculation on the nature of union with God. In book 6 of his *In Hierarchiam caelestem* he insists that it is love rather than knowledge that is the means of our union with God,[33] and two of his spiritual opuscula, *De amore sponsi ad sponsam* and *Soliloquium de arrha animae*, freely use the imagery of union of lover and beloved found in the *Song of Songs*.[34]

That great systematizer, Richard of Saint Victor, is also wary of using the term *unio* in his two great "how-to" treatises on contemplation, though these include detailed discussions of the relation of love and knowledge in mystical ascent. *The Twelve Patriarchs*, or *Benjamin Minor*, lays out a map of the gradual perfecting of the affective and intellectual powers of the rational soul up to the level of the birth of Benjamin, or ecstatic contemplation. Marital imagery suggesting union is used,[35] but Richard's interest centers on *excessus*, the passing beyond and above reason. The *Benjamin Minor* is particularly important for its teaching about the relation of love and knowledge in the path to ecstatic contemplation. Richard insists throughout that love and knowledge have mutually supporting roles as the ascent proceeds. "So the more Judah [i.e., ordered love of celestial things] grows . . . the greater there burns in Rachel the desire to give birth, which is the pursuit of knowing."[36] And even if the birth of Benjamin involves the death of Rachel, his mother, it is still significant that it is from Rachel *(ratio)* and not Leah *(affectus)* that he is born.[37]

In *The Mystical Ark (Benjamin Major)*, Richard concentrates on the divisions of contemplation, especially its highest stages, in greater detail and with more use of erotic imagery.[38] Again, no explicit treatment of union occurs, though attention is given to the mutuality of love and knowledge in the journey to God.[39] Like Bernard, Richard finds the *unus spiritus* formula of *1 Corinthians* 6:17 a perfect expression for the joining of human and divine that takes place in the marital embrace.[40]

It is only in turning to some of the Victorine's shorter treatises dealing with *caritas* that we find explicit treatment of the nature of the union suggested by the erotic imagery found in the other works. The treatise *De quatuor gradibus violentae caritatis*, that profound discussion of the paradoxical relation of sacred and profane love, does not spend much time discussing exactly what the "total transition into God" might be;[41] but it is interesting to see that the primary example used for the third, or marital, level is that of the liquefaction of an iron bar in fire,[42] one of the traditional metaphors used by Bernard in his discussion of union of wills in the *De Diligendo Deo*. The Pauline *unus spiritus* text also appears.[43] In the brief treatise *De gradibus caritatis* we find an extended treatment of what kind of *unitas* the soul enjoys with God.[44] It should come as no surprise that here Richard is in fundamental agreement with Bernard's understanding of *unitas spiritus*[45] and that he makes use of another of the standard union images, that of the drop of water diffused in wine.[46] Richard goes beyond Bernard in joining his use of fire imagery to the *cor liquefactum* of *Psalms* 21:15, seeing the text as implying an interior melting into God in love that is superior to any exterior *raptus*.[47] The Victorine agrees with William of Saint-Thierry in analyzing the relations between love and knowledge. Love is the superior "eye" of the soul in that it can "wound" God,[48] but love and knowledge work together on the mystic path in such a way that "the more we recognize the grace of perfection, the more ardently we also desire it, and the wider we burn for love, the more perfect our illumination to recognition."[49]

Conflicts over Mystical Union in the Later Middle Ages

Mystical union and its relation to love and knowledge were widely discussed, both implicitly and explicitly, in the thirteenth century.[50] The great heir of the twelfth-century mystical theology concerning union and the path to it was Bonaventure, the Franciscan doctor, especially in his masterpiece, the *Itinerarium mentis in Deum*.[51] Although the seraphic doctor's favorite terms to discuss the goal of the spiritual ascent are *raptus* with respect to this life and *beatitudo* with respect to the life to come,[52] he can also describe this goal in the language of union adapted from chapter 1 of Dionysius's *De mystica theologia*.[53]

Good Scholastic that he was, Bonaventure had a precise understanding of the different ways in which union is to be understood, as a glance at the treatment of the mode of union of the Incarnation found in his *Commentaria in quatuor libros sententiarum* shows.[54] The *Sentence Commentary* also makes it clear that the affective joining of God and human that is brought about through charity never takes away the dignity of our personhood.[55] Thus, we can never be said to be "one with God" in a univocal sense,[56] because any affirmation of oneness with the divine nature is incorrect without the addition of some determination or qualification, like *unus "spiritus."*

How did the Franciscan conceive of the relation of love and knowledge to the *raptus* experienced in mystical union? Bonaventure's intricate map of the ascent of the soul's six powers to God in the *Itinerarium* is well known. All the intellectual powers are brought to bear in this journey, but affectivity goes beyond intellect: "In this passing over, if it is to be perfect, all intellectual activities must be *left behind* and the height of our affection *(apex affectus)* must be totally transferred and transformed into God."[57] It is evident that the *apex affectus*, or *apex mentis*, the sixth and final level of the ascent, surpasses the *intelligentia* that can know the Divine Unity identified with *esse* and the Trinity as *bonitas*.[58] This suggests that in comparison with his twelfth-century predecessors, Bonaventure took a more negative view of the role of any form of knowing in the experience of union. But some scholars have argued that the Franciscan's thought about the role of knowledge in the mystical goal still contains a subsuming aspect, that is, that the transcendent love of *unitas spiritus* includes a transformed presence of its intellectual foundations. Étienne Gilson claimed that for Bonaventure *excessus mentis*, while primarily affective, could be characterized as a kind of "intellectualized affectivity."[59] A text from the third book of the *Sentence Commentary* suggests this when it says, "This is the most excellent knowledge *(cognitio excellentissima)* which Dionysius teaches. It consists in ecstatic love and it transcends the knowledge of faith according to the common mode."[60]

Nevertheless, the ambiguity of Bonaventure's thought on the presence of knowing in the unitive experience raises a significant issue in the history of Christian mysticism. It has been commonplace among scholars to detect a turn toward greater emphasis on affectivity and a growing distrust of reason and intellect in later medieval mysticism.[61] To evaluate the legitimacy of this view, it will be helpful to set forth some general theses about the roles of loving and knowing in Christian mysticism before turning to an investigation of some representative authors.

Christian mystical theology is based upon the twin premises of the unknowability of God on the one hand and his accessibility to love on the other. It is extremely difficult to find any Christian theology of mysticism that is not affective in the sense of giving love an important role in human striving toward God. Few, if any, Christian mystical theologies can be described as purely intellectual, as the discussion of Meister Eckhart will show. Thus, the way to understand the variation to be found among Christian mystical theologians is not through any simple division between affective and intellectual mystics but through a study of how they understand the *relations* between love and knowledge on every stage of the mystic path. The following four propositions can help guide such investigation:

1. God is unknowable in the sense that the divine nature cannot be grasped through rational discursive thought.
2. Love has a special access to God because God is love and because he bestows his own form of loving on human persons so that they may love him in return.
3. The love by which we grasp or attain God includes a form of intuitive "knowing" *(intelligentia, intellectus)* superior to reason *(ratio)*.
4. This form of knowing *subsumes* the lower aspects of the reasoning process into the higher, transformed state.

The first proposition is shared by most forms of theistic mysticism, however differently they may express it. The second is common to Christian mystics but also has notable analogies in many non-Christian forms of mysticism, especially in Judaism and Islam. The third proposition has often been thought to mark a division between early medieval mystics (who would admit it) and the new "affective" mystics of the later Middle Ages (who would not). However, a close look at two of the most influential of the late medieval affective mystics suggests that in most cases it is on the basis of the final proposition that one can distinguish some important changes in later medieval mystical theory.

Thomas Gallus, who became abbot of Vercelli and died in 1246, is one of the overlooked figures in the history of Christian mysticism.[62] This last great Victorine was a prolific commentator who began his writing career with reflections on the vision of the sixth chapter of *Isaiah* and finished it with extensive *Explanationes* of the Dionysian corpus and two large commentaries on the *Song of Songs*. Gallus gives the soul a hierarchical structure in which the highest level, the Seraphic, is designated as the *affectio principalis*. Basing his position on a text from *De divinis nominibus* 7.1,[63] he holds that there are two distinct ways of knowing God: the *theoricus intellectus*, by which we know intelligible things and through them God as cause; and the *affectio principalis*, or *apex affectionis*, where *unitio* with God takes place. The former is the world of rational theology, which even the pagans could attain;[64] the latter belongs to the realm of *theologia mystica*, which has two main divisions and essential textbooks: the *theorica*, or negative aspect, based on the writings of the Pseudo-Dionysius, and the *practica*, or positive aspect, based on the language of love found in the *Song of Songs*.

Two things should be noted about this influential system. First,

Gallus's language about the relation of knowing to loving in the ascent to God frequently stresses a rather sharp separation, or cutting off, of all intellectual operations,[65] although he is still ready to speak of the high point of love as a *superintellectualis cognitio*.[66] For Gallus and his followers, affective union no longer seems as interested in subsuming the lower forms of intellectual activity as it is in kicking them downstairs. The change is perhaps a subtle one, but on the mystic path subtle shifts can have far-reaching results. The second thing to note is how Gallus understands *unio*, or *unitio*, as he prefers to call it. A study of his use of the word in the *Song of Songs* commentaries indicates that he takes it, not in terms of ontological unity with the divine being, but rather to indicate transcendent union of wills, as the constant imagery of love suggests.[67] In other words, Gallus's understanding of the relation of God and the human person in union is quite traditional, despite the innovations we find in his teaching about the roles of love and knowledge.

However important Gallus's place in the creation of an "antirational" understanding of the path to union with God in the later Middle Ages, we must not exaggerate the differences between this tendency and that of the major authors of the twelfth century. A failure to discriminate between the issues involved in the third and fourth propositions previously outlined has led to many skewed presentations of the development of late medieval views on the relation of love and knowledge to *unio mystica*. Gallus disagrees with earlier authors on the fourth, not on the third, proposition, and the same holds true in more subtle fashion in the case of one of the masterpieces of late medieval mysticism, *The Cloud of Unknowing*.[68]

Like Thomas Gallus, the anonymous author of the *Cloud*, writing around 1370, was heavily dependent upon the Dionysian corpus; like Gallus, too, he interpreted the Pseudo-Dionysius in an affective way. A rapid reading of the *Cloud* might easily lead to the conclusion that the author is rigidly anti-intellectual, not only because of his insistence that "it is love alone that can reach God in this life, and not knowing,"[69] but also because of his at times sharp attacks on theologians.[70] But a close reading of this text, as well as of the other treatises of this great English mystical theologian,[71] shows this to be a mistaken view. William Johnston has discussed the issue in detail,[72] showing that the *Cloud* author both appreciated the role of reason in its own sphere and also maintained at least some intellectual aspect to the "dart of love" that alone can penetrate the cloud of unknowing that stands between us and God.[73] Still, it seems there are differences that set off the writings of the *Cloud* author from the Cistercian and Victorine mystics he knew so well. Even Johnston admits a tendency toward searching for a clear line of division between the role of intellect and of will not found in twelfth-century mystical writers,[74] and the issues may well go deeper than that. As an heir to the Aristotelian Scholastic world with its heavy emphasis on the discursive role of *ratio*, the power of conceptualizing sense impressions, the *Cloud* author appears to have had less appreciation for the higher dimension of human knowing that the twelfth-century mystical theorists had discussed under the Platonic epistemological terms of *intellectus* and *intelligentia*. One can sense at times in the *Cloud* and related writings an ambivalence in vocabulary that makes it more difficult for the author to express the role of supereminent understanding and its relation to more lowly forms of human desire for truth.[75] It is also telling that the author parts company with many earlier authors, including Thomas Aquinas, on the superiority of the mixed life of action and contemplation in relation to the life of pure contemplation.[76]

The *Cloud* contains profound reflections on the nature of the union that love can attain in this life. Bernard would have approved the careful way in which the author analyzes the Pauline *unus spiritus* in chapter 67.[77] Although the description of union in chapter 68 as an encounter with the Nothing that is Everything in a spiritual nowhere is reminiscent of the apophatic language of the new conception of *unitas indistinctionis* to be discussed later,[78] the *Cloud's* treatment of union, like that of Gallus, emphasizes an operational identity of willing and loving rather than any ontological or substantial merging.[79] In chapter 71 the author advances an important distinction between two kinds of union presented in the figures of Moses and Aaron—the first experienced God in ecstasy after the effort of climbing the mountain; the second, as a priest in the temple, could taste the divine presence at any time.[80]

The traditional character of the *Cloud* author's understanding of union is worth noting, because a new and suspect view of *unio mystica* had arisen in the thirteenth century and was much discussed throughout the later Middle Ages. This new tendency emphasizing essential or ontological union between God and the soul is remarkably close to the conception of union found in the writings of Plotinus and Proclus, but once again there is no evidence that acquaintance with old texts was what inspired important changes in the history of Western Christian mysticism. Rather, we may surmise that Neoplatonic notions of the union of identity or indistinction provided helpful experiential and explanatory categories for some thirteenth-century mystics and their interpreters.

The teaching authority of the Church was uncomfortable with this new understanding of union. A group of heretics present in Swabia in the early 1270s were attacked, among other things, for claiming "that the soul is taken from God's substance."[81] In the early fourteenth century papal authority condemned Meister Eckhart and the Free Spirit heretics, and in the fifteenth century Jean Gerson claimed that such views originated with the heretic Amalric of Bène (d. 1209).[82]

This new tendency did not begin with Eckhart, though he is its foremost theoretical exponent. We find it in some of the woman mystics of the thirteenth and early fourteenth centuries, such as the three Beguine vernacular writers, Hadewijch of Brabant, Mechthild of Magdeburg, and Marguerite Porete.[83] A brief look at these representative women has much to tell us about this decisive change in Western Christian mysticism.

Hadewijch, a Netherlands Beguine active about the middle of the thirteenth century, was not only a literary genius in both prose and verse but also a woman of considerable theological education and sophistication. The teaching on *unio mystica* contained in her letters, visions, and poems reveals itself as a highly charged affective, indeed erotic, relation between God and the soul. Letter 9, for instance, speaks of the "wondrous sweetness [with which] the loved one and the Beloved dwell one in the other, and how they penetrate each other in such a way that neither of the two distinguishes himself from the other." But, like Bernard, she goes on to insist that "they are both one thing through each other, but at the same time remain two separate selves."[84] Letter 16 calls love the glue "whereby God and the blessed soul are united together."[85] Numerous other texts clearly express the traditional notion of union as *unitas spiritus*[86] or else may be said to imply it.[87]

There are some passages in her writings, however, that speak of "becoming God" in rather untraditional and more daring ways.[88] Hadewijch's concrete and frequently erotic visions are also at times described as leading to a height where all sense of difference or distinction between Lover and Beloved is lost.[89] In one vision she speaks of union in terms of "flowing back *(regiratio)* through the

Godhead itself,"[90] language that suggests the Neoplatonic understanding of *unitas indistinctionis* that was to be developed by Meister Eckhart.

Mechthild of Magdeburg (ca. 1207–ca. 1282) received her mystical vocation at a young age and lived a long life, first as a Beguine and in her later years as a Cistercian nun at the famous convent of Helfta.[91] Her writings collected as *Das fliessende Licht der Gotheit (The Flowing Light of Godhead)*, are impressive witnesses to the Frauenbewegung, or women's movement, of the thirteenth century.[92]

Mechthild frequently speaks of union *(einunge, vereinicheit, herzeeinunge)*, using a wide variety of images and metaphors that had a rich history in Middle High German mystical literature.[93] Like Hadewijch, she is an unwearied advocate of the importance of love on the path to God. One of the poems scattered through the generally brief chapters of her work apostrophizes love as: "O blessed Love, whose mission was and is/To unite God to the human soul."[94] Unlike the Dutch Beguine, who had a highly developed understanding of the relation of love and knowledge at least in part dependent on twelfth-century sources, Mechthild shows little theoretical treatment of issues involving faculty psychology. Although she always insists that pure love is superior to all knowledge and learning,[95] some passages mention an illuminated knowledge *(bekantnisse)* that Divine Love reveals to the soul. This indicates that she probably would not have denied that "amor ipse notitia est."[96]

Mechthild's descriptions of *unio mystica* are highly imagistic and poetic, with particular fondness for metaphors of fire,[97] though more abstract terms and discussions are not totally lacking. She insists that union with God is a uniting with the three Persons of the Trinity, and hence it is not surprising that *Das fliessende Licht* contains some profound reflections on the Trinitarian character of *einunge*.[98] The erotic descriptions of the union of the human bride and the divine Bridegroom generally conform to the *unitas spiritus* motifs found in the Cistercian and Victorine authors,[99] but there are also passages that suggest some form of substantial union between God and the soul.

Book 1, chapter 44, is an allegorical love drama in which the Soul converses with her servants (the five Senses), God the Holy Spirit, and Christ, the youthful Bridegroom. In the midst of what is basically an erotic description of union, God tells the soul, "Dame Soul, you belong to my nature to such a degree that nothing at all can come between you and me."[100] In defending this suspect language against attack in a later chapter, Mechthild appealed to the preexistence of all things in the divine "enclosure" *(klote)* before creation, a move not unlike Meister Eckhart's defense of his notion of indistinct union through invoking the virtual existence of all things in the divine Principle.[101] Although there are also some texts in book 3 of *Das fliessende Licht* that go beyond traditional expressions,[102] by and large Mechthilde's teaching on union hints at rather than develops a new understanding of union.[103]

A third Beguine mystic of the late thirteenth century was more daring and paid with her life for her dangerous teaching. Marguerite Porete was burned as a relapsed heretic at Paris in 1310 because she had continued to promulgate her book *Le Mirouer des ames simples (The Mirror of Simple Souls)* subsequent to its condemnation at Valenciennes by the bishop of Cambrai.[104] Despite Marguerite's fate, *Le Mirouer* enjoyed a considerable reputation in the later Middle Ages, when it was translated into a number of languages and read as the work of less suspect mystics such as Jan van Ruusbroec.

Le Mirouer offered more than enough ammunition for condemnation on less abstruse issues than that of the nature of *unio mystica*. Marguerite's insistence that the higher stages of ascent demand leaving the virtues behind[105] and her distinction between "Holy Church the Little," governed by reason and the clergy, and "Holy Church the Great," ruled by love and the spiritually adept,[106] would have been provoking themes in any era.

Le Mirouer is digressive, at times even confusing, so any brief account of Marguerite's thought is subject to qualification. As in the case of the two older Beguines, her insistence on the superiority of love is set forth in a poetic and frequently erotic language influenced by the courtly literature of the later Middle Ages. She goes beyond them—in tone if not in theory—in the force and frequency of her attacks on reason. It is not until Soul has managed to "slay Reason with Love" that real progress to the higher stages of the mystical life can begin.[107] Although she insists that it is Divine Love entering into the annihilated will that alone brings the Soul to God, "Amour" is often associated with a higher form of knowledge usually called "Entendement d'Amour," which is something like the *intelligentia amoris* of the twelfth-century mystics.[108]

Chapter 118 of *Le Mirouer* lays out Marguerite's map of the sevenfold ascent of the soul to God.[109] The fourth stage is described as a "concordance of union," but the true heights of *unio mystica* are found above it. In traditional fashion, Marguerite reserves the seventh stage for the life hereafter, so stages five and six contain the heart of her teaching on the possibility of union in this life. In the fifth stage the Soul realizes that God has given her free will as "her own" and that until all willing is abandoned she can never be completely one with her Divine Lover. In giving up all willing, even the willing of the good,[110] the Soul begins to attain the Divine Goodness: "Now she is all, and so she is nothing, for her Lover makes her one."[111] Finally, in the sixth stage, the Soul is so united with God that initially she sees neither herself nor him. "But God sees himself in her through the Divine Majesty by which he glorifies this Soul, so that she sees there is nothing outside God himself, 'Who is,' from whom everything is."[112] Thus, the transformation into Divine Love described in *Le Mirouer* seems to go beyond the level of *unitas spiritus*.[113]

The insistence on giving up all willing of any kind in order to attain the most complete union with God is one of the themes that brings Marguerite Porete's mysticism close to that of Meister Eckhart, who was teaching in Paris shortly after her execution. Recent scholarship has argued that one of the most profound statements of Eckhart's notion of *unitas indistinctionis*, that found in his vernacular Sermon 52, shows direct contact with *Le Mirouer*.[114] There are, indeed, a number of close parallels in thought and expression between passages in the Beguine's work and this and other Eckhart sermons. Especially striking are texts stressing how the Soul's annihilation of will returns it to a preestablished level of union with God where no distinction can be found between the Soul's willing and God's willing, or the Soul's seeing and God's seeing, since now it is where it was before it was created. Chapter 91 puts it thus:

> Now he [God] possesses the will without a why in the same way that he possessed it before she [the Soul] was made a Lady by it. There is nothing except him. No one loves except him, for nothing is except him, and thus he alone completely loves, and sees himself alone completely, and praises alone completely by his being itself.[115]

Although the language used in this and similar texts is not as metaphysically dense or sophisticated as it is in Eckhart, the similarity of thought is striking. It is possible to argue that in this, as in other important mystical themes, Eckhart's thought represents both an appropriation and a correction of some of the elements of Beguine mysticism.[116]

Other passages and themes in *Le Mirouer* also suggest a substantial understanding of *unio mystica*,[117] though, to be sure, the book also uses language associated with the standard teaching on unity as an *unitas spiritus* with God.[118] Marguerite Porete, however, even more than Hadewijch and Mechthilde, shows that the germs of the new mysticism of *unitas indistinctionis* were present, especially among female mystics, prior to Meister Eckhart.

If the Pauline *unus spiritus* is the leitmotif of the mystical theorists of the earlier Middle Ages, it is a series of Johannine texts, especially the *Prologue of the Gospel* with its teaching about existence "in the Beginning [or Principle]" *(in principio)*, that may be said to be the scriptural warrant for Eckhart's views.[119]

We can begin from Eckhart's formula that "God's ground and the soul's ground are one ground,"[120] that is, that there is in the soul a "spark" *(vünkelîn)*, "castle" *(bürgelîn)*, or "ground" *(grunt)* that is identical with God.[121] This formula is the foundation for Eckhart's claim that the deepest reality of intellectual being is its *indistinct union* with God.[122] This is not a totally untraditional doctrine, since all Christian theologians admitted that created reality enjoyed a superior form of preexistence in the divine ideas. There was far less agreement, however, on how to explain the relation between this virtual or ideal existence in the divine mind and the formal existence of individual substances in the world.[123] Eckhart's metaphysics put virtual existence in God as principle *(in principio)* at the center of his thought, as can be seen from a glance at the two essential themes of his mystical teaching, the birth of the Son in the soul of the just man and the "breaking-through" *(durchbrechen)* to the divine ground. These notions are dialectical ways of spelling out what the Meister meant when he insisted that true union with God must be union without a medium *(sine medio, âne mittel)*.[124]

Hugo Rahner has shown that the birth of the Son in the justified soul, first in baptism and later understood in what we may call more mystical terms, was an ancient theme in Christianity.[125] Writings of the German theologian Henry of Friemar tell us that in Paris around 1310, the same year that Marguerite Porete was burned as a heretic for her errors, there was considerable discussion—some of it erroneous, Henry thought—on this theme.[126] Eckhart boldly cited the controversial idea in his public preaching, especially in the vernacular sermons he delivered in Strassburg and Cologne from about 1313 on.

The Meister's understanding of the union achieved by the birth of the Word in the Soul goes far beyond a *unitas spiritus* level toward metaphysical claims whose daring implications he was all too glad to spell out to an audience that we can imagine as alternately puzzled, shocked, or deeply moved. Because God's ground and the soul's ground are in deepest reality one ground, then not only "must God's existence be my existence and God's is-ness my is-ness"[127] but also, just as the Father is giving birth to the Son from all eternity, so "He gives me birth, me, his Son and the same Son."[128] This identity of the soul with the Only-Begotten Son in the Trinity was the source of the numerous passages where Eckhart applied scriptural texts concerning Christ and his divine activities to any justified person, that is, to the just person "insofar as he is just," as the Latin works put it.[129]

Not content with this treatment, Eckhart plunged ahead into even more daring formulas. If the soul is identical with the divine ground in its principle, then it is not only identical with the Son being born but also with the Father begetting[130] and with the Holy Spirit proceeding from both.[131] Further, since the divine ground, the absolute unity beyond the Trinity, has a certain priority, albeit a dialectical one, in relation to the three Persons, Father, Son, and Holy Spirit, the ultimate mystical goal can be described as a "breaking-through" to indistinct oneness with the Godhead. As he puts it in German Sermon 48, the spark in the soul is not content with the Trinity of Persons, not even with the simple divine essence, "but it wants to know the source of this essence, it wants to go into the simple ground, into the quiet desert into which distinction never gazed, not the Father, nor the Son, nor the Holy Spirit."[132] There God has promised to speak to the soul "with one, one from one, one in one and in one still one everlastingly."[133] Throughout his works, but especially in the vernacular sermons, Eckhart insists upon the absolute oneness of God and the soul: "Between man and God, however, there is not only no distinction, there is no multiplicity either. There is nothing but one."[134]

There is no space here for a full analysis of the union of indistinction that Eckhart holds out as the essence of mystical awareness,[135] but in terms of our theme it is important to consider two further questions. First, what are the roles of love and knowledge in attaining union? And second, in what sense, if any, are love and knowledge present in the union of indistinction itself?

It is customary to see Meister Eckhart as an intellectual mystic. He frequently spoke about God as "Pure Intellect,"[136] and, like Thomas Aquinas, he insisted that the beatific vision resides primarily in the intellect rather than in the will.[137] In his sermons he claims that it is knowledge rather than love that makes us one being and not just one activity with God.[138] Since to understand is to become one or indistinct with what is understood, "to rise up then to intellect, to be attached to it, is to be united to God," as Latin Sermon 29 puts it.[139]

But anyone who has ever read much Eckhart will know how much attention he gives to the role of love in attaining union with God. A substantial number of the Latin and vernacular sermons take love (*caritas, minne*) as their major theme,[140] and one can find passages in which he insists "the perfection of beatitude lies in both: Knowledge and love."[141] Even more significant are the texts in which he associates love with indistinction, thus showing that both love and knowledge have a part to play in gaining *unitas indistinctionis*. "God is indistinct, and the soul loves to be indistinguished, that is, to be and to become one with God."[142] Other places he insists that the soul becomes identical with the love that is the Holy Spirit[143] and that the "living without a why" that characterizes the detached person who dwells in awareness of indistinct union with God is maintained by love: "He who lives in the goodness of his nature lives in God's love, and love has no why."[144]

Everything that Eckhart says about the roles of love and knowledge in gaining union, however, must be qualified by his continuing insistence that the kind of union he is speaking of lies beyond *both* love and knowledge, at least as we conceive and experience them. "Some teachers claim that the spirit takes its happiness from love; others claim it takes it in seeing God. I say, however, it takes it neither from love nor from knowing nor from seeing."[145] The pure detachment that he praises as superior to both humility and charity in the treatise *On Detachment* also surpasses knowing: "And when this detachment ascends to the highest place, it knows nothing of knowing, it loves nothing of loving, and from light it becomes dark."[146] Such formulas are typical of Eckhart's self-reversing dialectical language (e.g., when *esse*, or "existence," is affirmed of creatures, it must be denied of God, and vice versa). In this case it may be taken to suggest that even if there is some kind of transcendental love and transcendental knowledge present in indistinct union, there is no way of describing these under the rubrics taken from the lower forms familiar to us.

To summarize, Eckhart's paradoxical view of *unitas indistinctionis* has a complex relation to both love and knowledge. Despite his insistence on the superiority of intellect over love, *caritas* is given an important role in the German Dominican's writings. Both love and knowledge, at least as we ordinarily experience them, are surpassed in union. In speaking of the manner of life lived out of the awareness of this union, however, Eckhart still uses the language of love, though admittedly only sparingly and in far different tones from the glowing affectivity of a Bernard, a Bonaventure, or the three Beguines previously discussed. In the case of Meister Eckhart, we might wish to reverse the traditional formula "amor ipse notitia est" into "intellectus ipse est amor" in order to suggest how the Dominican recognized a dual aspect to the way in *unio mystica* fulfills both the intellectual and the affective dynamism of the human spirit, though in a transcendental way that breaks the limits of language.

Eckhart's notion of the union of indistinction was attacked during his lifetime and posthumously condemned.[147] The Meister's defense of his controversial teaching, amply set out in the documents from both the Cologne and the Avignon proceedings, rests in essence on his teaching about God's distinct/indistinct relation to creation[148] but more explicitly on what we can call the *inquantum* principle, or to put it in his own way, "the words 'insofar as' *(inquantum)*, that is, a reduplication, exclude from the term in question everything that is other or foreign to it according to reason."[149] What this principle means in practice is that Eckhart defended his statements about union by arguing that they were true of the soul insofar as it has its true being *(esse virtuale)* in the divine principle, but they were not true of the soul in its concrete formal existence *(esse formaliter inhaerens)*.[150] Eckhart also pointed to many places in his works where he had upheld the necessary distinctions between God and man. The Meister's judges at Avignon misunderstood the *inquantum* principle, and it is also clear that they refused to accept his explanation of the relation between God's being and our being. In the bull of condemnation *(In agro dominico)* issued by John XXII in 1329, no fewer than seven of the twenty-eight articles (10–12, 20–22, and 1 of the appended articles) involved his teaching on union.[151]

Eckhart's condemnation made the situation difficult for his followers. Although they continued to use the language of indistinct union and to defend the Meister, implicitly or explicitly, their understanding of indistinction departs from his teaching in a number of ways. John Tauler used the language of unity and indistinction in his sermons, but he cautiously added, "I do not say that all difference between God and the soul disappears, but that the soul loses its sense of difference."[152] Henry Suso's *Büchlein der Wahrheit (Little Book of Divine Truth)* is at once a defense, clarification, and at times modification of the Meister's teaching on union, one of the most penetrating discussions of the theme in medieval mystical literature.[153] In a number of places in this text, as well as in his autobiographical *Leben (Life of the Servant)*, Suso discusses the "breakthrough" and its state of freedom from willing in deeply Eckhartian ways. Some passages mingle Eckhart's themes with directly erotic language, as when God says of detached souls: "I will so kiss them interiorly and embrace them lovingly that they are me and I am they, and we two will ever more remain eternally one Only One" (cf. *Jn.* 17:21).[154] Such texts must be interpreted in the light of three traditional qualifications Suso always insisted upon: first, that union does not involve a merging of essences;[155] second, that union removes the consciousness but not the ontological reality of distinction;[156] and third, that the soul becomes God by grace and not by nature.[157]

Perhaps the most interesting later treatment of union without distinction occurs in the Flemish mystic Jan van Ruusbroec (d. 1381), not only because Ruusbroec had a clear sense of the difference between true and false mysticism (which included keeping his distance from Eckhart), but also because his theories on union were not always satisfactory to later critics like Jean Gerson.

Ruusbroec discusses union throughout his works. In the third book of *The Adornment of Spiritual Marriage*, he speaks of a union of essence that takes place in the Godhead above the distinction of Persons in a way that seems remarkably close to Eckhart.[158] Similar passages occur in other places.[159] The Flemish hermit holds that passage into this state takes place above reason, "lifted up by love into the simple bareness of our intelligence," as *The Sparkling Stone* expresses it.[160] In the very next chapter of the same work, however, he insists on the infinite distinction that must always accompany and succeed the experience of union.[161]

In the *Little Book of Enlightenment*, Ruusbroec summarized his understanding of union in order to confute false mystics. Union with God consists of three levels: union with an intermediary, union without an intermediary, and union without difference or distinction.[162] Union with a medium is achieved through God's grace, given in the sacraments and through the virtues;[163] union without a medium happens when a person is "exalted through love and dies in God to himself and to all his works."[164] We can say that for Ruusbroec this is the level of the Bernardine *unitas spiritus;*[165] it is also the level where the soul participates in the life of the Trinity.[166] Finally, union that is *sonder differentie ochte onderscheet* is described as taking place "where the three Persons give way to the essential unity and without distinction enjoy essential beatitude. . . . There all the elevated spirits in their superessence are one enjoyment and one beatitude with God without difference."[167] To clarify how Ruusbroec wished these levels to be understood, we must remember his insistence that the three are not successive stages, but they always coexist both in this life and the next.[168] We can also note that Paul Mommaers in his introduction to the new edition of the *Little Book of Enlightenment* holds that Ruusbroec uses *essence* in two senses: first, in the familiar Aristotelian and Scholastic way and second, as signifying a manner of being or a presence.[169] If it is possible to understand the third level, that of union without distinction, in the latter way, this would further distance the Flemish mystic's notion of union from any essential identity.

The condemnation of Eckhart had taken place in the midst of growing fears about the claims and the activities of mystics on the part of the ecclesiastical leaders. Historians today rightly question whether anything like a concerted movement of heretics of the Free Spirit ever existed,[170] but there can be no doubt of the perception of danger on the part of many, even among the mystics themselves. During the fourteenth century, theologians like William of Occam and Jordan of Quedlinburg attacked the language and images used by the mystics to describe *unio mystica*,[171] and disputes about the correct way of understanding union with God were rampant in the fifteenth century.

Jean Gerson was at one time chancellor of the University of Paris and among the most influential theologians of his day. As a commentator on Dionysius, he knew and praised Thomas Gallus highly; he also criticized Amalric of Bène, Jan van Ruusbroec, and even Bernard for their mistaken views on union. In his *De mystica theologia speculativa* of 1402 Gerson outlined three mistaken views of what he calls the *amorosa unio cum Deo*, the goal of mystical theology.[172] The first is the absorption back into virtual existence in God, which, as we have seen, is essential to Eckhartian metaphysics. Gerson mentions Ruusbroec's *Adornment of the Spiritual Marriage* by name in this connection,[173] though noting that the author appears to have corrected himself in other writings.[174] The examples make it clear that Gerson may also have had Tauler in mind, whether directly or indirectly.[175] The second example is Peter Lombard's formal identity between the love of God in us and the Holy Spirit. The third mistaken view is more interesting. The Parisian chancellor takes on those who wrongly employ corporeal examples to describe *unio* or *spiritualis transformatio*. Seven examples are discussed, much to the detriment of Bernard.[176] Gerson rejects the drop of water in the vat of wine analogy and that of food converted into nourishment because both suggest a change of substance. He criticizes a Bernardine text from the *De praecepto et dispensatione* that some had interpreted along the lines of a complete passing over of the soul into God, and he also repudiates the analogy of transsubstantiation, for which Eckhart had been condemned.[177] Gerson is more cautious about the analogies of burning iron and illuminated air (both traditional) and that of the union of form and matter (more Eckhartian),[178] which he seems to think can be interpreted in a legitimate sense if some necessary metaphysical distinctions are made.

Despite his attack on some of the abbot of Clairvaux's formulas, it is evident from the forty-third consideration that Gerson stands in a tradition close to that of Bernard. His definition of mystical theology as "experimental knowledge *(cognitio)* of God attained through the union of spiritual affection with Him"[179] indicates that knowledge still plays a role in the mystic's goal. Not only does Gerson cite the Gregorian dictum "amor notitia est,"[180] but he also teaches that the love union that forms the height of mysticism subsumes rather than rejects the intellectual path to God.[181]

Gerson's carefully argued case is evidence that the traditional understanding of the relation of love, knowledge, and union forged in the twelfth century was by no means dead in the fifteenth. In the 1450s, the debate over Nicholas of Cusa's *De docta ignorantia* once more raised the issue of whether the love that attains union with God is devoid of all knowledge.[182] Cusa's response, like Gerson's, was traditional: "Therefore, in every love by which one is carried into God there is a cognition *(cognitio)*, even though one remains unaware of what it is one loves. Thus there is a coincidence of knowledge and ignorance, or a learned ignorance."[183] One could also pursue these issues in the writings of the Renaissance Platonists, such as Marsilio Ficino, whose thoughts on the mutual interaction of love and knowledge are highly intricate.

Mystical Union in the Classical Spanish Mystics

This essay cannot consider every treatment of love, knowledge, and mystical union in the centuries under consideration. But even such a limited sketch must take note of the understanding of union with

God and its relation to love and knowledge found in the Spanish mystics of the sixteenth century, Teresa of Ávila and John of the Cross. The extent of the dependence of Teresa and John, as well as the other Spanish mystics of the sixteenth century, on their medieval forebears has been well established.[184] Their position as the recognized "doctors of mystical theology" of the Roman Catholic church gives them a special status for our theme.

Teresa's two major works, the *Vida,* or *Autobiography* (1562–65), and the *Moradas,* or *Interior Castle* (1577), show considerable, though not unresolvable, differences. In the earlier work, filled as it is with direct descriptions of the experience of God, union is seen as a lower state than that of rapture or ecstasy, primarily because union is conceived of in terms of an intermediate state of prayer ("the prayer of union" described in chapter 20), whereas rapture is a superior divine seizure of the soul. The description of the prayer of union as the "highest point" where the "faculties are lost through being closely united to God" reflects the language of the experience of the union of wills found in the medieval mystics.[185]

In the *Interior Castle* the picture is more complex. Here the prayer of the "sleep of the faculties," or "prayer of quiet," occurs in the fifth dwelling place, or mansion,[186] but a more careful distinction of two kinds of union helps explain what this means. *Castle* 5.3.3 discusses the union of our wills with the divine will as the necessary ground that leads to the "true or delightful" union experienced in the prayer of quiet. Although the higher sixth and seventh mansions are presented primarily under the erotic images of betrothal (or rapture) and marriage, Teresa is now willing to speak of the highest stage also as a union, the "union of spiritual marriage" in which the soul or spirit "is made one with God."[187] In 7.2.4–5 of the *Interior Castle* she even makes use of the full range of the traditional metaphors describing union of wills that we have seen as early as Bernard, as well as the *unus spiritus* text from *1 Corinthians* 6:17.[188] For all the originality of her pyschological analysis of mystical states, Teresa adds little that is new to the main line of theological understanding of union.

No Christian mystical theologian gave more careful attention to issues of the relation of love, knowledge, and union than John of the Cross, particularly in his *Spiritual Canticle* (1579–85).[189] What follows is a brief survey of the highlights of his views as set forth primarily in this work.

Individual passages in the writings of the great Carmelite taken out of context might suggest that he understands unity as indistinction,[190] but any extensive reading shows that despite his rich and at times hyperbolic language, John insisted that the ultimate loving union with God that can be partly experienced in this life and will be completed in heaven involves no fusion of substances but only complete uniformity of wills. Here below, union with God begins intermittently in the "betrothal" stage that characterizes the illuminative way and reaches its culmination in the "spiritual marriage" of the unitive way. In both manifestations it can be said of God and the soul that "each is the other and that both are one."[191] Hence, the Spanish mystic makes considerable use of the language of transformation into God, or deification, throughout his works. These statements, however, are always qualified by his traditional insistence on the lasting difference of substances—"this thread of love binds the two . . . with such firmness and so unites and trans-forms them and makes them one in love, that, although they differ in substance, yet in glory and appearance the soul seems to be God and God the soul."[192] In one place in the *Spiritual Canticle* John provides one of the most careful formulations of the *unus spiritus* tradition in Christian mysticism: "When this Spiritual Marriage between God and the soul is consummated, there are two natures in one spirit and love *(son dos naturalezas en un espiritu y amor)*, even as says Saint Paul, making this same comparison and saying, 'He that is joined unto the Lord is made one spirit with him.' "[193] Like Bernard before him, who also insisted on the absolute dis-tinction of substances between the divine and human lover, John makes use of a wide variety of the traditional images and symbols that to the unwary reader might suggest a fusion of essences rather than an inexpressible harmony of wills.[194] Misinterpretations, however, must rest with the reader in the case of an author who took such care to provide a theologically nuanced exegesis of his own poems and images.

There is no space here to enter into some of the more subtle and profound issues in the Spanish mystic's doctrine of union, such as the way in which he relates the Christological and the Trinitarian aspects of the soul's loving fusion with the Divine Lover.[195] Directly relevant to our theme, however, is the way in which John under-stands the role of love and knowledge as both preparation for and characteristic of the union of the soul with God.

Despite his dependence on Thomistic theology in many par-ticulars, not least in his notion of the beatific vision, John of the Cross adhered to an older, Augustinian understanding of the three powers of the soul—memory, understanding, and will—as the anthropological basis for his understanding of the path to union. The active and passive nights of purgation cleanse all three powers, and all three are also involved in union. John insists that only love, that is, the operation of the will, can unite us with God in this life: "Properly speaking God does not communicate himself to the soul through the flight of the soul—which is, as we have said, the knowledge that it has of God—but through the love that comes from that knowledge."[196] This union of love perfecting the will (the power in the soul that corresponds to the Holy Spirit, the bond of unity in the Trinity) also involves both the understanding (corresponding to the Son) and the memory (corresponding to the Father).[197] The "knowledge" that is given to the understanding and the "recreation and delight" granted the memory in the fusion of wills are, of course, quite unlike those that are gained naturally. This new knowledge of God is substantial, nondiscursive, passively received not actively gained, and, above all, incommunicable.[198] Like the author of the *Cloud of Unknowing*, John insists that "every apprehension that has form and figure are all lost and no longer known in that absorption of love"; but, like Bernard and other proponents of the subsuming tradition, he also holds that the habits of the acquired sciences are not lost. "When a small light unites with another that is great, it is the greater that overwhelms the lesser and gives light, and the smaller is not lost but perfected."[199] John of the Cross always insists upon the mutuality of love and knowledge both in the union enjoyed in this life and in the Beatific Vision in heaven.[200]

Conclusion

On the basis of this survey, the following conclusions can be advanced. The first, already noted above, is that in Christianity at least the contrast between intellectual and affective mysticism is too general to be very helpful.[201] "God is love," according to *1 John* 4:8, and the first and greatest commandment is to love the Lord God with one's whole heart and mind and soul. To label a mystic like Meister Eckhart intellectual is to risk not doing justice to the important role that love plays in his thought, as well as to lose sight of his claim that union is deeper than both knowing and loving. To describe Bernard of Clairvaux or John of the Cross as affective mystics because of their emphasis on love as the unifying bond with God minimizes the role that subsumed understanding has for them. Where Christian mystics do differ is in their varying conceptions of the roles that *both* intellect and love play in the path to and enjoyment of union.

During the period between the twelfth and the sixteenth centuries, in Latin Christianity at least, two views about the nature of union with God (*unitas spiritus* and *unitas indistinctionis*, as I have called them) interacted with at least three tendencies in the way in which mystical theologians understood the roles played by love and knowledge in relation to union.

The real, if at times subtle, differences emerge over the question of the relation of the goal, that is, mystical union however conceived, to the lower stages of human knowing. One tendency, well expressed in classic Cistercian and Victorine mystical theory but found in many later authors, especially John of the Cross, emphasized the continuous dynamic activity by which Divine Love subsumes all spiritual activities toward a union with God where love and knowledge form one transcendent reality.[202] Another tendency, represented by Thomas Gallus and the *Cloud of Unknowing*, was inclined to look with suspicion on the lower aspects of human intellectual activity and thus sought to establish a clear line of demarcation and separation between these aspects and the ultimate loving union lest human discursive and conceptual thinking egotistically try to invade a realm where it could only do more harm than good. Finally, Meister Eckhart's insistence on the radical transcendence of union led him to emphasize that all loving and knowing (at least as we experience them) are negated in the *unitas indistinctionis*. Perhaps each of these tendencies will always be present in Christian mysticism, but it is especially important for theologians and historians of mysticism not to lose sight of the "subsuming" tradition as a corrective to those who have viewed mysticism as an anti-intellectual, purely emotional, and obscurantist phenomenon.

Since the time of Gregory the Great, the majority of Western mystics have insisted that "amor ipse notitia est." No one has expressed this more beautifully than John of the Cross in stanzas 26–27 of his "Canciones entre el alma y el esposo," the poem that forms the basis for the *Spiritual Canticle:*

> Deep-cellared is the cavern
> Of my heart's love, I drank of him alive:
> Now, stumbling from the tavern,

No thoughts of mine survive,
And I have lost the flock I used to drive.
He gave his breast; seraphic
In savour was the science he taught;
And there I made my traffic
Of all, withholding naught,
And promised to become the bride he sought.[203]

Bewildered Tongue: The Semantics of Mystical Union in Islam

MICHAEL SELLS

I become the hearing with which he hears, the seeing with which
he sees, the hand with which he grasps, the foot with which he
walks.[1]

These words take the form of a *hadīth qudsī* (transcendent hadith), an extra-Qur'anic pronouncement in the divine voice. They
are the foundation text for Sufi understanding of *fanā'*, the "passing
away" of the self, and *baqā'*, the "remaining" of a consciousness
that can be said to be divine within the human or human within
the divine. Together, *fanā'* and *baqā'* correspond to what in the
West is called mystical union, if union is understood in a special
sense. Although some Islamic terms such as *jamˁ* might fit the standard definition of *union* as a "conjunction of two entities," such a
conjunction is not what is meant by the theologically more explicit
language of *fanā'* and *baqā'*. When one of the entities (the human)
passes away, the other (the divine), insofar as it can be considered
an entity at all, fills its psychic space, becoming its hearing and
its seeing. To become empty of self, to pass away, is to become like
a polished mirror reflecting the divine image and to become one
with the divine in that image. This moment of union is manifested
in language through a transformation of normal reference and the
divisions between subject and object, self and other, reflexive and
nonreflexive, upon which language is based.

87

In Islamic literature there is no adjective such as "mystical" to distinguish the Arabic terms from their use in other contexts. The topic of mystical union confronts us immediately with a central aspect of classical Islamic culture: the interpermeability and interfusion of discursive and cultural worlds such that each is reflected within the other. The challenge in an essay of this kind is to allow not only the central terms of Sufism but the language contexts in which they are embedded and without which they are stripped of meaning to show through and, in showing through, to contribute their own distinctive perspective to comparative mysticism. I have organized the essay thematically, with five sections corresponding to five major language worlds or modes of discourse. Because such thematic division occasions some chronological skipping back and forth, I present here a topical outline of the five sections:

> *Section 1:* the poetic archetype of lover-beloved union, and the critical relation between the classical poetic tradition and Sufi language of union.
>
> *Section 2:* Qur'anic themes and theological controversies appropriated and transformed within Sufi language of union.
>
> *Section 3:* the mythic ascent through the heavenly spheres to the divine throne and the Sufi discovery of a symbolism of union within this mythic cosmos.
>
> *Section 4:* the Sufi "bewildered dialogues" of union in which distinctions between subject and object, speaker and hearer, begin to melt.
>
> *Section 5:* the new discourse of mystical dialectic, transformation of philosphical discourse by mystical union, and simultaneous transformation by philosophy of mystical expression.

The dynamic character of the Arabic and Islamic language of union is a result of the interplay among the five modes. Certain themes (remembrance of the beloved, love-madness, bewilderment, and the moment of truth) and theological issues (free will and destiny, divine unity and divine names, the ambivalent nature of the self encountered in union) form channels of interaction and allusion among modes, giving the Islamic language of union its distinctive configurations and tone.

In all five language worlds union is a secret or mystery *(sirr)* that even in expression remains paradoxically unrevealed. The poetic and erotic moment lies unfathomably deep within the poetic remembrance. Complete theological expression of unity lies beyond the dualities of language reference and discursive thought. In the ascent to the divine throne, the hero proceeds from and returns to a self beneath or beyond the individuated consciousness of the ego. Since *fanā'* occurs only insofar as the self passes away, conversations from within union involve essential paradoxes concerning the identity (in both senses of the term) of the two parties. Finally, when union becomes the central principle of a mystical dialectic, a transreferential *aporia* or perplexity is built within language, transforming its normal functions and structure.

I have focused upon texts that are Arabic or can be related to the Arabic tradition of Sufism. To do justice to the non-Arabic traditions, both in their own cultural integrity and their interactions with the Arabic tradition, would not be possible in an essay of this length and kind. The discussion will need to go beyond the various terms for *union* to their multiple, partially interfused, and constantly interacting cultural and linguistic contexts in a manner that may seem at times to digress from the topic of union more narrowly defined. It is the intertextual play across language worlds that gives the Sufi semantics of union its nuance and intensity. Union is the *dynamis*, the generative and guiding principle within all five modes, never expressed, moving the discourse into ever deeper semantic levels.

Union, Secret, and the Bewildered Lover

> Last night the Saqis' flagons brimmed over.
>   May our life be like last night
> until the day of resurrection![2]
>
>   *   *   *
>
> We drank in memory of the beloved a wine
>   that intoxicated us before creation.[3]

These two Sufi verses are among the many that play upon the themes of drunkenness and love. How are we to know that the beloved alluded to is the divine beloved, that the wine brought by the Saqi, or wine bearer, is the wine of mystical intoxication? How are we to know that references to the eternal or to the day of resurrection are not the irreverent hyperboles of the wine poets?[4] Although the distinction is sometimes made later in a Sufi poem, or in a poet's commentary, the poet will often heighten and play upon the ambiguity rather than clarify it.

Sufis are said to have found in the wine song and love poetry a vehicle to express an episode of mystical union experienced independently. However Sufis adopted and transformed not only the themes of wine and love but also the full range of motifs, conventions, and images from classical poetry. In addition, the poetic and the Sufi traditions share a semantics of allusion governed by intricate rules of behavior and expression *(adab)* and of literary and psychological sensitivity or taste *(dhawq)*. Poetic and Sufi sensibility are most closely intertwined at the moment of union. To consider one the vehicle of the other is to lose the resonance and power brought about by the interfusion of the two language worlds.

The poetic tradition of pre-Islamic Arabia had at least as strong an influence on much of later Sufism as the *Song of Songs* would have upon Jewish and Christian mystical literature. This may seem surprising. Islamic writers refer to pre-Islamic Arabic culture as the Jahiliyya (period or condition of moral ignorance), and the Qur'an places itself within the prophetic, Abrahamic tradition. However, while critical of much of the Arabian ethos and identifying itself with the tradition of Abraham, the Qur'an also insistently and emphatically calls itself an *Arabic* Qur'an, marking its immanence within the cultural-linguistic world that developed with or through the oral tradition of Jahiliyya poetry.[5] Rather than rejecting this heritage, early Islam recorded it in one of history's greatest philological endeavors. The harshest critique of pre-Islamic society did not prevent the preservation and appropriation of its deeper symbolic patterns.

The ode, or Qasida, the classical form that bequeathed its language, themes, and structure to Sufi literature, was divided by medieval literary critics into three major movements: (1) the *nasīb*, or remembrance *(dhikr)*, of the lost beloved; (2) the journey (a movement that in some way prefigures the major Islamic journey of the Hajj); and (3) the boast. Remembrance of the beloved is the wellspring of both the poetic and the Sufi voice. A brief listing of the conventions and motifs of the poetic remembrance, or *nasīb*, that will be echoed, appropriated, and transformed within Sufi literature would include the following: (1) the traces of the lost beloved's abodes; (2) the blaming of the lost beloved for her continually changing forms and moods *(ahwāl;)* (3) the stations *(maqamāt)* of her journey away from the poet; and (4) images of fertility and tranquillity that memory of her conjures in place of the desolate ruins of her campsite, images that open onto the underlying archetype, beloved as lost garden.

The classical *nasīb* engendered two independent genres. The Ghazal would contribute to Sufi literature a rich set of topoi (dalliance and murderous glances from the beloved, for example) and a sophisticated use of double-entendres. The ᶜUdhri love poem would portray the poet-lover as driven mad (*majnūn*, literally "Jinned" or possessed by Jinn) out of love for the beloved, as *hā'im* (wandering aimlessly), as perishing *(hālik)*. The beloved is portrayed as constantly changing in form (a quality attributed to the Jinn), appearing in miragelike visitations that lead the poet off the path to destruction. The most famous ᶜUdhri lover, Qays, is better known as Majnun Layla, "driven mad" for Layla. In the ᶜUdhri tradition the conjunction within the classical *nasīb* of eros, madness, and inspiration (all symbolized by the Jinn by whom the poets were said to be inspired) is intensified.[6] The *nasīb* continued to find new expression. From the new style *(badīᶜ)* poetry of the Abbasid age to the Andalusian tradition exemplified by Ibn Zaydun (d. 463/ 1071), from the reworking of the Majnun Layla tradition in romance and folk literature to the treatises on courtly love, *nasīb* sensibility filtered through the Islamic world.

To divulge or describe the secret of the relation between lover and beloved would be a betrayal. The pre-Islamic poet ᶜAlqama (sixth century C.E) begins an ode by addressing his own persona, then shifts into a third-person reference to the beloved:

> Is what you knew
>   given in trust
> still secret? Or was her bond to you
>   broken, the day she left you far.[7]

To divulge the secret is a violation of *adab*, a word that can be translated as "sensitivity" or "discretion" but which is so central it comes to mean "literature." Although the lives and mores of the early poets were different from the Sufis, both poet and Sufi refused to entertain a certain kind of questioning about the relationship with the beloved. An example of the identity of expression between Sufis and poets can be found in the verses just cited. The "entrusting" of the secret is one of hundreds of poetic terms found within Sufi literary and psychological vocabulary. In the first section of the Qasida, the central and secret nature of union *(wasl)* creates a semantics of allusion, beginning with the intricacies of temporal and spatial relations, of affective moments, of stations and moods. Although the later sections might seem more remote from the theme of union, it is remembrance of union that governs them. In the journey and boast, manifestations of fate as inexorable time *(dahr)* and as the alloted moment of death *(maniyya)* resonate powerfully with the fate that has separated lover and beloved in the *nasīb*. In the wine song the poet proclaims how well he has forgotten the beloved, but the more he proclaims he has forgotten her the more he belies his own proclamation. Union with the beloved, never described, transcending all forms of direct reference, is immanent within all sections of the ode, opening it onto an expanding and textured depth.[8]

Although the Qasida movement, from *nasīb* to journey to boast, is often kept by Sufis on the formal level, the theological relocation of union creates a simultaneous reversal of direction. Instead of beginning with the loss of union, engaging in a trial, journey, and encounter with death, and finally reintegration with society, the Sufi leaves the community, enters a period of *khalwa* ("isolation"), often in scenes of confrontation with mortality and self that cannot help but recall the journey of the Qasida,[9] and finally approaches union. The stations *(maqāmāt)* of the beloved's journey away from the poet become stations *(maqāmāt)* of the Sufi's journey to the divine beloved. The changing moods and states *(ahwāl)* of the beloved become also the changing "graces" of the divine beloved and the changing spiritual states of the Sufi. The remembrance that guided the poet away from the beloved becomes the remembrance guiding the mystic toward him or her. Similarly, the intention and motivation *(himma)* that led the poet out of remembrance, away from the beloved and back into tribal life leads the Sufi toward union with the divine beloved. The wine song that forms a consolation for the loss of the beloved and an initiation into the world deprived of her becomes the celebration of mystical intoxication in which self and rationality are transcended. The love-mad poet, wandering and perishing in the desert, becomes the Sufi, driven mad by divine love, transcending the imprisonment of reason, society, and ego. Even the battle boast *(mufākhara)* and the ritual taunting of the enemy *(hijā')* become Sufi conventions. The *munāqara* (spiritual joust), a Sufi master's self-glorification and simultaneous vilification of his rival, is a puzzling phenomenon among those who seek to leave behind the vanities of the ego-self *(nafs)*. It becomes comprehensible when seen as a play upon its pre-Islamic paradigm.[10] And when Sufis describe the final phase of mystical union as the effacement of the trace *(rasm)* of individual self, they evoke the effaced traces of the beloved's abode with which the Qasida begins. Beneath the formal poetic movement from a past union through a journey to an affirmed world of separation, the Sufi theological relocation of union from an irretrievable past to a future often opening onto a moment of eternal now creates a counterpoint subtext.

Insofar as the Sufi "achieves" *fanā'*, or passing away, there is no individual human subject anymore who can be said to achieve union. Union involves not only a passing away of self *(nafs)* but also a loss of discursive reason *(ᶜaql)* that functions upon the principle of the self-identity. A similar paradox confronts the poet; union involves a loss of the normal boundaries of self. The poet is driven out of his reason *(ᶜaql)* both by union with and separation from the beloved. Out of the poetic tradition grew courtly love manuals, in which love *(ᶜishq)* was portrayed as resulting in madness, fainting (less metaphysical than, but analogous to, Sufi "passing away"), loss of intellect *(ᶜaql)*, and the increase in spirit *(rūh)*.[11]

In the preface to his *Interpreter of Desires (tarjumān al-ashwāq)*, Ibn al-ᶜArabi (d. 638/1240) discusses the divine appearances *(ẓawāhir)* in the context of the poetic motif of the Jinn-like, constantly changing manifestations of the beloved. The ephemeral nature of the appearances of the beloved, and consequently of the lives of the viewer who lives only through her presence, is a source of *halāk* (perishing of the lover) and of bewilderment *(hayra)*, and, most strongly, of love-madness. In a commentary on his own reference to famous poet-lovers Ibn al-ᶜArabi writes that Allah had afflicted them with human love "as a rebuttal to those who claim to love him, but are not in like manner driven mad with love. Love deprived them of their wits. It made them pass away from themselves at the sight in their imagination of the beloved."[12]

In section five I discuss theological implications of Ibn ᶜArabi's love-mad Sufi perishing among the changing appearances of the beloved. I cite this passage here in a poetic context to emphasize that the precise correlation of Sufi theology and the poetic tradition is not merely an allegorical use by Sufis of poetic themes. Ibn ᶜArabi is speaking out of both the poetic and the theological traditions and is doing full justice to each. The common distinction between profane and Sufi love is difficult to make on the basis of the respective treatments of love. In each case the love is erotic, less in the popular sense of sexual than in the psychological phenomenology, the loss of reason, identity, sense of self. Especially in regard to the pre-Islamic *nasīb*, where the symbolism of the lost paradise and the sacrality of the sacred traces are at their strongest, it would be difficult to separate the *ᶜishq* of the poets from the *ᶜishq* of the Sufis by appealing to the profane nature of the poetic union.

The Persian poets Hafiz (d. 792/1390) and Omar Khayyam (d. ca. 517/1123) succeeded in both contexts so completely that the controversial decision concerning the Sufi or non-Sufi nature of their poetry usually rests on appeals to biographical data and a biographical view of authorial intent:

> On this road there are conversations which melt the soul.
> Each man has such a quarrel that it's beyond telling.[13]
>
> *   *   *
>
> Neither you nor I understand the secret of eternity.
> Neither you nor I can solve this riddle.
> From behind a veil is our conversation.
> When the veil drops, neither you remain nor I.[14]

The frequent refusal on the part of Sufis to distinguish mystical union from the love union of the poets might be illuminated by an analogy with a similar problem that occurs in apophasis, or "negative theology." There, a moment of nothingness is demanded, a giving-up of all notions of a referentially determined divine being. At this moment it is impossible to distinguish verbally between this nothingness beyond being and mere nihilistic nothingness. This idea will be pursued in more detail in section five. Here I only wish to point out how the apophatic refusal to give up a moment of nothingness, to concede a "something," echoes the refusal by Sufi poets of easy distinctions between poetic love union and mystical union.

From the ninth through the twelfth century c.e. Sufi psychology, theology, and mystical philosophy underwent a remarkable development. From the beginning that development was influenced by the poetic forms and the poetic sensibility that the Sufis inherited. Perhaps *influence* is a misleading term. The melting of the soul in the lovers' conversation and the disappearance of the two parties when the veil is dropped may or may not be interpreted mystically. At this moment no interior distinction can be drawn between the experience of the poet-lover and that of the mystic-lover. However great the range and development of the other aspects of Sufism discussed in the following sections, and however much they may be in tension with the poetic tradition in certain areas, they seem to align with the psychologically and literarily refined poetics of union. With the lightest touch, the sublest play upon syntax or vocabulary, a Sufi writer can evoke the full power of the poetic tradition.

Unity, Fate, and Theological Bewilderment

> When the skies are torn apart
> When the stars are strewn
> When the seas boil over
> When the tombs burst open
> Then a person will know what she has given
>   and what she has held back[15]

The poetic mode stresses the dissolving of reason and language at the point of union. Although the poetry can be highly intellectual, the rhetoric and the phenomenology of union stress the dissolution of intellect (ʿaql). But the theme of love-madness does not rule out theology. Sufi language of union is as intermeshed with the disputations of the scholastic theologians as it is with the odes of the poets. The love-madness of many Sufis was achieved not through the abandonment of intellectual and theological endeavor but within that endeavor. This section traces two intertwined issues, divine unity and human destiny, from their Qur'anic source through the debates of theologians and philosophers to their reappearance within the Sufi language of mystical union.

The Qur'an refers to itself as a remembrance or reminder (dhikr). The early Meccan passages present that reminder in the context of the yawm al-dīn, the "day of reckoning" or "moment of truth." On that day or in that moment, what seems real and secure (the mountains and the earth; wealth, status, and lineage; the cosmos itself) is ripped away. What seems insignificant (a "mote's weight" of kindness or meanness) is revealed to have absolute ontological value.

At this moment the secret hidden within the earth, behind the cosmic spheres, within the human heart, and within the grave, will be revealed. The Jahiliyya paradise was to be found in an inaccessible past. The Qur'anic paradise lies, at least on one level of discourse, in the future. But the future is a function of the human perspective. From the divine perspective the secret is known. Several Qur'anic divine names relate to this knowledge: al-samʿī (the all-hearing), al-basīr (the all-seeing), al-ʿalīm (the all-knowing), and especially al-khabīr (the one skilled in knowing the innermost heart of the human being). The eschatological moment also reflects the precreative moment, the Qur'anic primordial covenant *(mithāq)* between Allah and the as-yet-unborn progeny of Adam, a covenant in which their destinies are said to be fixed.[16]

The mystery of destiny and of divine knowing, seeing, hearing, and willing of that destiny within the inner recesses of each human heart is central to the deeply textured Qur'anic language. The Qur'anic articulation of this issue, so difficult to bring across in its full power in translation, is reflected in Islamic disputational theology *(kalām)*. Qur'anic tensions between human free agency and divine omnipotence, between divine unity *(tawhīd)* and the plurality of divine attributes (the all-seeing, the all-knowing), generated a profusion of theological positions that for the Sufis heightened the sense of *hayra*, the perplexity or bewilderment that the theologians had aimed to dispel. Sufi language of union would turn on its head the theological sense of *hayra*, finding in the irreducible character of the enigma a key to the language of mystical union. But this revalorizing of bewilderment was not an abandonment of theological disputation. In many instances Sufi language of mystical union interiorizes within its own movement both sides of the arguments.

To account for a free and responsible human agency is as difficult in Islam as it is in any tradition that maintains a personal deity both omniscient and omnipotent: how can a human make a choice other than that already foreseen and forewilled by the all-knowing, all-powerful deity? The Qur'anic articulation of the issue becomes particularly profound when, in regard to the moment of truth, the divine voice announces that had Allah wished, the outcome could have been otherwise and that Allah guides whom he wills and leads astray whom he wills.[17] In these passages the meditation on destiny resonates with the meditation upon *dahr* (fate or time) in the pre-Islamic poetry. A *hadīth qudsī* admonishes the human not to curse *dahr* "for I [Allah] am *dahr*."[18] The will of Allah replaces pre-Islamic *dahr* as the focus for the paradoxes of predestination and free will. This change from an impersonal fate to the foreordaining of a personal deity gave theological urgency to discussions of free will. Controversies arose between those who asserted a free human agency and those who opposed it as contradictory to divine omnipotence, between those who put limits on divine power and will—the divine must be just according to an impersonal, rational standard of justice—and those who defined the good and just as what the divine wills.[19]

These disputes were intertwined with the controversy over

unity and attributes. Divine attributes (hearing, seeing, knowing, willing, etc.) can lead to anthropomorphism (if the divine sees and hears, does it then have sense faculties?). Or they can threaten a rigorous understanding of divine unity. If the attributes are eternal, there is implied a plurality of eternal forces, a form of *shirk*, or associating other gods with the one God. If the attributes are not eternal, there is a split in the deity between essence and attributes, with the implication that the attributes are contingent.

On both Neoplatonist and Aristotelian grounds Islamic philosophy took a strong reading of *tawhīd*. Al-Farabi (d. 339/950) upheld the absolute unity of attributes in the divine essence, affirming the identity of divine knowing with divine willing, for example.[20] Ibn Rushd (d. 595/1198) insisted that divine activity cannot be expressed through choice, will, or deliberation on the grounds that such attributes imply change, passivity, or lack, all of which are incompatible with an omnipotent, impassive deity.[21] Particularly strong in its insistence upon *tawhīd* was the Arabic Plotinian school reflected in the pseudepigraphic writings of al-Shaykh al-Yunani, the "Greek Master." The Greek Master's writings differ from the more widely known Arabic Plotinian text, *The Theology of Aristotle*, in their emphatic and radical affirmation of the formless, attributeless, nondelimited aspect of the divine and provide a succinct formulation of the unity of attribute and essence. The Greek Master repeats again and again that the first originator has no form, did not create after any forethought, created through its very is-ness *(anniyya)* rather than through any contingent attribute, and is the object of love *(ᶜishq)* on the part of the rational intellect, a love that is beyond proofs *(ᶜillal)*.[22]

An intimation of theological and philosophical controversy serving as a basis for Sufi language of union can be found in the dispute over the Ashᶜarite school's statement of *tawhīd:* "God knows by a knowledge that is not distinct from his essence." The Maturidi school objected to this formulation on the grounds that the instrumental force of the word *bi* (by or through) threatens the integrity of divine powers (knowledge, power, will) with the suggestion of contingency. The value of such disputes over "mere semantics" lay in the resultant critique of language, down to the subtlest detail of its most minute components. The Sufis would follow the Maturidi school in posing a rigorous critique of all predicative or instrumental understandings of the divine attributes. They would then retrieve the attributes in a noninstrumental mode as "realizations" (simultaneous understandings and actualizations).

This move is taken up in detail in sections four and five of this essay. Here I wish only to suggest that much was at stake. Recent studies of the importance of the metaphors implied in apparently innocent terms like *through*, and the subtle and powerful effect upon consciousness of such hidden metaphors, allow a reevaluation of scholastic concerns as being far more than mere hair-splitting.[23] Despite Sufi antischolastic polemic, Sufi formulations of mystical union were in part the result of careful and sustained attention to the intricacies of *kalām* disputation.

The precision with which Sufi language of mystical union is calibrated with such debates can be seen in the controversy over a hadith describing Adam as "made in his image" *(bi sūratihi)*. How can Adam be made in the form or image *(sūra)* of Àllah if a rigorous understanding of divine transcendence and unity is incompatible with the notion of Allah having a form or image? The Ashᶜarites suggest that the term *his* refers not to Allah but to Adam: Allah creates Adam in Adam's [own] image.[24] Such a reading is grammatically ingenious but redundant: we are not really being told much more than that Allah created Adam. We are left between the horns of the classical dilemma. The philosophical insistence that the divine can have no form, image, or plurality of attributes upon which a creature could be modeled puts into question the status of creation language and the divine names, risking a stripping *(taᶜtīl)* of the divine of its Qur'anic attributes. The traditionalist insistence upon a plurality of attributes risks anthropomorphism *(tajsīm)*, the creating of a finite god in a human image.

The interpretations by al-Hallaj (d. 309/922) and Ibn ᶜArabi of an important Qur'anic story can be seen as two distinct Sufi responses to this dilemma. In the Qur'anic account of Adam's creation, Allah announces to the angels that he will create the human being to be his *khalīfa* (regent) on earth. The angels ask, "Will you create one who will spill blood and corrupt the earth?" The divine voice replies by asking the angels whether they know the "names." When they respond that they only know what they have been taught, Allah commands Adam to teach them the names. The angels are then commanded to prostrate themselves before Adam. All obey except for Iblis (Satan), who refuses and is exiled from the heavens.[25]

Hallaj interprets Satan's refusal to bow before Adam as a refusal to worship the image of the divine rather than the divine itself in its absolute, imageless unity. The order to bow was a test. Iblis refused the explicit command, obeying instead the interior, secret divine will. At one point Iblis suggests that his disobedience was itself predetermined by that same inner will. He acts out of pure love, oblivious to rewards and punishments, willing to endure eternal exile from the beloved as well as eternal opprobrium from all beings, rather than betray that love. The love-madness exemplified in Majnun Layla recurs here intertwined with theological reflections upon destiny and unity, as the suggestion that Iblis's action has been predetermined pulls against the heroic, willful passion of his refusal to bow to Adam. In the following verses Iblis explains his refusal of the divine command as his affirmation *(taqdīs)* of the divine transcendence of any mere image such as Adam. The last verse is constructed so as to leave two equally plausible readings.

> My disavowal in you is *taqdīs*.
>   My reason in you is befuddlement.
> Who is Adam, other than you?
>   And the one in between is *Iblīs*. [or]
>   And to distinguish one from the other, who is
>   *Iblīs?*[26]

At the point of Iblis's exile, nearness and separation are brought together in a *coincidentia oppositorum*: "I have attained certitude that distance and nearness are one."[27] Iblis was the guardian of the divine throne, the creature most intimate with the creator. As one approaches union one approaches the *coincidentia oppositorum*, which can be expressed either as a simultaneous presence of contradictories or, in narrative, as a violent oscillation between them. Rather than seeking a logical mean or compromise between the two extremes, the Sufi logic of Hallaj pulls the two sides of the paradox to their limit.

The second interpretation, by Ibn ʿArabi, favors Adam over Iblis, seeing Adam as the archetype of mystical union. Iblis should have prostrated himself before Adam. Adam is the image of the divine, and through his knowledge of the names, that is, the divine attributes, he is more complete than the angels. The cosmos and the human heart are the mirror of the divine, but that mirror is clouded. In *fanā'* the Sufi's own ego-self that clouds the mirror is obliterated and the heart becomes like a polished mirror reflecting the divine image or like a prism in which the undifferentiated light of divine unity is refracted into all the various attributes. At this moment the individual Sufi realizes the primordial nature of Adam.

In such a reflection and refraction the true referent of the *his* in "his image" is revealed.[28] Were we to use the convention of capitalizing pronouns with a divine referent, we would have to write that Adam was created "in His/his image." Rather than trying to solve through standard logic the debate over the antecedent of *his*, Ibn ʿArabi finds in mystical union a paradoxical logic in which the term refers to both the human and divine party. Self and other, reflexive and nonreflexive, are semantically fused. Divine attributes, rejected as instrumental predications, are retrieved as realizations within the union of divine and human.

The following section of this essay will take up the symbolic manifestation of the ambivalence over this "image." Sections four and five will examine how Sufis apply the *coincidentia oppositorum* exemplified by the interpretation of Hallaj and the reference fusion exemplified in the interpretation of Ibn ʿArabi to a range of dialogical and dialectical language of union. Anticipating that discussion, I suggest here that, though bewilderingly paradoxical, Sufi language of union responds with precision to the arguments of the scholastics. Disputations over questions such as the *his* in "his image" revealed for the Sufis the breaking apart from within of normal language and logic when confronted with dilemmas of divine unity and human destiny. Many traditionalists felt that the divine attributes should be accepted as a mystery, *bi lā kayfa* (without asking how), not explained away through sophisticated allegorical interpretations. The secret nature of *qadar* (destiny or fate) was deeply embedded within Islamic culture, as numerous sayings testify: "Do not speak about destiny. It is God's secret; do not give away his secret"; "Disclosure of the mystery of God's lordship [i.e., his setting of destiny during the primordial convenant] is *kufr* [unbelief]"; "Whoever knows the secret of destiny is an atheist"; "Destiny is a deep sea. Do not sail out on it."[29] Insofar as they held to the pre-Islamic poetic value of maintaining the secret, insofar as they criticized the claim of theology to dispel the perplexity surrounding divine unity and human destiny, and insofar as they objected to allegorical explaining away of divine attributes, Sufis were allied with the traditionalist critics of rationalism. But unlike the traditionalists, they would not interpret the necessity of preserving the mystery as a demand to accept "without asking how" *(bi lā kayfa)* Qur'anic statements on the nature of the divine. Eschewing the scholastic ambition to dispel bewilderment by finding a dogmatic position between anthropomorphism *(tajsīm)* and stripping *(taʿṭīl)* the divine of attributes, between divine will and human freedom, Sufis would use the increasingly sophisticated arguments of the theologians to stretch the two sides of the paradox to the limit. Both sides of the theological disputes were interiorized and taken up into Sufi language of union. In this logic of extremes, the greater the original tension, the more compelling the moment when willer and willed, divine and human, pretemporal eternity of covenant and posttemporal eternity of the moment of truth, come together in union. At this moment one "drowns" in the deep waters of destiny and passes away in *fanā'*. Bewilderment becomes the active principle leading ever deeper into the irresolvable questions of destiny and divine unity to the point where the standard logic and the referential structures of language are transformed.

Ascent to the Throne: Bewilderment Amidst the Reflecting Tiles

> Then he occupied *(istawā ʿalā)* the throne, directing what was at hand *(yadabbiru al-amr)*.[30]

The Islamic world inherited a cosmology and mythology, variously call Gnostic, hermetic, or protomystical, that included a primordial human being fallen into mortality and suffering, as well as a cosmos of concentric spheres through which the primordial human has fallen and through which he ascends in order to be reunited with the divine world. The myth is embedded in a complex language world of alchemy, astrology, numerology *(jafr)*, and magic. Or rather, since these terms give the misleading impression of wholly separate esoteric sciences, we might speak of one language world in which the stars and planetary spheres, minerals, geometric shapes, letters and their numerical equivalents, members and humors of the body, four primal elements, religious and mythic figures such as angels and prophets, and various geographical, climactic, social, and psychological states were all part of an intricate system of interactive correspondences. While the heavenly journey can be seen as an ascent from the sublunary world of mortality to the divine throne, it can also be seen as a progressively deeper descent into the self. In this sense it is a process of remembrance *(dhikr)* and of symbolic and transformative interpretation *(ta'wīl)* from the exterior reality *(zāhir)* to the interior and hidden *(bātin)*. This mythic cosmos was found in Batiniyya Shi'ism, in the Sabaean Gnostic culture at Harran in Iraq, in Jewish Hekhalot texts, and in the Mi-

ʿraj story.[31] In the Miʿraj accounts, Muhammad is taken on a night journey *(isrā')* to Jerusalem and then on a heavenly ascent through seven spheres to the divine throne. The legend was early and deeply implanted within Islam, although in the Qur'an the reference to the night journey is vague and no explicit mention of a heavenly ascent is made at all.[32] The same mythic cosmos was appropriated by Sufis, and the journey to the divine throne became a paradigm of the journey toward mystical union.

Standard features like the hierarchy of spheres with the divine throne at the summit, or the seventy thousand angels or veils protecting the throne, or the use of letters, numbers, and angelic names as meditative devices revealed a common way of thinking but not a standard doctrine. They set the contours for a dialogue and polemic across philosophical and religious boundaries, carried out through subtle changes within the structuring of the hermetic cosmos. The issue of the "guardians" of the seven planetary spheres (and sometimes three spheres of fixed stars as well) can illustrate how this worldview functions as a symbolic language. The guardians might be malevolent servants of fate locking the human being into the mortal world, or they might be benevolent, helping the human initiate rise beyond that world. They might be intellects (*ʿuqūl*, as in the philosophically centered versions), angels (as in the Gnostic versions and some early Sufi appropriations of them), spirit entities (*ruhāniyyāt*, as in the Sabaean writings), or prophets (as in the Miʿraj story and some later Sufi appropriations of it).[33] In the choice of sphere guardians what was at stake was the nature of mystical transformation as the process of becoming more intellectual, more spiritual, or more deeply human. Whether seen as Muhammad (as in the Miʿraj story accounts), Idris (Enoch, Hermes), or another figure, the heavenly voyager leads the reader through a complex web of correspondences and a continual contemplation of the central issues of destiny and free will, divine unity and the world of plurality.

The tension is strongest near the culmination of the ascent, where the journeyer encounters the divine throne and often finds a figure sitting upon it. Is the figure god, human, angel, demon, or idol? This ambivalence shows up in the Jewish Sufi text attributed to David b. Josue Maimonides, in which the author appropriates, with a telling revision, a passage from Abu Hamid al-Ghazali (d. 505/1111). In the original passage, Ghazali had taken up the Qur'anic account of Allah's breathing the spirit into Adam and Adam's role as *khalīfa* as well as the "in his/His image" hadith. In his reformulation of this passage, David cites *Genesis* 1:26 ("Let us create the human being in our image") and *Ezekiel* 1:26 ("On this likeness of a throne was a likeness like the appearance of a human above it"). He then warns against the anthropomorphism *(tajsīm, tasawwur, tashbīh)*, the making of comparisons for the incomparable, that can result from a misinterpretation of such mysteries.[34] This reformulation of al-Ghazali's text highlights the central worry over the ambiguity and the dangers of misinterpretation inherent in the biblical passages and the "in his/His form" hadith, the Qur'anic notion of Adam as *khalīfa*, and the imagery of the throne and merkavah found in the Qur'an and *Ezekiel*. In each case stable boundaries between divine and human are revealed to be problematic. In each case the result is bewilderment and fear of misinterpretation. Especially compelling is the similarity in the reduplication of the term *likeness* in the *Ezekiel* passage ("On this *likeness* of a throne was a *likeness like* the *appearance* of") and the Qur'anic affirmation of transcendence ("*like* his *like* there is nothing").[35] It is easy to neglect the reduplication and to translate the statements along the more natural lines of "On this throne was the likeness of a human" or "There is nothing like him," but in both cases the notion of likeness is held at a double-remove in a linguistically contorted fashion that turns the entire question of likeness into an indefinitely self-replicating enigma.

In the Qur'anic tradition the danger of anthropomorphism was located by the philosophers and theologians in the Qur'anic divine attributes, especially in the Qur'anic verses concerning the creator occupying the throne and "governing."[36] The Greek Master discussed earlier states emphatically that the divine does not practice "governance" through any attribute but through its being *(anniya)* alone. This ambivalence over the form on the throne and the anthropormorphic activity of "directing" or "governing" *(tadbīr)* is reflected in other texts. In the Hebrew Hekhalot text 3 *Enoch*, the enthroned figure Enoch-Metatron is alternately glorified and punished, leaving his status unresolved.[37] In some Sufi texts there is a play upon the Qur'anic story of the queen of Sheba's bewilderment in the palace of Solomon (she lifts her skirts thinking the polished tiles are water). The throne room bedazzles and bewilders the visitor by the brightness of its reflecting tiles, a bewilderment of reflections that test the journeyer's entitlement to such a station.[38] The same theme is present in Hekhalot interpretation of the Talmudic account in which Rabbi Akiva warns the mystic that when he reaches the tesselated walls of the divine palace he should not shout "water, water."[39] In both Sufi and Hekhalot texts the sense of drowning is aligned with the identity confusion brought about by the reflections. The drowning theme resonates with the warning, quoted above in section two, that the issue of destiny is a deep sea and with Qur'anic reference to the divine throne being upon water.[40]

In the Miʿraj story and in later Sufi adaptations of it, much of this mythic cosmos reappears, but the intellects of the philosophers and the spirit entities and angels of the Gnostics are made subservient to the prophets. The Sufi location of mystical union at the summit of the ascent can be seen in the reformulation of Muhammad's Miʿraj attributed to Abu Yazid al-Bistami (d. 261/874). In the classic account of Ibn Ishaq, Muhammad is taken through seven spheres, occupied by Adam, John and Jesus, Joseph, Idris, Aaron, Moses, and Abraham.[41] Of the encounter with Abraham, the text states: "Then to the seventh heaven and there was a man sitting on a throne at the gate of the immortal mansion (al-bayt al-maʿmūr). Every day seventy thousand angels went in not to come back until the resurrection day." Instead of displacing the angels from the spheres in the manner of Ibn Ishaq, the Bistami account keeps them as guardians of the various heavens but places the prophets above them, beyond the throne. At each heaven Bistami encounters an angel or host of angels who offer him gifts "no tongue can describe." Each time he refuses a gift, the angels who had appeared in such awesome majesty are reduced to the like of mosquitoes. After passing through veil upon veil, kingdom after kingdom, Bistami comes to an angel seated on a chair, passes through the various seas on which waves were colliding with one another (another allusion to the drowning, dissolution, throne-upon-water topos), and finally arrives at the throne of the compassionate (ʿarsh al-rahmān). There the divine voice invites him to see the subtleties (latā'if) of the creation. Beyond the throne, Bistami attains union. He melts like lead, is given a drink from the spring of "pure intimacy," and encounters the souls of the prophets, finally reaching the precreative state of beyond being: "until I became as I was when there was no being. And reality (al-haqq) was without being, relation, position, or quality, great his glory and transcendent his names."[42]

In the Miʿraj account of Farid al-Din ʿAttar (d. 617/1220), Muhammad reaches the royal hall, at which point his guide, the angel Gabriel, must stay behind. The once-glorious angel recedes to the figure of a wren. Again union is to be found beyond the throne:

He saw no place, direction, intellect, or perception,
No throne, no ground, no earthen sphere.
He saw the non-place without soul and body—
He saw himself concealed there.

After this vision of his concealed self, the Prophet passes out
of his own persona and gazes into the real. He is struck speechless,
at which point he engages in a dialogue (!) with the divine voice,
each of which states that only one party can now exist. The distinctions of lover and beloved, human and divine, and self and other
pass into total bewilderment.[43]

Ibn ᶜArabi offers several ascent accounts based upon the Miᶜraj.
In one, he describes a philosopher (sāhib al-naẓar) and a follower
(tābiᶜ) of the prophetic tradition. The two rise up through the
spheres, but the philosopher must content himself with interro-
gating the spirit entities (rūhāniyyāt), while the follower gains
deeper secrets and ultimately leaves the philosopher behind.[44] A
second account reaffirms both how standard the basic features of
the ascent were and how subtle and complex the variations could
be. Just as Bistami refused the offering of each angel, so Ibn ᶜArabi
counsels the seeker to avoid stopping at any one level of ascent.
After receiving secrets of the mineral, vegetal, and animal worlds,
the Sufi passes through progressively more intense stages. They
oscillate from the terror of the "surface signs" in which the fixed
forms of delineated reality melt into one another, to the "overflow
of languor and tenderness and compassion in all things." The seeker
passes beyond the highest heaven, and sees into "the gardens." As
in Bistami, union is yet further on:

> And if you do not stop with this, he reveals to you the world of
> dignity, serenity and firmness; the ruse (makr), the enigmas and
> secrets. And if you do not stop with this, he reveals to you the
> world of bewilderment, helplessness, and inability, and the trea-
> suries of works. This is the highest heaven.
> And if you do not stop with this, he reveals to you the gardens:
> the degrees of their ascending steps, their blending into one an-
> other, and how they compare to one another in pleasure. And
> you are stopped on the narrow path and brought to the brink of
> Jehennam. . . . And if you do not stop with this, he reveals one
> of the sanctuaries where spirits are absorbed in the divine vision.
> In it they are drunken and bewildered. The power of ecstasy (wajd)
> has overcome them, and their state beckons you. . . .
> And if you do not stop with this, he reveals the forms of the
> sons of Adam, and veils are lifted, and veils descend. They have

a special praise which upon hearing you recognize, and you are not overcome. *You see your form among them, and from it you recognize the moment which you are in.* And if you do not stop with this, he reveals to you the throne of compassion. . . . You will know your destination and place and the limit of your degree, and which divine name is your lord and where your portion of gnosis and sainthood exists—the form of your uniqueness. . . .

And if you do not stop with this, you are eradicated, then withdrawn, then effaced, then crushed, then obliterated. When the effects of eradication and what follows are terminated, you are affirmed. . . .[45]

The prelude to union is the vision of one's precreated self and the recognition of one's "lord." This term, along with the phrase "forms of the sons of Adam," suggests the primordial covenant in which each person recognizes his or her "lord," precreative self and destiny. This moment is aligned in the same passage with the "moment of truth," or the eschatological revelation of one's destiny and true self. This moment of inversion, in which one's inner essence or self is seen as projected outside, recalls later Sufi theories of the afterlife in which what is manifest and apparent in this world becomes interiorized and what is interior and secret in this world becomes manifest.[46] The interconfessional importance of this mode of mystical union as a psychic turning-inside-out can be seen by comparing the passage from Ibn ʿArabi to a similar passage by a Palestinian disciple of the prophetic Jewish mystic Abraham Abulafia (d. ca. 1291). The passage begins with a description of "jumping" *(dillug)*, a free-associative stage of Gematria-like meditation upon the letters. The motion of the consonants "heats the thinking" and annihilates desire for any other activity. Passing beyond the control of his natural mind, the meditator now cannot stop the thinking even if he wishes to do so. He continues to "draw thought forth from its source" until:

Through sheer force that stage is reached where you do not speak nor can you speak. And if sufficient strength remains to force oneself even further and draw it out still farther, then that which is within will manifest itself without, and through the power of sheer imagination will take on the form of a polished mirror. And this is "the flame of the circling sword", the rear revolving and becoming the fore. Whereupon one sees that his inmost being is something outside of himself.[47]

With Ibn ʿArabi, union begins with a vision of the Qur'anic

paradise and one's inner self, the encounter in a moment *(waqt)* of "eternal now," the destiny of the preeternal primordial covenant and the posteternal moment of truth. In the Abulafian text it is at the "flame of the circling sword," interpreted as the sword of the angel guarding paradise, that the innermost self is seen projected outside as in a polished mirror, a mirror simile that also occurs in Ibn ʿArabi's accounts of *fanā'*. In both texts, the semantic ambivalence seen in theological disputes over Adam's being made "in His/his image" is reflected on the mythic level. Is the inmost "self" that the meditator finds projected outside and confronting him as if from a polished mirror, divine or human, the divine reflection within the human heart or the human reflection within the divine mind?

In discussing Jewish apocalyptic,[48] Ithamar Gruenwald has suggested that the hero rising through the spheres uncovers two kinds of secrets, the secret of the cosmos and the secret of justice, the two kinds of secrets that the divine voice tells Job are not to be sought by humans. In accounts like those cited above, the secret *(sirr)* and subtleties *(latā'if)* of creation and justice are offered at first in terms associated with earlier apocalyptic: visions into the levels of reward and punishment and the subleties of creation. Beyond this understanding of secret, the more mystical texts open onto a point where both the secret of destiny and justice and the secret of unity, or *tawhīd*, are revealed in encounter and union with the inner self, human and divine, or transcending the duality of human and divine, self and other. Still, the secret is in another sense not divulged since the party *to whom* it is revealed is now one with the revealer and the act of revelation. The secret transcends the duality between acceptance and rejection, union and separation, right guidance and going astray, temporal moment and eternity. As one nears the divine presence such considerations are obliterated by the intensity of the witness *(shahāda)* or self-witnessing, as standard boundaries between self and other, between deity, idol, angel, Satan, and Prophet, between worship and idolatry begin to dissolve, and standard certainties are drowned or dissolved in a moment, dangerous and promising, of the most profound ambiguity. The encountering of the secret is not so much a resolution of mystery through a comprehensive knowledge as it is a deepening of mystery through unresolvable paradox:

> When I witness, O!-the-one-who-has-no-likeness
> Guidance and error are the same to me.

The self knows it, encounters it face to face,
and witnesses it in the moment *(waqt)* and in
eternity.[49]

Mystical Union and Bewildered Conversation

The self in the final station drowns in its love to the point that
it has no more feeling of itself or even of its love. The lover arrives
at a station in which he says: I am my beloved. My beloved
is I.[50]

The subtle channels connecting the language of mystical union
to the various language worlds of the Islamic world were clearly
and early on reflected in the Sufis' description of their own meditative practice. By the time of Abu Talib al-Makki (d. 386/996),
psychologically refined systemizations of Sufi moral and meditative
stages had been created.[51] ᶜAyn al-Qudat Hamadhani (d. 525/1131)
builds upon this development when he lists a catalog of major Sufi
terms that must be understood before one can evaluate and judge
controversial Sufi statements concerning mystical union and the
stations leading to it.[52] The terms play upon nuances in the various
forms of nearness and farness, expansion and contraction, ecstasy
and night of the soul, consciousness and extinction of conscious
thought. In demanding that those who would condemn Sufi sayings
understand such terms, ᶜAyn al-Qudat demands that they develop
dhawq (taste), a cultivation of ever more refined degrees of experience in love, love-madness, union, and bewilderment.

Bewilderment results from the union of subject and object implicit in the "union hadith" ("I become the hearing with which he
hears. . . . "). Seeing, hearing, and other perceptions become the
sole domain of the Qur'anic all-seeing *(al-basīr)* and all-hearing *(al-
samīᶜ)*, the divine perception of the secret of destiny within each
human heart. These intensive gerunds are commonly translated
with the locution "all-," but at this point a term like "all-seeing"
would mean not only "seeing everything" but "everything that
really sees." At the moment of mystical union, the divine covers
the human faculties with its perceptive activity. In the paradig-
matic text attributed to the sixth Imam Jaᶜfar al-Sadiq (d. 148/
765), Moses expresses astonishment at the divine self-revelation at
the burning bush ("I am I your lord," *Innī anā rabbuka):*

It is not proper for anyone but Allah to speak of himself by using
these words *inni ana*, "I am I." I was seized by astonishment

(dahsh), and passed away (in *fanā'*). I said: "You! You are he who is and who will be eternally, and Moses has no place with you nor the audacity to speak unless you let him subsist by your sub-sistence *(baqā')* and you endow him with your attribute." . . . He replied to me: "None but I can bear my speech, none can give me a reply; I am he who speaks and he who is spoken to, and you are a phantom *(shabah)* between the two, in which speech takes place."[53]

Junayd (d. 298/910) uses the union hadith in a manner that reflects the phantom nature of the self in *fanā'*, interpreting divine names such as "the all-conquering" as references to the divine overwhelming of the human faculties of the mystic. Normal human identity, perception, and knowledge are obliterated, and the vestige or trace *(rasm)* of the human personality is effaced. The mystic re-turns to that state of *fanā'* "in which" he was created at the pre-temporal covenant with Allah. The status of such an existence, and of the individual personality of the mystic who achieves it, is am-biguous:

> Then he unveiled over me an overwhelming vision and a clear manifestation. He annihilated me in generating me as he had originally generated me in the state of my annihilation. I cannot designate him because he leaves no sign, and I cannot tell of him because he is the master of all telling. Did he not obliterate my trace with his attribute? Did my knowledge in his nearness not pass away with my obliteration? He is the originator as he is the one who retrieves.[54]

The divine reveals itself in the obliterated and then divinely oc-cupied faculties of the Sufi in the phase of return or remaining *(baqā')*. Here the pretemporal eternity and destiny of the primordial convenant is revealed as one with the posttemporal eternity of the return or retrieval. To approach the divine presence is to lose con-sciousness of one's own nearness in the "annihilation of annihi-lation," namely, the annihilation of the consciousness of the undergoing of annihilation. Insofar as the "I" in the text has re-turned to his human selfhood this passage is fairly straightforward. The haunting quality of the prose is a result of an implication that the "I" is really the phantom *(shabah)* referred to in the text of Jaʿfar, an "I" that is in the process of declaring its own nonexistence. Despite his annihilation, Junayd's phantom self remains. Having tasted union, life becomes a torment (ʿadhāb, an allusion to the torments of hell) and a trial (balā'). Insofar as the lover is separated from the beloved, all "taste" for life has gone.

While in this text the ghost of the self speaks of its own annihilation, the reverse occurs in the genre of ecstatic utterance known as the *shath*. This term was traced by Abu Nasr al-Sarraj (d. 378/988) to the concrete senses of being shaken like sifted flour in the shaking house (al-mishtāh) that then spills over its edges or to overflowing like water from a stream.[55] The two most famous *shathiyāt*, anā al-haqq ("I am the real") of al-Hallaj and *subhānī* ("glory to me") of al-Bistami, have been interpreted by later Sufi commentators according to the doctrine of the divine covering of the human with divine attributes: from the point of view of *fanā'*, the passing away of the ego-self, it is not Hallaj or Bistami who speak but the divine voice clothing them or speaking through them. Like Junayd and Jaʿfar they have passed away, but rather than speaking as phantoms of their own nonexistence, the real declares its own complete existence and reality through them. In both the phantom speech of Junayd and the intoxicated utterances of Hallaj one is sometimes unsure whether the pronoun refers to the human or the divine—whether there are still two parties or whether one has reached the point where speaker and hearer are the same. Referential and predicative structures are pulled apart or fused by the presence of union within or beneath the text.

One notices also that pronouns tend to become separated from their antecedents. As a pronoun (huwā, or he; anta, or you) continues to recur without specific reintroduction of the antecedent (Allah, the human lover), the language takes on a charged, personal feeling, a feeling that increases in intensity as the human lover approaches the divine beloved. Many Sufi fragments consists of references to "him" without any nominal antecedent, references that establish an intimacy of texture, as well as an intimacy of relation between reader and the author who is speaking of the deeply personal. The affective charge of the language is in direct proportion to the distancing of these pronouns from their nominal antecedents. This existence of a charged, personal discourse within a highly abstract philosophical framework recalls the philosophical doctrine of the Greek Master wherein the intellect is said to be attached by bonds of love (ʿishq) to that which is beyond form and beyond all proofs. With Hallaj and other Sufi writers, the discursive treatment of a theological or philosophical theme can subtly shift toward the erotic dialogue, then back again to the discursive level, through the tightening or loosening of the pronoun from its antecedent. As the pronoun is progressively distanced, the impersonal declarative mood shifts to the vocative and the pronoun begins to take on the force of an interjection. Rational and affective elements, intellect and desire, are juxtaposed, intertwined, and fused in accordance with this play of pronoun, antecedent, and referent. Whenever the elements become particularly personal, the world of Arabic love poetry reappears, with its themes of love-madness and bewilderment.[56]

A particularly compelling series of bewildered conversations, far less well known in the West than those of Hallaj, are to be found in the *Book of Mystical Standings (Kitāb al-Mawāqif)* by Niffari (d. 354/965). A *waqf* ("standing" or "staying") is Niffari's term for the state of being riveted, as it were, in a particular place at the divine presence. The term resonates with the Qur'anic "standing" of each person before the revelation of her destiny during the apocalyptic moment of truth. It also echoes the poet-lover's standing before his fate of separation from the beloved at the *ghadāt al-bayn* (morning of her departure). In a single "standing" Niffari condenses a full range of language worlds and a complexity of referential and antecedental play.

The Standing "Who Are You and Who Am I"

He stood me in place, saying
   Who are you and who am I?

I saw the sun, moon, stars, and all the lights

He said to me
   In my sea stream nothing remains you have
   not seen

Everything came toward me—
   Nothing remained that did not—
     Kissed me between the eyes
      Blessed me
       And stayed in the shadow

He said
   You know me but I know you not

I saw him clinging to my robe not me

He said to me
   This is my devotion

I did not incline   Only my robe
   Inclined He said

Who am I?

Sun and Moon were veiled
The stars fell
The lights died out
All save he enveloped in darkness

My eye did not see
My ear did not hear
My perception failed

Everything spoke saying
Allahu Akbar!

Came toward me lance in hand

He said to me: Flee!
I said: Where?
He said
Fall into the darkness

I fell into the darkness
And beheld myself

He said
Behold yourself only yourself forever

Never will you leave the darkness

But when I release you from it
I will reveal myself

You will see me
And when you do
You will be the farthest of those most far[57]

This passage defies any single interpretation.[58] It may be helpful to begin with a schematic, though admittedly subjective, reading from the point of view of *fanā'*. The initial dialogue structure assumes the stability of identities: apparently divine statements that occur after the phrase "he said" are juxtaposed with apparently first-person references to mystical experiences ("I did not incline," "I saw"). After being "stood," Niffari has a vision of the planetary spheres and lights. Nothing remains (*yabqā*, perhaps an allusion to the mystical remaining of *baqā'*) that he hasn't seen, and he is blessed by everything in a moment of peaceful ecstasy. The divine voice states, "You know me but I know you not," perhaps an allusion to the famous Sufi dictum "Who knows his self, knows his lord."[59] Still, why would the voice deny divine knowledge of the human? The next line seems to provide a clue. The divine clings to the robe, "not to me." Is this another phantom discourse, as with Junayd, in which the self of the speaker has been annihilated, even in the moment of inclining toward the beloved, in which the divine clings to the robe of the phantom *(shabah)* of Junayd? The heavenly lights then die out in an echo of the Qur'anic moment of truth ("When the skies are torn asunder, and the stars are strewn. . . ." quoted earlier). The human faculties fail ("My eye did not see / My ear did not hear"), a direct play upon the union hadith ("I become the seeing with which he sees, the hearing with which he hears"). After the annihilation of *fanā'*, the peaceful ecstasy of the first part of the passage is replaced by a very different state. What had kissed him between the eyes now comes toward him lance in hand. The voice tells him to fall into the darkness where he "beholds himself," a self-beholding reminiscent of that mentioned by Ibn ʿArabi and quoted in section three. The passage also brings to mind Hallaj's words concerning Iblis's refusal to worship Adam and his exile from the heavens: when the *ʿayn* (essence, eye) changed on Iblis, he "fled from its gazes into the secret."[60] A final paradox occurs when the divine voice announces that when it releases him from the darkness, and he sees the divine, he will be the farthest of those most far. This may refer to the error of duality: insofar as one sees the divine (sees the "other" as an object), one is outside the union. Only in union is there the vision, or rather self-vision, of the divine.

Just as some Sufis interpreted the Satan story to mean that the being closest to Allah is somehow in farthest exile, so a similar *coincidentia oppositorum* takes place at the end of this passage: the closest approach to union is one with the extreme of alienation and rejection. From this point of view the shift from nearness to extreme separation may be less the result of a mistake than it is a reflection of the cosmic paradox exemplified by Iblis, the most intimate guardian of the divine throne and therefore the most radically rejected. Such a position would fit in well with the interpretation of ʿAyn al-Qudat Hamadhani, who articulated a view of Iblis in which separation was seen as a more advanced stage than union, since it results in a more dynamic relationship.[61]

This perspective can be seen as a reflection of the position of Junayd whereby *baqā'*, the remaining or return of consciousness, the tortured consciousness undergoing continual trial *(balā')* of divine jealousy after the extinction of *fanā'*, is considered a higher station than that of *fanā'*. But Hamadhani's expression can also be seen as an extension of Hallaj's emphasis upon Iblis's experience of separation at the point of closest intimacy. The movement of extremes is intermeshed with the poetics of separation and union, and the poetic tradition, with its moments of love-madness, be-wilderment, separation from the beloved, and night journey, res-onates throughout the passage. What may be occuring here is an oscillation between the existence of the individual outside union, an existence that causes the consciousness of separation and the passing away of the individual in the union. This dynamic oscil-lation is expressed in the classic verses attributed to love poetry and appropriated by the Sufis: "If I am absent he appears / If he appears, he obliterates me."[62]

The ambivalence concerning the divine and human occupant of the throne recurs here in a different context. The Iblis figure, never mentioned here explicitly but alluded to through the radical play of union and separation, recalls other figures such as Metatron or Hermes (Idris), who insofar as they approach union are subjected to the extreme of separation. In this language of bewildered con-versation, what is elsewhere expressed through the ambivalent na-ture of the figure upon the divine throne is brought out through the most subtle and most powerful play of pronoun, antecedent, and reference ambiguity.

One of the qualities of the Qasida poetic form is the inter-permeability of the various sections. An entire Qasida can be writ-ten as a wine song, with its own *nasīb*, journey, and boast, or as a *nasīb*, within its own journey, boast, and wine song. Each major section or movement can contain the others with its own distinctive modality. This trait of the Qasida is also found within Sufi liter-ature. Each language world, poetic, theological, hermetic, and dialogical, can contain the others. In this brief Sufi dialogue, the Qur'anic, poetic, hermetic, and theological language worlds are contained, and a rich interpretation of the dialogue could be given from each of them.

In all of the texts discussed in this section, standard distinc-tions—of subject and object, first person and second person, second person and third person, first person and third person, self and other, divine and human—have been seen to dissolve at the moment of union with a variety of linguistic consequences. The dislocating effect of the Niffari passage is augmented by the radical but some-what indeterminate effects of such fusions. The syntax and parallel dialogue structures of the Niffari passage suggest a clear distinction between the divine and human parties. But the intensity of the experience seems to pull at those divisions. Can we really be certain that it is Allah who clings to Niffari's robe (an anthropomorphic image) and not Niffari clinging to the divine robe? The title of the standing, "Who Are You and Who Am I," also gives us cause to wonder about the security of a consistent and clear division of the two parties of the dialogue. Could the persons be reversed at key moments? Could it be Niffari who clings to the divine robe? Could it be Niffari who is known by but does not know the divine? One has the sense that beneath a seemingly consistent and clear division, another kind of oscillation occurs, an oscillation not so much of states (union to separation) but of references. The "I" that began as the human party seems to flow or overflow, momentarily, into the "he" that began as the divine party; the two referential motions run past or through one another, as it were.

Mystical Union and Bewildered Discourse

> He reveals through him/Him his/His secret to him/Him
> It reveals through it/self its/own secret to it/self[63]

The dialogical language of union in Junayd, Bistami, Hallaj, and Niffari leaves the question of the relationship of the mystical union to the rest of society unresolved. The phantom discourse of Junayd offers an indelibly compelling evocation of union but does not attempt to integrate union into a wider cultural or philosophical world. The *shathiyāt* of Hallaj and Bistami confront the diverse members of society with an invitation to live on a similar edge of existential heroism. In Niffari the intensity of the language is in direct proportion to its intimacy.

By the time of Ibn ᶜArabi, Sufism's place in Islam had changed. Al-Ghazali's political and polemical activity had contributed to a new political center, with Sufism included and rationalist philosophy excluded. Organized networks of Sufis embracing various strata of society were forming around the names of earlier figures such as ᶜAbd al-Qadir al-Jilani (d. 560/1166). The relocation of mystical union within a wider society and a broader language is reflected in the writings of Ibn ᶜArabi, the grand master *(al-shaykh al-akbar)* of Sufi philosophy. In his voluminous *Meccan Openings (al-Futūhāt al-Makkiyya)*, he treats all branches of exoteric and esoteric learning from jurisprudence, hadith, grammar, and theology to poetry, alchemy, astrology and numerology. In his *Ring Settings of Wisdom (Fusūs al-Ḥikam)* he covers similar ground but in a language centered on philosophical rather than on hermetic principles. In either case, a mutual transformation has occurred. Sufi language of mystical union is opened onto a more discursive field, the world of third-person scientific and philosophical language, but Sufi mystical union is placed at the center of the language, transforming it from within. The move from the *dialogical* language of union found in the Hallaj and Bistami to the mystical *dialectic* of Ibn ᶜArabi need not be seen, as it often has been seen, as a decadent movement from genuine experience to intellectual abstraction. In mystical dialectic, the reference shifts and fusions of mystical union were not lost in intellectual abstractions. They were integrated into a third-person discourse of mystical philosophy, the guiding principle, or *dynamis*, of which was union. Mystical union transforms philosophical and other objective or scientific discourse, even as the philosophical language offers a new dimension of critical self-awareness and logical precision to the mystical.

The dialectic begins with a relentless critique of what Ibn ᶜArabi calls "binding" *(taqyīd)*. The divine manifests itself in various images refracted through the delimitations of language, philosophy, and cultural heritage. The number of possible images is infinite, and the manifestations are in a state of continual flux. While it is natural and proper to bind the divine in the sense of seeing it as manifested in an image, there is a human propensity (binding in the negative sense) to claim that that particular image or manifestation, what Ibn ᶜArabi calls the "god of belief," is in fact the divine essence itself. The result is anthropomorphism (taking the Qur'anic attributes as predications), idolatry (worship of the image in the place of that which is transcendent to its images), and infidelity (the denial of the divine as it appears in other beliefs, manifestations, and images). If left at this point such a critique would be liable to the charge of *taᶜtīl*, the stripping of the divine of all substance and all relation to the world, the charge that was leveled against those philosophers and theologians whose emphasis upon unity threatened a meaningful role for the Qur'anic divine names or attributes. Mystical union provided the central force for a positive movement, a retrieval of the divine names as realizations. These realizations, which had been reflected in the earlier Sufi dialogues, now become part of a wide-ranging interdisciplinary discourse. In Ibn ᶜArabi's works, the mystical dialectic reveals itself in four interlocking themes: the myth of the "breath of the merciful," the metaphor of the polished mirror, the archetype of the complete human being *(insān kāmil)*, and the moment of eternal now *(waqt)*.

In Ibn ᶜArabi's creation myth, the seven principal divine names (called doorkeepers, or *sadana*, reflecting the hermetic terminology and number) find themselves in a state of tension. The world and humankind have not yet been created, and without them the names really have no existence. Names such as the "hearer," "the seer," and "the just" take their meaning from language, which is intertwined with the world it reflects and with human consciousness.[64] The names present themselves before Allah, the comprehensive divine name, and complain that they do not exist and feel "tense." Allah orders the name "the overflowingly bountiful" *(al-rahmān)* to breathe *(nafasa)* the world into existence, thus relieving *(naffasa)* the names. The world is created through the breath of the merciful and serves as a mirror and prism for the divine, reflecting and refracting the divine light into the multiple divine names. But without Adam, the world is like an unpolished mirror. To complete the process human consciousness is needed to serve as the polishing of the mirror.

This creation myth can be seen as a metaphysical joke with a serious point. The absurdity of the divine names complaining to Allah that they do not exist dramatizes the anthropomorphic quality of conventional language of creation, even when creation language is attempting to avoid such a quality. Creation language uses names that can only be refractions of and results of the very process they are described as preceding. In some texts Ibn ʿArabi begins with the divine "willing" to see its names refracted and reflected in a cosmos. But "will" can only exist as a distinct name or attribute within that refraction. Thus to speak of the divine "willing to see its reflection" is to speak of will as a cause of a process of which it is the result. Language of creation spirals into an infinite circle of paradox. The names are retrieved only insofar as the mirror is polished in mystical union. At this moment the names that had been shown to be absurd as predications are retrieved as realizations.

The focal point of this retrieval is the figure of Adam as the complete human being *(al-insān al-kāmil)* based upon the Qur'anic account of the angels prostrating themselves before Adam because Adam knew the "names" and was the *khalīfa* (regent) of the divine. Implying that Adam's knowledge was knowledge of both the names of creatures and the divine names, Ibn ʿArabi makes Adam, archetypal human consciousness, the medium of reflection and refraction of the divine names. He plays upon the term *insān* (human, pupil of the eye) to indicate the human function as a locus for divine self-manifestation in the multiplicity of its names.

In his homage to the complete human being *(insān kāmil)* Ibn ʿArabi maintains that the *insān kāmil* is more *kāmil* than Allah. This apparently outrageous claim marks a redefinition of what it means to be *kāmil*. For many Sufis, most notably Junayd, *kāmil* might best be translated "perfect," the perfected state that is reached only by the transformation of the lower *nafs*, or soul, and through a progressive spiritualization until one arrives at a state approximating that of the angels. For Ibn ʿArabi, *kāmil* refers not to such spiritualized perfection but rather to "completion," to a twofold universality embraced by Adam: the universality of existing on all strata of reality, from the spiritual to the elemental (thus forming a *barzakh*, or interface, between element and spirit), and the universality Adam has as locus of refraction and reflection of the divine names. By using an expression that if understood in the older sense of perfection would seem outrageous, and by not spelling out specifically his redefinition, Ibn ʿArabi guarantees his redefinition a high symbolic and religious charge.[65]

Unlike Hallaj, Ibn ʿArabi saw Iblis's refusal to prostrate himself before Adam as an error. Although angels are more perfect than humans, more powerful, unencumbered by the grosser layers of bodily and mortal existence, Adam's role in the cosmos is more central. Adam was made the *khalīfa* of the divine, the regent, the microcosm. By embracing all strata of reality, and by knowing the divine through the plurality of the divine names, Adam is complete *(kāmil)*. The asceticism of early Sufis like Hallaj and hermetic writers like the Sabaeans, in which the individual attempts to shed not only the egoism of the *nafs* but also the human condition itself, is for Ibn ʿArabi an undervaluing of the human role in the universe. The human being, *as human*, is the locus of the divine self-reflection. The attempt at transcending the lower *nafs* is not abandoned, but the metaphysical role and value of the human, in accordance with which that attempt takes place, has been changed. This tension between the spiritualists (those who advocated a progressive angelization of the human) and the humanists (those who advocated a deepening and completion of human, as opposed to angelic, qualities) is reflected particularly in the differing interpretation of the Satan-Adam relationships and especially in the meaning given in specific contexts to the term *kāmil* (i.e., perfect or complete).

The human roles as *insān* (pupil of the eye) and *khalīfa* (regent) are intertwined. Human regency can be seen as a recognition that any attempt to refer to divine governance is necessarily anthropomorphic in its language and can only reflect human categories.

However, the individual human, inhabiting a world of space and time, cannot reflect all the names simultaneously. Each human is guided by a particular name and tends to bind the divine into the name or image and to deny other names and images, betraying his or her universality. Even the prophets were in some sense limited to a particular vision. In *fanā'*, such binding can in one sense be overcome. The heart of the Sufi becomes the polished mirror, polished insofar as it is void of its own images and projected names. The "ascent" visions of the bedazzlement within the throne room, and the vision of an image which is one's deepest self, form a subtext at this point. Ibn ᶜArabi hints throughout his writings that the throne is nothing other than the human heart. In the hermetic text, the *Poimandres*, the divine looks down upon nature and sees its image reflected within it. Falling in love with that image, the divine attempts to embrace it and is thus caught within the mortal embrace of nature.[66] The *Poimandres'* use of the mirror metaphor as a narcissistic fall into one's own image is reversed in Sufi ascent and Sufi use of the mirror metaphor in which the individual gives up its own images and self-infatuation and upon doing so becomes one with and in the divine image reflected in the polished mirror. Although the parallel is not complete, since Ibn ᶜArabi does not accept the negative valuation of nature and body that is present in the *Poimandres*, in some sense Ibn ᶜArabi can be said to be both appropriating and reversing the motif. The mirror metaphor forms the central paradigm for both the fall and the return, and at the more intense moments of union, the procession and the return are revealed as one.

At this point we return to the theological controversy over the notion that Allah created Adam in "his" image, and the claim of one school that *his* cannot refer to Allah since the divine is beyond form and image, and thus must refer to Adam. To translate Ibn ᶜArabi's passages dealing with the mirror metaphor and the creation of Adam, I have been forced to some experimental means for expressing the reference fusion that occurs. English demands that a choice be made between reflexive and nonreflexive pronouns. If we say, "He saw him reflected in the mirror," it is assumed that the *him* refers to someone other than the subject of the sentence. Arabic does not so insistently require such a distinction. At the moment of mystical union, of reflection in the mirror, the reflexive and nonreflexive possibilities are fused:

yuzhiru bihi sirrahu ilayhi

> he reveals through him/Him his/His secret to him/
> Him

or if we take the impersonal side of the pronoun (either "it" or "he"
can be implied in the Arabic pronoun):

> it reveals to it/self through it/self its/own secret[67]

These prepositional and pronominal contortions are found in earlier
writers such as Hallaj:

> Love *(ishq)* in the eternity of eternities from the primordial
> in it/him, by it/him, from it/him appearing
> and in it/him a beginning.[68]

In this case the pronoun *hu* can refer to the love as an impersonal
or to the divine beloved as a personal. This piling up of preposi-
tional-pronominal phrases was listed by Sarraj as one of the standard features of Sufi language of union, and it has been recently
related to the literary techniques of the *badi^c* school of poetry, which
developed at the same time as early Sufi literature.[69] Nevertheless,
in earlier Sufi writings, even writings as highly pitched as those
attributed to Hallaj or those mentioned by al-Sarraj, the ambi-
guities in reference and antecedence seldom overwhelm the stability of the initial divine-human division on the purely grammatical level, however radically they might challenge it on the
thematic level. In Ibn ^cArabi, this buildup of pronouns and prepositions occurs within the context of the mirror metaphor and the
mythic background in a manner that achieves a more radical and
complete referential fusion. The question of who sees whom in
whom, like an image in a double mirror, refracts into an infinitely
receding double set of possibilities: the divine sees itself in the human; the human sees itself in the divine; the divine sees itself in
the polished mirror, which, insofar as it is polished, is void of the
human qua human *(nafs)*. The statement "created in his image,"
which had been such a problem for the theologians, now reveals
within a grammatical fusion of antecedents a double meaning in-
corporating both of the theological positions: the *his* refers both
to the divine and to the human. Were it to refer to the human alone
(as suggested by the Ash^carites), the statement would be semantically flat. Were it to refer to the divine alone, the statement would
imply an anthropomorphic notion of divinity. The statement be-

comes meaningful only in the mystical union of *fanā'*, in which the reflexive (its own image) and nonreflective (the other's image) collapse into one another. The issue of destiny undergoes a similar transformation. No longer does the question pit human free will and agency against divine omniscience and omnipotence. At the moment of union, the one actor is both the human and the divine. In the moment of mystical union the choice between a tyrannical, arbitrary deity or a deity limited by human free agency (both of which involve, as was seen earlier, intractable theological problems) is taken up into the reference fusion. The power of the revelation of the secret of destiny in the Qur'anic *yawm al-dīn* (moment of truth) receives a compelling mystical interpretation. The attributes (knowing, willing, seeing) are no longer anthropomorphic predications of an exterior deity but realizations (i.e., simultaneously understandings and actualizations) reflected within the mirror of human/divine union. The willer is the divine reflected in the human or the human reflected in the divine. At the conjunction of this double reflection is the *lordship*, the inner destiny acknowledged at the primordial covenant and revealed at the moment of truth. One only realizes this self that was seen projected outside as in a mirror insofar as normal self-identity is given up. Like the question of destiny and free will, the question of the individuality or universality of this self is not answered but taken up into the reference fusion.

At this point the danger is greatest. Since for the individual in space and time, the images and manifestations of the divine must be constantly changing ("in every moment he [Allah], is in a [different] state"),[70] to hold on to the image that appears in the polished mirror is the prime temptation. To bind the divine in it is to fall into worship of a static and delimited image, with all the attendant dangers of intolerance and spiritual stagnation. The response to this danger is a perpetually transformative conception of *fanā'* based upon a new version of the *waqt*, or moment. In his account of the mystical ascent discussed in section three, Ibn ʿArabi spoke of a point just before the culmination in mystical union where the mystic sees the "forms of the sons of Adam," namely, the preexistent souls at the moment of the primordial covenant sealing their destiny. He then said, "You see your form among them and from it you recognize the *waqt* you are in." The *waqt* here is the eternal moment in which the pretemporal eternity of the convenant and the posttemporal eternity of the moment of truth are realized in their unity. Ibn ʿArabi's notion of *waqt* has a wide set of intertextual resonances. To deny that the creator was subject to laws of natural causality, the scholastic theologians had claimed that in every moment *(ān)* the creator destroys and re-creates the world. Early Sufis had attempted to be "sons of their moment " *(abnā' al-waqt)*, living only for the moment and making no provision for the future. The poets had claimed that in every moment the beloved changed her mood, condition, and form, trapping them in a continual flux of emotion and image. In a play upon all three notions, Ibn ʿArabi outlined his understanding of the eternal moment. In every moment one should pass away, become one with the divine in the mirrored image, and then give up that image to pass away again. The individual can approach the universality of the complete human *(insān kāmil)* only through the process of *taqallub* (perpetual transformation), not binding himself or herself to any image, belief, philosophy, or dogma. Ibn ʿArabi speaks of *taqallub* in a pun on the word *q-l-b* (meaning both "heart" and "change"), and it is this notion of heart as seat of transformative wisdom, as opposed to the analytical knowledge of the ʿaql (intellect, a term whose root meaning is "binding"), that is at the center of his famous verses:

> Marvel, A garden among the flames.
> My heart has become receptive of every form.
> It is a meadow for gazelles, a monastery for monks,
> An abode of idols, the Kaʿba of the pilgrim,
> The tables of the Torah, the Qur'an.
> My religion is love—wherever its camels turn
> Love is my belief, my faith.
> We have a model in Bishr, Hind, and her sister,
> In Qays and Layla, Mayya and Ghaylan[71]

At this point we return to the passage cited in section one of this essay (p. 93), where Ibn ʿArabi explains the reference to the famous lovers of the poetic tradition at the end of the above verses:

> [Allah] afflicted them with love of human beings as a rebuttal to those who claim to love him, but are not in like manner driven mad with love. Love deprived them of their wits. It made them pass away from themselves at the sight in their imagination of the beloved.

We also recall the verses of the Persian poet Hafiz: "On this road there are conversations which melt the soul/ Each man has such a quarrel that it's beyond telling." When discussing the creation of Adam in the context of the reflection in the polished mirror, Ibn ᶜArabi does not assert as a theological doctrine that the *his* in the "his image" refers both to Adam and to Allah. His language realizes or enacts such fusions or slides of reference of reflexive and non-reflexive, self and other, human and divine. The fusions or slides occur often. The following passage concerns the attempt to achieve a new moment *(waqt)* of as short a duration as possible, so that the Sufi is continually experiencing union and separation, *fanā'* and *baqā'*, extinction and reconstitution within a new image. The shortest moment is the breath. In each breath a *dhikr*, or remembrance, is recited. In each inhalation the Sufi achieves a new form. In each exhalation the Sufi gives up the form. Through antecedence fusion, the breath of the mystic is aligned with the eternal divine "breath of the compassionate" that was breathed and always is being breathed into Adam:

> The seeker continues to say with every breath
> "My lord, increase me in knowledge"
> as long as the sphere of the universe turns in His/his breath
>
> So that he attempts to make his moment his/His breath[72]

Again the locution his/His is needed to show the fusion that occurs in the original Arabic. The reference to the sphere of the universe turning in "his" breath has a dominantly divine reference. But by the time one reaches the second reference to his/His breath the fusion is complete, and the "his" fits equally well the divine and human referent. Depending upon position and context, a pronoun's reference and antecedent may 'slide' (a dominant reference yielding to an alternate possibility) or it may involve a complete fusion in which both possibilities are equally present.

Union is perpetually reenacted. The lover perpetually finds and perpetually separates from the beloved. Similarly, mystical dialectic does not bind meaning but continually moves from the referential delimitation of an object to an apophatic moment and back again to referential intentionality. The reference fusion discussed earlier in two cases recurs often in the Andalusian Sufi master's writings in a wide variety of contexts, and in each case it serves to transform closed hierarchies, doctrines, and formulations into open-ended movements.[73] Because the divine names and attributes are not predicates but realizations or reflections in the mirror of mystical union, they are not meaningful outside of union. A writer cannot disclose the secret of union, cannot disclose "what" is encountered there, anymore than a Sufi writer can distinguish what occurs in mystical union from what occurs in the erotic union of the poets. What is revealed in union is communicated only to one who passes away.

This does not imply that mystical union is reserved only for the spiritually and ascetically heroic. For Ibn ʿArabi the highest stage of the mystical ascent was the station of "no station," in which the notion of hierarchy is transcended. From the perspective of no station every moment of passing away from an old image and remaining or returning in a new image, however humble or insignificant such an act might seem as an experience, is the one polishing in the mirror that always has occurred and always is occurring.

Many of the themes and linguistic effects were to be echoed by Sufis writing in other languages and combined with the contributions those Sufis brought from their own deep traditions. The role of mystical union within those literary traditions is another story. It seems fitting to end the discussion with Ibn ʿArabi, who in many senses can justifiably be said to have been the "seal," if not of the saints (as some interpreters believe he claimed to be), at least of the classical formulators of mystical union within the Arabic tradition.[74]

Unitive Experiences and the State of Trance

DANIEL MERKUR

When the term *unio mystica,* "mystical union," was borrowed from
Roman Catholic theology for academic application in the comparative study of religions, the theological category was assumed
to be a culture-specific phrasing of a psychological category that
was valid cross-culturally. Although the validity of comparative
studies of mysticism rests, in part, on this assumption, it is very
much an assumption. The nature of mystical union has been the
subject of a lively debate for over a century. The present contribution seeks to understand what mystical union is, both in the experience of the mystics and from a psychoanalytic point of view.
The former no less than the latter is a reductive procedure; an apophatic, or negative, theology cannot be otherwise.

The Common-Core Hypothesis

Upon the rise of medical psychiatry in the mid-nineteenth century,
various Christian mystics—including several traditional saints—
were diagnosed as morbid personalities. The diagnoses were challenged, first by Roman Catholic writers and next by Anglicans, who
simultaneously revived the practice of mysticism in their churches
after a lapse of some two hundred years.[1] Because of the discon-

The author would like to thank the Lady Davis Fellowship Trust for a post-
doctoral fellowship at the Hebrew University of Jerusalem in 1985–86.

tinuity of the living practice in Western Christendom, modern knowledge of traditional Catholic mysticism depends on historical reconstructions. As may be expected, factual errors have not been few.[2]

Comparative perspectives played an understandably large role in the Christian mystical revival. Living mystical traditions were investigated for insights that would elucidate the writings of Christian mystics. The Hindu Yogic emphasis on the Atman-Brahman equation and the Buddhist preoccupation with Nirvana were compared with the emphases that some Christian mystics had placed on *unio mystica*. Modern theologians simultaneously discouraged the revival of other Christian mystical practices—the apparitions and visions that had been classified since Augustine as corporeal and imaginative visions[3]—because they were no longer prepared to defend their religious validity.[4]

Academic studies of comparative mysticism, which arose late in the nineteenth century to further Christian concerns, favored comparably restrictive definitions. In an influential formulation, Evelyn Underhill suggested that "mysticism, in its pure form, is . . . the science of union with the Absolute, and nothing else, and . . . the mystic is the person who attains this union."[5] Emphasis was placed on experience to the exclusion of ideology but at the expense of a value judgment that denied spiritual authenticity to experiences other than union. The inherently theistic implications of the term *mystical union* have since been avoided by references, for cross-cultural purposes, to *the mystical experience*. The definite article perpetuates the assumption that only one variety of religious experience is properly termed mystical.

When Gershom Scholem pioneered the academic study of Jewish mysticism, he adopted a contrary position, claiming that whatever the historical Jewish mystics experienced was, by definition, mystical. Scholem emphasized that visionary practices had dominated Jewish mysticism from its origins throughout the twelfth century.[6] Comparable arguments may readily be mounted on the evidence of Christian, Muslim, Hindu, and Buddhist mysticism. In no culture have mystics been limited to unitive experiences. Neither have unitive experiences been limited to mystics. For example, although shamans favor visionary and/or auditory experiences that suit the needs of their seance practices,[7] shamans occasionally have unitive experiences[8] and may even base part of their worldviews on them.

Academic research also inherited a second unearned premise

from the Christian mystical revival: the assumption that mystics' writings about unitive experiences referred to an experience that is everywhere one and the same. In his classic but rudimentary account of mysticism, William James proposed six invariants of mystical experience: a sense of union;[10] a "consciousness of illumination [which] is . . . the essential mark of mystical states";[11] and the subsidiary features of ineffability, noetic character, transiency, and passivity.[12] By *ineffability*, James referred to the mystics' claims that they cannot adequately explain their experiences in words. Because language is inherently contextual and referential, mystics are at least partially unable to explain their experiences to the uninitiated, much as the blue of the sky cannot be explained to the unsighted, the melody of a symphony to the deaf, or the taste of a pear to a person who has never eaten the fruit.

James's claim that mystical experiences invariably have a noetic—in modern idiom, a cognitive—aspect has been much disputed; we shall return to the problem later. Passivity is definitely a variable feature. It is found in Christian mysticism but not, for example, in Buddhism.[13] As for transiency, most mystical experiences vary in duration from several minutes to perhaps as much as two hours; but a few mystics have known unitive states of a type that will be later described as "personal" and that lasted during all of their waking hours for years.[14]

James maintained that mystical experiences were highly variable and contingent on what he termed "overbeliefs": religious conceptions that a person brings to a religious experience, not only postexperientially in the process of its interpretation and reportage, but also preexperientially as a contribution to the experiences' contents.[15]

> The mystical feeling of enlargement, union, and emancipation has no specific intellectual content whatever of its own. It is capable of forming matrimonial alliances with material furnished by the most diverse philosophies and theologies, provided only they can find a place in the framework for its peculiar mood.[16]

All in all, James referred the "common core" of mysticism to the "subconscious." Mystics' conscious experiences were highly variable because their overbeliefs were integrated within "the mystical feeling of enlargement, union, and emancipation."

The older psychologists of religion fostered a debate between the uncommunicating positions of medical psychiatry and academic theology. James wrote in explicit refutation of the hysteria theory of mysticism,[17] while G. A. Coe, J. B. Pratt, R. H. Thouless, and J. C. Flower allowed no more than that mysticism and hysteria sometimes overlapped.[18] The psychological consensus arose in response to theologians' emphasis of a neglected fact. Several Catholic mystics had actively engaged in detailed and protracted practices of meditation in whose consequence they had experienced progressively increasing oblivion to both the perceptible world and the interior life of the mind. At the height of their meditations, the mystics passively experienced contemplations that subjectively seemed to infuse consciousness in spontaneous and involuntary fashions. Translating these findings into the language of their own discipline, the psychologists concluded that, although mystical union is sometimes a spontaneous symptom of psychopathology,[19] it is not necessarily pathological, because its occurrence can also be induced through meditation. Meditation was recognized as a religious form of autosuggestion, and the resultant psychic state was identified as self-hypnosis.[20] This consensus, which originated among the older psychologists of religion,[21] was later accepted by both psychoanalysts[22] and hypnotherapists.[23] The theory has since been confirmed by experimental psychological research. Mystical experiences, encompassing a loss of personal identity, followed by a sense of infinite being, and finally a consciousness of nothing, have been produced in deep hetero-hypnotic states.[24]

An example of the type of experience that the common-core hypothesis addressed may be observed in the following report by Alfred, Lord Tennyson.

> I have never had any revelations through anaesthetics, but a kind of waking trance—this for lack of a better word—I have frequently had, quite up from boyhood, when I have been all alone. This has come upon me, as it were out of the intensity of the consciousness of individuality, individuality itself seemed to dissolve and fade away into boundless being, and this not a confused state but the clearest, the surest of the surest, utterly beyond words— where death was an almost laughable impossibility—the loss of personality (if so it were) seeming no extinction, but the only true life. I am ashamed of my feeble description. Have I not said the state is utterly beyond words?[25]

Tennyson induced his experience through monotonous, repetitive meditation—a classic technique for bringing about both hypnotic trances and mystical experiences. During his experience, consciousness of both external reality and personal identity disappeared. What remained was a sense of "boundless being." It was an experience of existing, an experience not of "I am" but simply of "am." All else was forgotten.

An important feature of the trance state may be observed when Tennyson's unitive experience is contrasted with its analogue during an LSD experience.

> It was indescribable, glorious, ineffable. Most of the time I was beside myself! I was carried, tossed on the creative sea of Being. . . . There was no limit to anything. It was infinite, timeless, boundless, and I was part of it. I was penetrated and permeated with the many splendored beauty of creation. I merged with it. All was unity. There were no barriers, no separations, no possibility of death—only transformation and an expanding consciouness of the creative wonder of eternity. The human mind and heart could not contain it. . . . Through all this, something in the center of me held firm and unshaken. . . . I wept for joy that this inner vision was so wonderful.[26]

What in Tennyson's experience seemed to be an objectively real expansion of the self to become "boundless being" occurred instead in the LSD experience as an "inner vision" of the "infinite, timeless, boundless" with which the drug taker was united. A sober or realistic sense of self, what the drug taker calls "something in the center of me," persisted and knew that the experience, though profoundly meaningful, was nonetheless imaginary. As it is a function of the trance state to reify imaginations,[27] the hypnosis theory of mysticism was able to explain the confusion of imagination with reality that is responsible for the irrationality of most mystics. Reference to psychopathology was unnecessary. The need remained, however, to account for the difference between mystical union and other religious uses of hypnosis (visions, voices, locutions, stigmata, spirit possessions, etc.). Also unexplained were the features of mystical experience that are rational and nonrational as distinct from irrational.

With the rise of psychoanalysis, the orthodox Freudian school of depth psychology, the unitive factor in mystical union was attributed to manifestations of ordinarily unconscious psychical materials of a unitive character. Psychoanalysis has since been followed by medical psychiatry in regarding the unconscious materials as regressions to—or relivings of—extremely early modes of experience. Two major candidates were proposed. Mystical experiences of a serene, solitary state of timeless and boundless being were interpreted as regressions to intrauterine experience. *Ex hypothesi* the fetus does not as yet know that anything else exists, does not yet differentiate the self by contrast with the not-self, and has no clear idea of whether the body terminates.[28]

The second formulation was offered by Sigmund Freud, who depended on a slightly defective self-report of what has since come to be termed the *oceanic feeling*. It is a different type of unitive experience. Rather than a sense of boundless being, the experience consists of a sense of the unity of all physical reality. The following self-report is from James's collection.

> I felt myself one with the grass, the trees, birds, insects, everything in Nature. I exulted in the mere fact of existence, of being a part of it all—the drizzling rain, the shadows of the clouds, the tree-trunks, and so on.[29]

Because the experience includes definite perceptions of physical realities beyond the body, Freud interpreted the union as a regression to immediately postnatal experience, when the infant "does not as yet distinguish his ego from the external world as the source of the sensations flowing in upon him."[30]

Both variants of the psychoanalytic theory suggested that the unitive factor in mystical union is a matter of outlook, rather than of the object(s) being viewed. Because the unitive outlook is thought with, rather than thought about, it causes mystics to feel identical to or united with whatever may be the objects of their thought. The unitive factor proceeds at the level of apperception, the non-verbal process of knowing, understanding, and recognizing by which the raw data of sense perceptions are organized into coherent and meaningful patterns.

Another strength of the psychoanalytic theories is their treatment of the hypnotic state and the unitive factor as independent features. Either may occur in the absence of the other. Although classical psychoanalysts rarely emphasized this belief, their theories warranted a diagnosis that psychoanalytic writers began to endorse in significant numbers only in the 1960s. Mystical experiences, occurring in the absence of trance, may contain no irrational elements. On medical criteria, the experiences must be recognized as benign, even by writers unwilling to acknowledge them as beneficial and desirable.

Carl G. Jung wrote extensively of the images in mystics' visions but almost not at all of their unitive experiences. His few remarks were generalizations based on his personal acquaintance with Hindu Yoga alone.[31] For their part, pastoral psychologists embraced the Freudian model but with the caution that "the question must be raised whether the elements which grasp the unconscious are bearers of the Ultimate and whether they are received by the total personality instead of remaining strange bodies within it."[32] The relocation of the common core of mysticism in the unconscious was similarly given qualified endorsement in Underhill's influential writings.[33]

The Phenomenological Approach

The rise of the phenomenological school of the history of religions *(Religionswissenschaft)* ruled out of court all references to the unconscious and returned academic research to the status quo before James. Serious attention was accorded, however, to the varieties of mystical experience.[34]

Friedrich Heiler understood mysticism as an introvertive experience during which the body is fixed in "cataleptic rigidity and complete anaesthesia."[35] According to Heiler, there is "a perfect cessation of the normal conscious life."[36] Neither the world of external sense perception nor the mystic's "human personality" are experienced. The soul is wholly "absorbed in the infinite unity of the Godhead" or, in Buddhism, Nirvana.[37] Mysticism admits to two major types that differ in the absence or presence of emotional content during the experience.

> Ecstasy is the highest pitch of emotion. Although the suppression of the normal emotional life is its presupposition . . . it shares with the normal emotional experience the element of spontaneity, passivity, involuntariness, impersonality, brevity, and lasting effect. . . . Nirvana, on the contrary, is complete disappearance of emotion, a continuous, permanent state of profound quiet and perfect solitariness, a blessedness without excitement, transport, or storm, not a being possessed, but a being utterly self-absorbed.[38]

As an illustration of what Heiler meant by Nirvana, let us consider a report by Agehananda Bharati, a Viennese-born social anthropologist and a Tantric monk.

> One night when I was about twelve, it happened for the first time. I was falling asleep, when the whole world turned into one:

one entity, one indivisible certainty. No euphoria, no colours, just a deadeningly sure oneness of which I was the center—and everything else was just this, and nothing else. For a fraction of a minute, perhaps, I saw nothing, felt nothing, but was that oneness, empty of content and feeling. Then, for another five minutes or so the wall with the *kitschy* flowers reappeared, and the fire crackled in the large brick stove. But I knew it was One, and I knew that this was the meaning of what I had been reading for a year or so—the Upanisadic dictum of oneness, and the literature around and about it. I did not think in terms of God, *atman*, *brahman*, nor, strangely enough, in terms of having found fulfilment—I was just struck by the fact that I had not known this oneness before, and that I had kept reading about it very much as I read about Gaul being divided into three parts, or elementary Sanskrit grammar. Then after some time, no longer than half an hour I would think, things returned to whatever had been normal before.[39]

Although he appears to have stated that he felt an ultimate oneness or unity at the climax of his experience, Bharati, in a personal communication,[40] denies that his published self-report is to be so understood. The climactic moments of his "zero experience" consisted of a conscious state that was wholly lacking in cognitive contents. His published account asserts that the moments of zero experience were "oneness" and "One," not because they were so experienced, but because Bharati so interpreted their significance. His interpretations were made immediately after the moments of zero experience during the waning phases of the experience, when he resumed cognitive thinking and external sense perception.

Bharati also had a second zero experience in which euphoria was present.[41] Heiler contended that the difference is significant: a conscious state that lacks both cognitions and affects is not the same experience as a conscious state that lacks cognitions but involves euphoria. As an example of the purely affective experience that Heiler called ecstasy, let us consider a self-report by the German Dominican Henry Suso (d. 1366).

He went into an ecstasy and saw and heard what is ineffable. It was without form or shape, and yet it bore within itself all forms and shapes of joyous delight. His heart was hungry and yet satisfied, his mind joyous and happy, his wishes were calmed and his desires had died out. He did nothing but gaze into the brilliant light, in which he had forgotton himself and all things. He did not know whether it was day or night. It was a sweetness flowing

out of eternal life, with present, unchanging peaceful feeling. He
said then: "If this is not heaven, I do not know what heaven is,
for all the suffering that can ever be put into words, could not
enable anyone to earn such a reward and for ever possess it."
This blissful ecstasy lasted perhaps an hour, perhaps only half
an hour; whether his soul remained in his body, or was separated
from his body, he did not know. When he came to himself he felt
just like a man who has come from another world.[42]

During its climactic phase, Suso's experience lacked all cognitions
but had intensely positive affect. Cognitive thought resumed before
the experience ended.

Rudolf Otto, to whom a Buddhist monk had described Nirvana
as an experience of "bliss—unspeakable,"[43] treated both of Heiler's
categories together as "the Inward Way" or "Mysticism of Intro-
spection," which he contrasted with experiences of "the Outward
Way," whose "unifying Vision" apprehends the perceptible world.[44]
The report just cited in connection with Freud's account of the
oceanic feeling is an instance of Otto's Outward Way. The waning
phase of Bharati's experience, when he saw the phenomenal world
in all its multiplicity but understood it to be One, is another example.

W. T. Stace proposed the terms "introvertive" and "extrovertive" mysticism, respectively, for Otto's two categories. He explained that "the introvertive [experience] looks inward into the
mind . . . from which all the multiplicity of sensuous or conceptual
or other empirical content has been excluded," while "the extrovertive experience looks outward through the senses."[45]

As varieties of introspective mysticism, Scholem distinguished
mystical union and communion.[46] Johannes Lindblom rephrased
the distinction by contrasting the impersonal and personal character of the two experiences. The goal of "*mysticism of unity* or
impersonal mysticism . . . is complete oneness with the divine conceived of as a more or less impersonal substance."[47] In personal
mysticism, however, "the personality is preserved, both the personality of the divine and the personality of the religious man."[48]
What is at stake in Lindblom's formulation is personality, not personhood. Mysticism is not personal simply because the divine is
conceived theologically as a personal being. Martin Buber observed
that our experience of another person in the second person as a
"thou" differs from an experience of the same person in the third
person. The failure to be engaged with another person's personality
denies much of his or her personhood, reducing "him" or "her" to

an "it."[49] The converse is also true. By treating them in the second person, inanimate phenomena can be accorded personality, personalized, or personified. So understood, mysticism is personal whenever it involves both an "I" and a "thou" but impersonal whenever an "I-it" relationship occurs.

The following report is an instance of personal mysticism.

> The happiness of this eternal moment was given to me. . . . I had not willed it, but received it as a divine gift of some divine will.
>
> This peace that passed understanding, this joy that was like a tide of music flowing with a calm compulsion and from an infinite source through my whole being was the reality at the heart of life. And the only necessary aim in human life was to qualify to receive and express it, to prepare the self like a bride for the coming of the bridegroom, to make of the body and mind a temple of the Holy Ghost.[50]

The spiritual marriage, or mystical union, effected a bond of "peace" and "joy," while the personal identities of the mystic and the Holy Ghost remained distinct.

Personal mysticism may also occur as a vision in which unitive ideas are manifested in vivid pictorial forms. The Indian sadhu Sundar Singh, who converted from Hinduism to Christianity in 1904, wrote about several such visions.

> Christ on His throne is always in the centre, a figure ineffable and indescribable. The face as I see it in Ecstasy, with my spiritual eyes . . . has scars with blood flowing from them. The scars are not ugly, but glowing and beautiful. He has a beard on His face. The long hair of His head is like gold, like glowing light. His face is like the sun, but its light does not dazzle me. It is a sweet face, always smiling—a loving glorious smile. Christ is not terrifying at all.
>
> And all around the throne of Christ, extending to infinite distances, are multitudes of glorious spiritual Beings. Some of them are saints, some of them angels. . . . When they speak to me they put their thoughts into my heart in a single moment; just as on earth one sometimes knows what a person is going to say before he says it. . . .
>
> In these visions we have most wonderful talks. . . .
>
> Any one who has been there [in Heaven] for one second says to himself, "This is the place on which I have set my heart, here I am completely satisfied. No sorrow, no pain, only love, waves of love, perfect happiness. . . ."

> Streaming out from Christ I saw, as it were, waves shining and peace-giving, and going through and among the Saints and Angels and everywhere bringing refreshment, just as in hot weather water refreshes trees. And this I understood to be the Holy Spirit.[51]

In unitive visions of this type, the identities of the mystic and God remain distinct. Union proceeds through a bond of love, emanating from God, that thoroughly permeates the mystic.

Although the phenomenologists' typological observations were empirical and valid, they were frequently seen not as providing a reason to acknowledge the historical diversity of mystical experiences but as arguing for the need to reformulate the common-core hypothesis. Perhaps because they disbelieved that any experience could lack both cognitions and affects, most scholars ignored the difference between zero and purely affective experiences, confounded their literary evidence, and identified the resultant fiction as the mystical experience.[52] The maneuver, which shifted the common-core hypothesis from a Hindu to a Buddhist standard, had a superficial plausibility. Mystical experiences had everywhere to be one and the same because complete absences of cognition cannot differ from experience to experience.

The Current Debate

Few scholars appreciated the irony that defining the mystical experience as a purely affective experience made the term mutually exclusive with unitive experiences, which include cognitions of union. The common-core hypothesis retained general subscription until Aldous Huxley claimed that psychedelic experiences were mystical.[53] Theological writers responded by abandoning the ecumenicism that had informed the common-core hypothesis.

The current debate takes its point of departure from R. C. Zaehner's proposal that differences among mystics' doctrines reflect actual differences in the phenomenologies of their experiences.[54] Scholars had previously treated mystical experiences and religious doctrines as independent variables, with single types of experience accommodating several doctrinal interpretations, and vice versa. Zaehner's first category encompassed mystical experiences of the unity of external physical reality. Not content to characterize the experiences as extrovertive, Zaehner specified that "nature mysticism," in which "all creaturely existence is experienced as one and one as all," is a "pan-en-hen-ism," meaning "all-in-one-ism." It has no theistic content and is improperly termed pantheism; it cannot constitute mystical union, but it does account for psychedelic experiences.[55] Zaehner next distinguished all experiences of "the soul contemplating itself in its essence" as "monism." Monistic mystical experiences involve a "state of pure isolation of . . . the uncreated soul or spirit from all that is other than itself." These experiences of "detachment . . . from all purely physical and psychic, and . . . temporal elements" contain no theistic element.[56] Theistic mystical experiences, by contrast, entail "the simultaneous loss of the purely human personality, the 'ego', and the absorption of the uncreated spirit, the 'self', into the essence of God, in Whom both the individual personality and the whole objective world are or seem to be entirely obliterated." In theistic mysticism, "the soul feels itself to be united with God in love." Zaehner reserved the term *unio mystica* for theistic mystical experiences, for they alone entail "the return of the 'self' to God."[57]

Zaehner's methodology—which invented psychological categories on the basis of doctrinal evidence—led him to err on all three counts. Extrovertive mysticism can indeed be theistic, as shown in the following self-report by the Franciscan mystic Angela of Foligno (ca. 1249–1309).

> After this I went into the church, and there did the Lord speak most sweetly and graciously unto me, whereat all my mind did greatly rejoice and take comfort. He said, "My beloved daughter," and many other things better still, and added, "No creature can console thee, only I alone, who desire to reveal My power unto thee."
>
> And immediately the eyes of my soul were opened and I beheld the plenitude of God, whereby I did comprehend the whole world, both here and beyond the sea, and the abyss and all things else; and therein did I behold naught save the divine power in a manner assuredly indescribable, so that through excess of marvelling the soul cried with a loud voice, saying, "This whole world is full of God!" Wherefore did I now comprehend that the world is but a small thing; I saw, moreover, that the power of God was above all things, and that the whole world was filled with it.
>
> Then said He unto me, "I have shown thee something of My power."[58]

In Angela's extrovertive mystical experience, God was both transcendent and omnipresent. She experienced not panenhenism but panentheism.

Zaehner's category of monistic mysticism is no less misinformed; it can be fairly applied to experiences of "boundless being." However, Ninian Smart rightly criticized Zaehner for treating both Hindu and Buddhist doctrines as monistic when the differences between the two are as great as those between monistic and theistic doctrines.[59] Hindu doctrines can accommodate experiences as various as those of Tennyson, Bharati, and Suso. Buddhism is more restrictive and has historically debated whether Nirvana is void of both cognitions and affects or cognitions alone.[60]

As for theistic mysticism, Zaehner's methodology did not do justice to the complexity and subtlety of the mystics' accounts. Ernst Arbman established a more convincing analysis of impersonal theistic mysticism in a magisterial study of religious trance that is undeservedly little known outside Scandinavia.

Arbman emphasized that mystical union has a gradual onset. The experience may commence quite early in the path to contemplation while the mystic is still able to perceive external reality. It invariably climaxes in deep trance, when both external perception of the sensible world and internal perception of the mind have been inhibited.[61] The process starts with the mystic experiencing a faint sense of the invisible presence of God. As the experience progresses, the divine presence becomes increasingly intense and compelling until, at climax, it is the exclusive content of consciousness.[62] Concurrent with this intellectual and, to some extent, kinesthetic dimension to mystic union is its emotional side. Both the mystic's emotional devotion to God and God's love for the mystic increase until, at climax, God's love alone is experienced.[63] A self-report by Mechthild of Magdeburg (ca. 1207–ca. 1282) illustrates this phenomenon:

> My body is in long torment, my soul in high delight, for she has seen and embraced her Beloved. Through Him, alas for her! she suffers torment. As He draws her to Himself, she gives herself to Him. She cannot hold back and so He takes her to Himself. Gladly would she speak but dares not. She is engulfed in the glorious Trinity in high union. He gives her a brief respite that she may long for Him. She would fain sing His praises but cannot. She would that He might send her to Hell, if only He might be loved above all measure by all creatures. She looks at Him and says, "Lord! Give me Thy blessing!" He looks at her and draws her to Him with a greeting the body may not know.[64]

Mechthild described an initial phase during which she experienced a process of being attracted to God. She cooperated in this process by remaining passive, giving herself to God, and avoiding speech. An impersonal union followed, but then ceased. During the "respite," she experienced not God's love for her but her own for God. She was now sufficiently introverted that she was unable to sing. She was able, however, to conceptualize a wish and then mentally to request God's blessing. Impersonal union then resumed.

The great systematizers of Roman Catholic mysticism developed generalizations that, as generalizations, are necessarily idealizing accounts. They attest, however, to similar transitions from personal to impersonal union as the experiences proceed from onset to climax. The following account is by Richard of Saint Victor (d. 1173).

> The Beloved is forced to wait a moment and a moment in all of these places. . . . He is heard by memory; seen by understanding; kissed warmly by affection; embraced by applause. He is heard by recollection; seen by wonder; kissed warmly by love; embraced by delight. Or if this pleases you better, He is heard by a showing; seen by contemplation; kissed warmly by devotion; drawn close for the infusion of His sweetness. He is heard by a showing when the whole tumult of those who make noise is quieted down and His voice only is heard as it grows stronger. At last that whole crowd of those who make a disturbance is dispersed and He alone remains with her [the soul] alone and she alone looks at Him alone by contemplation. He is seen by contemplation when on account of the sight of an unexpected vision and wonder at the beauty of it, the soul gradually glows, burns more and more, finally at last catches fire completely until it is thoroughly reformed to true purity and internal beauty. . . . She melts completely in desire for Him with a kind of ineffable infusion of divine sweetness and that spirit which clings to the Lord is made one spirit.[65]

The differences between the beginning and the climax of mystical union were such that Teresa of Ávila (1515–82) referred separately to the "spiritual betrothal" and the "spiritual marriage," respectively.

> In the union of the Spiritual Marriage. . . . The Lord appears in the center of the soul, not through an imaginary, but through an intellectual vision. . . . This instantaneous communication of God to the soul is so great a secret and so sublime a favour, and such

delight is felt by the soul, that I do not know with what to compare
it. . . . It is impossible to say more than that, as far as one can
understand, the soul (I mean the spirit of this soul) is made one
with God, Who, being likewise a Spirit, has been pleased to reveal
the love that He has for us by showing to certain persons the
extent of that love, so that we may praise His greatness. For He
has been pleased to unite Himself with His creature in such a
way that they have become like two who cannot be separated
from one another: even so He will not separate Himself from her.

The Spiritual Betrothal is different: here the two persons are
frequently separated, as is the case with union, for, although by
union is meant the joining of two things into one, each of the
two, as is a matter of common observation, can be separated and
remain a thing by itself. This favor of the Lord passes quickly
and afterwards the soul is deprived of that companionship—I
mean so far as it can understand. In this other favor of the Lord
it is not so: the soul remains all the time in that center with its
God.[66]

Teresa's spiritual betrothal was a personal mysticism that had
intermittent moments of impersonal union. Her spiritual marriage
was a sustained impersonal experience.

The climactic moments of mystical union consist of a loss—
not of consciousness but of self-consciousness. It is this process that
mystics have described metaphorically as death or annihilation.[67]
When dreaming or when absorbed in a book, a drama, and so on,
a person forgets that he is having an experience; he devotes the
whole of conscious attention to the experience itself. In mystical
union, the experience happens to be the presence of God.[68] Coin-
ciding with the absorption of attention by the experience, I suggest,
is an identification with its contents. Just as in a dream one may
observe one's image and feel it to be the locus of one's consciousness
and self, so too in mystical union there is both an external observation of an experience and an identification with its content. Because the content happens to be the presence of God, the mystic
feels at one with God.

Arbman emphasized that the union is invariably experienced
as the mystic's own deification.[69] John of the Cross referred explicitly to the soul's deification through experiences of mystic
union:[70] "They are indeed encounters, by which He ever penetrates
and deifies the substance of the soul, absorbing it above all being
into His own being."[71] As additional examples, Arbman cited *Sister
Katrei*, Angela of Foligno, Madame Guyon, and Pierre Janet's patient

Madeleine.[72] The evidence may readily be augmented. The Greek Fathers of Christianity conventionally spoke of the mystic's "divinization."[73] Symeon the New Theologian claimed that "by grace I am God." Catherine of Genoa spoke of being "changed completely into pure God." Maria Maddalena de'Pazzi saw herself "wholly united with God, transformed into God." Antoinette Bourignon wrote that "the purified soul transforms itself into him."[74] The fourteenth-century brethren of the Free Spirit were said to have laid claim to deification through mystical union.[75] Again, the kabbalah and Hasidism speak literally and not euphemistically of the mystic's "divine soul." *Yehidah*, "union" or "unification," is considered an experience of the mere "comprehension" of the self-evident fact.[76]

The monotheistic religions have regularly interpreted the mystical experience of deification as falling short of identity with God. Christian mystics have spoken of "divinization by grace" and rejected the reality of "divinization by nature." Kabbalists accept an identity of the soul with the sefirot, the emanations of the divine within the creation, while categorically rejecting the possibility of an identity with the *Eiyn Sof*, the uncreated Godhead. It is important to emphasize, however, that mystics experience very little of a cognitive character during the moments of union. There is an unelaborated intuitive idea of deification, but sustained cognitive thought forms no part of the experiential moment. Teresa explained that "the soul is wholly in the power of another, and during that period, which is very short, I do not think that the Lord leaves it freedom for anything."[77] For this reason, the Sufi mystics of Islam distinguish between the soul's intoxication during union and its subsequent reassertion of sobriety, while Catholic mystics speak of the soul's death during union and its rebirth upon God's withdrawal, and so on.[78] It is only after the moments of deifying union, during the waning phase of the ecstasies, that measured intellectual observations become possible and theological interpretation on the sense in which deification took place begins.

In final analysis, however, it is not the claimants of mystical deification but the apologists who command attention. In polemic against the Free Spirit movement, Henry Suso argued that because the self is experienced both before and after union, it cannot be destroyed but must instead persist during the experience of Nothing.[79] The subjective experience and its objective reality consequently differ. "The powerful transport into the Nothing casts out all difference in the ground, not according to our essence, but according to our perception."[80] Although the soul does not perceive itself, it is nonetheless present, as is proved by its capacity to perceive the experience. "Man can, in some measure, if he is rapt into God, be one in losing himself, and yet externally be enjoying, contemplating, and so on."[81] For Nothing to be experienced, there must be a soul, an observing self, that experiences the Nothing.

Suso further denied that "the creative Nothing that is called God"[82] is the same Nothing that the soul experiences in mystical union.

> A man may in this life reach the point at which he understands himself to be one with that which is nothing as compared with all the things that one can imagine or express in words. By common agreement, men call this Nothing "God", and it is itself a most essential Something. . . . But there is something more deeply hidden in Him. . . . As long as one understands thereby a unity, or such a thing as can be explained by words, one has to go farther inwards. The Nothing, however, cannot penetrate deeper into itself, but we can, as far as our understanding allows.[83]

The soul may experience Nothing, but this Nothing is necessarily an essential Something. Hidden within it is what alone truly cannot be described in words: the hidden Godhead. Union with the essential Nothing is possible in this life, but union with the hidden and utterly Indescribable is not.[84] During its absorption in the Nothing, the soul fails, however, to appreciate the distinction.

> The soul always remains a creature, but in the Nothing in which it is lost, it does not consider at all in what way it is then a creature, or what the Nothing is, or whether it is a creature or not, or whether it is united or not. But when one is able to reflect, one understands this, and it remains in us unimpaired.[85]

In addition to his extended discussion of impersonal mysticism, Suso also remarked briefly on personal mysticism, when self-perception persists.

> These men who are rapt into eternity, consider themselves and all things for ever as everlasting and eternal, because of their surpassing indwelling unity.
>   Question: Is there no otherness there?
>   Answer: Yes, he has it more than ever who knows it, and recognizes himself as a creature, not as sinful, but as united.[86]

Suso's account of mystical union was intended to explain experiences of both impersonal and personal types. Because he had himself experienced purely affective mysticism, he was not prepared to deny the actual phenomenon of impersonal mystical experience, but he was adamant in rejecting its apparent philosophical significance.

The Sufi mystics have similarly gone to the trouble of denying the reality of mystical deification. The following passage is from Abu Hamid al-Ghazali (d. 1111), the philosopher and mystic who secured the public respectability of Sufism.

> The mystics, after their ascent to the heavens of Reality, agree that they saw nothing in existence except God the One. Some of them attained this state through discursive reasoning, others reached it by savoring it and experiencing it. From these all plurality entirely fell away. They were drowned in pure solitude: their reason was lost in it, and they became as if dazed in it. They no longer had the capacity to recollect aught but God, nor could they in any wise remember themselves. Nothing was left to them but God. They became drunk with a drunkenness in which their reason collapsed. One of them said, "I am God (the Truth)." Another said, "Glory be to me! How great is my glory", while another said, "Within my robe is naught but God." But the words of lovers when in a state of drunkenness must be hidden away and not broadcast. However, when their drunkenness abates and the sovereignty of their reason is restored—and reason is God's scale on earth—they know that this was not actual identity, but that it resembled identity as when lovers say at the height of their passion:
> "I am he whom I desire and he whom I desire is I;
> We are two souls inhabiting one body."[87]

The testimony of Martin Buber provides further and unequivocal evidence of the experience of deification.

> Now from my own unforgettable experience I know well that there is a state in which the bonds of the personal nature of life seem to have fallen away from us and we experience an undivided unity. But I do not know—what the soul willingly imagines and indeed is bound to imagine (mine too once did it)—that in this I had attained to a union with the primal being or the godhead. That is an exaggeration no longer permitted to the responsible understanding. Responsibly—that is, as a man holding his ground before reality—I can elicit from those experiences only that in them I reached an undifferentiable unity of myself without form or content. I may call this an original prebiographical unity and

suppose that it is hidden unchanged beneath all biographical change, all development of the soul . . . existing but once, single, unique, irreducible, this creaturely one: one of the human souls and not the "soul of the All"; a defined and particular being and not "Being"; the creaturely basic unity of a creature.[88]

The very fact that Catholic, Sufi, and Jewish mystics have apologized for experiences that they did not wish to experience proves that the experiences were real. Deification is not an overestimation but the actual phenomenon or experience of impersonal theistic unions. Indeed, it cannot be otherwise. Impersonal theistic mysticism is invariably a conjunction of self and God. The experience commences as an interpersonal encounter, but God ceases to be felt as a distinct Thou when, at climax, one's normal or realistic sense of oneself is replaced by an ideal Self who is seemingly God.

Arbman further established that any or all of three subsidiary features of unitive experience may coincide with the climactic moments of deifying union: an emotional experience of intense love,[89] a visual experience of brightness or light,[90] and an intellectual experience of ideas that seem to the mystic to be thoughts of God that have now become his/her own.[91] These ideas, which may have either verbal or nonverbal form, impart an extensive cognitive content to the total experience but should not be confused with the extremely limited cognitive contents of the actual moments of union. Teresa stated that "we never . . . hear these words at a time when the soul is in union. . . . When this short period has passed, and the soul is still enraptured . . . divine locutions" occur.[92] The ideas, which are highly variable in content, may pertain to any topic of religious or theological interest. Arbman exphasized that they frequently have moral content. Teresa wrote: "They make us tremble if they are words of reproof and if they are words of love fill us with a love that is all consuming."[93]

Mystics who have written of the union of wills with God refer to their acceptance of moral values. Their own wills become one with, because they are subservient to, the will of God. Rebirth and passive transformation are metaphors for this moral regeneration.[94] This union of wills occurs after the climactic moments of deification during the waning, cognitively rich phase of the total experience. Angela of Foligno stated:

> When the soul is transformed in God and is in God, and hath
> that perfect union and fulness of vision, it is quiet and worketh

nothing whatsoever. But when it cometh again to itself it striveth to transform itself into the will of God.[95]

Arbman emphasized that at no time during mystical experience does the mystic's ego disappear. The conscious idea of self is forgotten, but the subjective experience of being an observer—the basic core of self—persists throughout. Nor is its experience vague or amorphous. Union is vivid, coherent, and completely memorable. It has been claimed to be vague and amorphous but only by writers who have vague and amorphous understandings of the experience.[96]

Impersonal theistic union may also occur in the pictorial form of a vision. The following self-report is by Hadewijch of Brabant, a thirteenth-century Flemish Beguine.

> The eagle, who had previously spoken to me, said: "now see through the Countenance, and become the veritable bride of the great Bridegroom, and behold yourself in this state!" And in that very instant I saw myself received in union by the One who sat there in the abyss upon the circling disk, and there I became one with him in the certainty of unity. Then the eagle said, when I was received: "Now, behold, all-powerful one, whom I previously called the loved one, that you did not know all you should become, and what your highest way was, and what the great kingdom was that you as a bride should receive from your Bridegroom."[97]

In the following self-report, Angela of Foligno described a vision of the same impersonal unitive type.

> Upon another occasion, as I was gazing at the Cross with the Crucified, and was looking at the Crucified with my bodily eyes, such a fervent love was suddenly kindled in my soul that even the members of my body felt it with great joy and delight. I saw and felt that Christ embraced my soul with the arm wherewith He was crucified, wherefore I rejoiced with a joy greater than I had ever had before.
>
> From this time forth there hath remained unto me a certain joy and clear enlightenment, whereby the soul knoweth and understandeth how it is that we see our flesh made one company with God.[98]

Experiences of this type consist of a vivid vision that commences with the mystic beholding both him/herself and God as discrete personal beings. As the vision proceeds, however, the two figures merge into one. What begins as personal mysticism thus ends as an impersonal union. God's personality abides but, in seemingly becoming an addition to the mystic's personality, ceases to be experienced in a personal manner as a Thou.

Because Zaehner's contentions linked the psychological analysis of mystical union with the philosophical problem of mystics' truth claims, he sparked a heated debate among philosophers and theologians. Methodological issues soon came to the fore. Ninian Smart emphasized that mystical experiences differ from the interpretations that mystics place on them, both during their occurrence and after the experiences have ended.[99] H. P. Owen also insisted that the mystics' beliefs, practices, and expectations contribute interpretive content to the experiences themselves.[100] Some consensus has developed that personal, cultural, and universal factors are interwoven in mystical experiences much as they are in nocturnal dreams.[101] With the exception of the moments of zero experience at the climax of occasional mystical unions,[102] mystical experiences invariably contain "incorporated interpretations" that are rooted in the cultures and eras of the mystics. In final analysis, "there are as many different types of mystical experience as there are incorporated interpretations of them."[103] The current consensus has thus at long last embraced a position close to that of William James and classical psychoanalysis—although without acknowledging the precedents.

Steven Katz, a force behind the current consensus, has further asserted that there "is no foundation for a phenomenology of mysticism or a typology of comparative mystical experience."[104] His contention is, I suggest, a necessary theoretical implication of the phenomenological method that has limited the academic debate since Heiler. This reasoning was most clearly articulated by Arbman, who theorized that the belief complex, or group of beliefs, that form the content of the meditations prior to a trance are converted by the trance state from objects of belief to objects of actual experience. Beyond its conversion of beliefs into experiences the alternate state contributes no doctrinal content to the experience. All differences among religious uses of trance states are consequently to be explained by reference to the preexperiential belief system.[105] Postexperiential doctrines ought therefore to be in perfect agreement with the preexperiential beliefs, and the varieties of unitive experience are as many as the preexperiential beliefs. Conversely, as long as the beliefs are constant—in the life of an individual and in an era of a culture—the experiences will be constant. As such, mystical experiences may be subject to valid diachronic generalizations that nonetheless preclude cross-cultural comparisons.

The flaw in the theory is its inconsistency with the facts.

The Postulation of the Unconscious

For methodological purposes, manifest psychic phenomena that cannot satisfactorily be explained by reference to the psychology of consciousness constitute a compelling reason to postulate the activity of one or more psychic factors that are not conscious and may thus be termed unconscious. Unconscious psychic activity is indicated, for example, in cases of theistic mysticism when mystics have had unwanted experiences of deification (as contrasted with deification experiences that may conform to traditional prebeliefs). Were mystics' preexperiential beliefs the exclusive determinants of their experiences, mystics disbelieving in self-deification would never experience it. They would not need to deny the apparent doctrinal consequences of their experiences. Some mystics have nevertheless experienced such deification despite consciously held religious beliefs to the contrary.

Further evidence requiring the postulation of the unconscious may be discerned in a self-report by Sundar Singh.

> When I used to practise Yoga there was no permanent refreshment, though the trance might be temporarily comforting. Indeed the great contrast between the state of Ecstasy and the Yogic states which I cultivated before becoming a Christian lies in the fact that in Ecstasy there is always the same feeling of calm satisfaction and being at home, whatever had been my state of mind before going into Ecstasy. Whereas in the Yogic state, if before the trance I was feeling sad, I used to weep in the trance, if cheerful I would smile. Also after an Ecstasy I always feel strengthened, invigorated, and refreshed. This result did not follow Yoga.[106]

The affective contents of Sigh's experiences of Yoga varied in keeping with his emotions prior to the alternate state. Once he had converted to Christianity, he experienced a highly positive feeling regardless of his mood prior to the onset of his ecstasies. Singh's ecstatic euphoria may not be traced to his Christian beliefs and expectations. Because his Hindu beliefs did not take precedence over his preexperiential mood during his Yogic states, we have no warrant to suppose that his Christian beliefs can have done so either.

Again, unitive experiences may be unanticipated and, as it were, adventitious consequences of trance induction. In a series of psychological experiments, Albert J. Deikman had his subjects sit in comfortable armchairs in a well-lit, neutrally painted and decorated room. Before them was "a blue vase ten inches high, which stood on a simple brown end table against the opposite wall." The subjects were given the following instructions concerning the technique of meditation.

> The purpose of these sessions is to learn about concentration. Your aim is to concentrate on the blue vase. By concentration I do not mean *analyzing* the different parts of the vase, or thinking a series of thoughts about the vase, or associating ideas to the vase, *but rather, trying to see the vase as it exists in itself*, without any connections to other things. Exclude all other thoughts or feelings of sounds or body sensations. Do not let them distract you but *keep them out* so that you can concentrate all your attention, all your awareness on the vase itself. Let the perception of the vase fill your entire mind.[107]

The experimental subjects meditated for five minutes on the first day, ten on the second, and fifteen on the third session and thereafter. Subjects wishing to prolong the sessions were allowed to do so; the sessions then lasted from twenty-two to thirty-three minutes before the subjects terminated them spontaneously.[108]

One subject reported impersonal unitive experiences from the first session onward but was frightened by the loss of her sense of reality.

> One of the points that I remember most vividly is when I really began to feel, you know, almost as though the blue and I were perhaps merging, or that vase and I were. I almost got scared to the point where I found myself bringing myself back in some way from it. . . . It was as though everything was sort of merging and I was somehow losing my sense of consciousness almost.[109]

The following is a report concerning the same subject's twenty-first session, during which she briefly passed beyond union to a complete lack of cognition.

> She reported that a diffuse blue occupied the entire visual field and that she felt merged completely with that diffuseness. She

had a sense of falling, of emptiness, of loneliness and isolation as if she was in a vacuum. Her sudden realization that there were absolutely no thoughts in her mind made her anxious and she *searched* for thoughts to bring herself back. "It was as if I leaped out of the chair to put the boundaries back on the vase . . . because there was *nothing* there . . . the vase was going and I was going with it. . . ."[110]

In her fifty-fourth session, the subject achieved a more complete union together with a distinct impression of the presence of a unifying, metaphysical force.

It was also as though we were together, you know, instead of being a table and a vase and me, my body and the chair, it all dissolved into a bundle of something which had . . . a great deal of energy to it but which doesn't form into anything but it only feels like a force.[111]

Deikman's subjects attempted to concentrate on their visual perception of the vase while excluding all other thoughts from consciousness. The voluntary restrictions induced trance states that converted them into increasingly restricted automatisms. Complete emptiness of consciousness was once experienced directly. Because the meditations did no more than restrict the normal contents of consciousness, the impersonal unitive experiences cannot be traced to the prior contents of consciousness. The experiences evidently filled the psychic emptiness that the meditation technique produced. Their source must be sought in the unconscious.

A Psychoanalytic Approach

Medical authorities today interpret an inverse causal relationship between psychopathology and unitive experiences. Nathaniel Ross writes: "It is quite common for schizophrenics to experience mystical ecstasies briefly before they plunge into the psychic depths. This would appear to represent a last desperate attempt to cling to the object world."[112] Paul Horton adds that in psychosis "the mystical experience . . . may . . . become a transitional phenomenon . . . [and] a special, potentially adaptive, ego mechanism of defense."[113]

It is my contention that unitive experiences act in a similar way in trance states that have been induced through meditations. In Deikman's experiments, the meditations were designed to provoke a conscious psychic emptiness, while the unitive experiences were unconsciously produced compensations for—better, defenses against—conscious mental paralysis. I suggest that this situation is the general rule. Trance is closely related to shock. In trance, as in shock, many of the normal functions of consciousness are repressed. As trance deepens, the normal functions of apperception, memory, sense perception of the external environment and the body, and in deepest trance even verbal thought itself are repressed with increasing completeness. In its own right, trance is contentless. Were it allowed to proceed without interruption, contentless states of trance-induced and trance-enforced unconsciousness would continue indefinitely until the body failed for lack of nourishment. As a defense against the potential danger of trance, unconscious thought supplies mental contents that break the hold of the trance. When the normal functions of consciousness are progressively inhibited during hypnotic trances, the unconscious psyche—specifically, the unconscious reach of the supergo—assumes the responsibility of mediating between ideas and actions.[114] *Ex hypothesi*, trance states that are so intense or deep that suggestion and its resultant automatisms are themselves partly or wholly repressed force the unconscious to resort to more drastic lines of defense. When nothing less will serve, the unconscious has recourse to unitive experiences, whose cognitive contents are so minimal that they tend to escape repression and whose intensely positive effects generally suffice to counteract the paralysis of trance itself. On this theory, it is unimportant whether a trance is a spontaneous manifestation of schizophrenia, mania, hysteria, or epilepsy or the voluntary consequence of hetero-hypnotic induction techniques, meditation techniques, or psychoactive drug use. As long as trance states are involved, unitive experiences function as defenses.

The relation of trance to shock should not be overestimated. The principal difference between the two—that one is voluntary and gentle while the other is involuntary and violent—requires that they be diagnosed very differently. The situation is analogous to pushing a large heavy object rather than being thrown rudely against it. Trance is potentially highly beneficial, but it is also potentially highly dangerous. Shock, by contrast, always has traumatic or pathogenic implications.

A psychoanalytic approach also allows us to construct a cross-cultural typology based on a selected number of structural features that reflect discrete processes or mechanisms of unconscious thought.

UNITIVE VISIONS. Personal and impersonal theistic visions may be regarded as subtypes of personal and impersonal theistic mysticism, respectively. Unitive visions are clearly variant forms of unitive ideas in which the ideas have undergone symbolization into pictorial form, much as ideas do during the dreams of natural sleep.

PERSONAL MYSTICISM. The psychic agency that Freud termed *das Über-Ich,* "the superego," is a systematic extension of the popular idea of conscience. The very superiority of conscience presupposes a capacity for self-observation, while its value judgments presuppose its possession, maintenance, utilization, and application of ideal values.[115] The superego is also capable of independent reasoning and problem solving.[116] For these reasons, the superego always conveys emotions, ideas, and the impression of a presence that collectively manifests a distinctive intelligence and personality other than the ego within consciousness. In its ideational form, personal mysticism, is, I suggest, nothing other than an intense and protracted manifestation of the superego.

IMPERSONAL MYSTICISM. Because impersonal mystical experiences invariably commence as personal mystical experiences, impersonal mysticism is best interpreted in parallel as a further manifestation of the superego.[117] When the deepening of the trance state causes increasing portions of the conscious ego to be repressed, the superego assumes increasingly extensive command of the psyche. Personal mysticism, in which the ego and the superego are separate but in communion, gives way, through the collapse of the ego, to impersonal mysticism, in which the superego and the observing function of the ego undergo a conjunction or fusion. Experientially, the ego's realistic sense of self is replaced by its sense of the superego. Impersonal mysticism is definitely not a manifestation of the ego alone. It includes a great deal of material, including large parts of the mystic's adult personality structure,[118] that is inconsistent with a theory of the ego's regression.[119]

Impersonal mysticism may be understood to encompass both the monistic experience of "boundless being" and the theistic experience of deification. The variable factor is a question, not of psychology, but of the overbeliefs consequent on one's philosophy: whether one interprets the superego as part of oneself or as an intrapsychic agency through which divine revelations occur. Monistic overbeliefs, incorporated within the experience, will determine that the ego's union with the superego will seem a union with one's higher self; theistic overbeliefs will cause the same union to seem a deification of the ego through its absorption into the love and wisdom of God.

ZERO EXPERIENCES. Because impersonal unitive experiences precede and/or follow moments of zero experience, the former are presumably preconditions of the latter. In zero experiences, the capacity of the trance state to inhibit the normal processes of consciousness apparently extends so far that the superego fails in its task of defense. As the trance state intensifies, it provokes and then represses an impersonal mystical experience, causing consciousness to be reduced to a zero experience.

It need scarcely be added that a truly contentless experience is a paradox that corresponds to no real psychic phenomenon. What mystics have experienced is, as Deikman has understood,[120] the bare minimum of the ego, its capacity to observe. Experientially, there is an experience of observing, but there is nothing to observe. Nor is there any experience of the idea that the ego is doing the observing. There is simply an act of observing that, from a psychoanalytic perspective, we may ascribe to the ego. The psychic condition is presumably just short of unconsciousness. Just as a word may remain on the tip of the tongue or a memory just beyond recollection, so psychic materials almost but finally do not manifest themselves consciously. Because they are pressing for consciousness, a conscious state occurs, but because they fail to manifest themselves, the state has neither cognitive nor affective contents.

AFFECTIVE MYSTICISM. Purely affective mystical experiences are presumably intermediate between impersonal unions and zero experiences. The trance state censors the cognitive content of an impersonal mystical experience but, for any of several reasons, does not additionally repress its affective content. The result is a purely affective experience.

EXTROVERTIVE MYSTICISM. Extrovertive mystical experiences are presumbly to be explained, in parallel, as manifestations of the superego that are akin to, yet differ from, the manifestations responsible for impersonal mystical experiences.[121] In introvertive mysticism, the ego identifies with the superego, experiencing it as though it were the ego's own identity. Extrovertive mysticism depends on the related process of "projective identification." The superego is both projected outward to encompass the perceptible world and identified with the ego. Because the superego serves as the intermediating link, external reality is experienced as an extension or part of the ego.

Conclusion

In all, there would appear to be at least three major psychological categories of unitive experience: (1) introvertive, personal mysticism; (2) introvertive, impersonal mysticism; and (3) extrovertive mysticism. There are also several subtypes. Both introvertive types may undergo symbolization and take form as visions. Impersonal mysticism may instead undergo partial or total repression, resulting in purely affective or zero experiences, respectively.

In its historical use by the Catholic mystics, *unio mystica* was a theological category. It was not a psychological term and cannot usefully be transformed into one. Some mystics applied the term to several different experiences; others limited its use to single psychic phenomena. Modern uses in comparative studies exhibit similar variations. It is not necessary to conclude, with Hans Penner, "that 'mysticism' is an illusion, unreal, a false category."[122] For academic purposes, mystical union may be usefully employed on historical principles as a general cover term in preliminary stages of research when gathering data. Mystical union's subdivision is necessary if the historical category is to be converted into scientifically valid, cross-cultural terms, but psychologically meaningful terminology can be applied with precision only as an outcome of the data's close analysis. Similar considerations are appropriate in the area of interreligious ecumenicism.

As for the psychological significance of mystical union, it cannot be too often repeated that the goal of mature religiosity is not religious experiences but the religious life. Unitive experiences are the most intensely pleasurable experiences that are possible for a human being. They are used hedonistically, as a narcotic, whenever they are made an end in themselves. Their unparalleled access to the deepest and most unconscious core of the superego can be used as a source of emotional and religious renewal when they are integrated within a responsible, socially active, practical, productive, moral, and empathetic way of life. Because the state of trance contributes an irrational factor over and above the unitive experiences themselves, unitive experiences that occur in the absence of trance are to be preferred to those that coincide with trances; else a rigorous, postexperiential reinterpretation is warranted if the benefits of the experiences are to be maximized.

Comments

Moshe Idel

A perusal of the present collection of papers invites some comparative comments, which were only tangentially addressed in the papers. First and foremost, the issue of the relative importance of the topic under examination remains an open subject. The authors have been able to establish the phenomenology of the expressions of *unio mystica* in the religions dealt with here, and the centrality of this type of religious experience in religious mysticism is indeed manifest. However, the "cruciality" of this type of mystical experience for religion in general and for mysticism in particular may still be an open issue. Is the existence of extreme unitive experiences a sine qua non for the flowering of mysticism, or is it possible to envision the development of mysticism without the impact of sharp unitive experiences? It is especially important to address the question of the contribution of the experiences designated by the scholars or the mystics themselves as unitive to the creativeness of the mystics.[1] Although any attempt at a definitive answer will always be conjectural, it seems that in some cases a certain correlation between the feeling of contact with the divine is expressly a catalyst for literary and other types of activity.

Beyond this question related to psychology (see Merkur's paper), a more sociological question seems pertinent: which of the writings concerning the most intimate relationship of a person belonging to the mystical elite, can, or did, contribute to society, or at least to the many? Elaborated answers to these types of questions will help to map the status of *unio mystica* within a large range of mystical experiences as a vital sociological factor, not just as an interesting case for religious phenomenology (see Dupré, pp. 7, 13–17, 21).

In the same line, we may ask what is the relative importance

157

of *unio mystica* in the three religions analyzed here? Even if the existence of a certain amount of discussion in a given religion is acknowledged, it is still important to address the problem of the initial openness this religion offers, or gradually develops, toward this type of religious phenomenon (see Sells, pp. 115–16). In Islam, expressions of *unio mystica* appear early in the first stages of the religion's development,[2] in contrast to the emergence of such types of expression—on experiences we can only speculate—in Christianity and Judaism at a later period. In Europe, Judaism and Christianity began their interest in mysticism with a moderate type of mystical expression, as twelfth-century Christian mysticism, the first half of thirteenth-century Jewish mysticism, and the theosophical-theurgical kabbalah demonstrate. In these religions, the explicit articulation of extreme types of mysticism seems to coincide with the emergence of more sophisticated philosophical vocabulary and concepts, whereas in Islam, the most extreme type of unitive expressions seems to depend less on the establishment of speculative trends of thought. For example, the influence of Neoplatonism seems to be crucial for Muslim mysticism, whereas the mystical implications of Aristotelian epistemology are less important. At the time when European mystics, Jews and Christians, expressed themselves in a growing movement and in bold ways, the bright colors of extreme mysticism in Islam had already begun to fade. This tendency corresponds to the abrupt descent of philosophy in the Islamic milieux, to use Sells's phrase, whereas in Europe, the thirteenth century saw a new and rich development of the Aristotelian and Neoplatonic trends of thought.

The early appearance of extreme types of expression in Islam may be one of the reasons for the phrases employed by some Muslim Sufis that Sells designates as "bewildered speech." Whereas Sufi literature describes the mystical experience with luxuriant paradoxes, the language of Jewish mysticism is austere, even meager insofar as the "bewildered" phrases are concerned. As I tried to show, Jewish mystics were substantially influenced by philosophical terminology, which entered Jewish culture earlier and which they employed to explain the nature of their experience to themselves and to others. This is, apparently, one of the reasons that the kabbalistic language is moderate in comparison with the Muslim one and, I assume, with that of Christian mysticism. Generally, mystical paradox that reaches the verge of blasphemy occurred when a highly sophisticated and agreed-upon terminology was absent or rejected by a certain mystic. As Islamic mysticism evolved, the "bewilderment" apparently diminished, though elements of paradoxical language still remained in use because of the incorporation of more speculative sets of terms and concepts (see Sells, pp. 116–17).

The temporal and geographical coincidences of the ascent of *unio mystica* expressions among Jewish and Christian mystics are indeed remarkable. If the existence of extreme expressions of unitive experiences in Jewish mysticism is recognized—in spite of the prevailing theory, which negates its existence in this body of writings—then a productive comparison of these expressions will become a desideratum for studies of medieval European mysticism.[3] Here only some preliminary remarks can be advanced.

As McGinn's paper demonstrates, the notion of essential union with the divine flowered from the second part of the thirteenth century onward. For example, extreme expressions occurred in the writings of Abraham Abulafia (1240–ca. 1291), only a small part of which was presented here.[4] But whereas these expressions first appear among people who cannot be counted among the intellectual and religious elite of the Christian world, Abulafia and some of his followers are of high status in the Jewish world. McGinn's paper (pp. 71, 74) emphasizes that it was only with the literary production of Meister Eckhart that extreme mystical expressions became part of the elite patrimony of Christian mysticism. The sharp reactions in early Islam to some mystics, culminating with the deaths of Hallaj and Suhrawardi, are paralleled in Christian mysticism by the death of Marguerite Porete. Animosity against extreme mysticism also emerged in Judaism, where Abulafia was accused of posing as a prophet, a term roughly corresponding in some medieval Jewish texts to "mystic." However, even Abulafia's most fierce opponent, Rabbi Shelomo ben Abraham ibn Adret, himself a kabbalist, did not insist, at least from what we know from the extant documents, on a death penalty for Abulafia.

Apparently, at least in the cases of Islam and Christianity, the powerful authorities backing the religious establishment restricted the flourishing of extreme mysticism by orchestrating efforts to extirpate expressions of deification among the mystics. The deification expressions found in Islam and Christianity may have included elements that were conceived of as heretical, for example, assumptions that could be understood as involving not only a spiritual but also a corporeal transformation in the deification processes. As far as Jewish texts are concerned, I am not aware of explicit or implicit claims that the human body, and not only the soul, underwent a deep transformation that could change its status. Furthermore, in Christianity and Islam the deification claims were not abstract pretensions; mystics who reached ultimate mystical experiences were convinced that they had transcended the ordinary religious requirements. These types of claims seem to be absent in Jewish texts, at least in explicit formulations.

Apparently, there is a certain correlation between the emergence of extreme expressions of *unio mystica* and women as mystics in Islam and Christianty. Although I would not push this correspondence too far, I assume that it is significant. Judaism has no parallels to the famous feminine figures who represent the two other religions; as Gershom Scholem has already remarked,[5] Jewish mysticism is exclusively a matter of males. Nevertheless, this fact does not seem to affect the emergence and diffusion of *unio mystica* expressions.

Jewish mysticism developed in two types of religious areas: Muslim and Christian. While mysticism in these two religions is transnational, including mystics who belong to different countries and nations, Jewish mysticism is uninational. Thus we witness a much more diversified typology of mystics in Christianity and Islam than in Judaism. What seems to be characteristic of Jewish mystical literature is its scholastic inclinations, that is, its tendency to follow models to a larger degree than in Christianity or Islam. We might expect that the coexistence of Jews with both Christian and Muslim mystics would contribute to a much more variegated picture. The history of kabbalah includes longer periods of creation in Christian countries, but as far as extreme types of mystical expressions are concerned, Sufi elements are much more influential on the kabbalah than any Christian beliefs. The gradual infiltration of technical devices, such as seclusion, concentration of mind, equanimity, and so on, can be traced to the Islamic milieux. These strong techniques apparently contributed to the emergence of more extreme types of experiences.[6] At least in some cases, the use of Muslim expressions for mystical union by Jews is undeniable.[7]

In the context of our discussion, it is important to point out the profound influence of the concept of *Ruhaniyyat*, discussed by Sells (p. 102), on Jewish mysticism. Union with the divine is portrayed as a spiritual force (Hebrew, *Ruhaniyt*) that descends upon the mystic.[8] This way of understanding unitive experiences is widespread in Jewish mysticism, mostly in Hasidism, an issue that was analyzed in detail elsewhere.[9] Significantly, the emergence of Jewish mystical groups directly influenced by Sufi models—for example, the Hasidic Sufism of thirteenth-century Egypt and possibly elsewhere in the Middle East—is unparalleled by meaningful examples in Christian areas. It seems Jewish philosophy was also more profoundly influenced by Islamic culture, including mysticism, than by Christianity.

Compared with Christian and Muslim mysticism, Jewish mysticism was relatively open, though the scope of its openness is very limited. While Judaism absorbed and transformed alien concepts, it did not recognize the legitimacy of other types of mysticism, including any mystical experience that transcended the boundaries of Judaism. (In Islam, by contrast, Ibn ʿArabi implied this; see Sells, p. 122.)

What seems to be partially comparable to a Christian model is eighteenth-century Polish Hasidism. Just as Meister Eckhart used the vernacular to propagate his mystical views, so the Hasidic Ẓaddikim resorted to Yiddish in their sermons, though the latter reached us only in their Hebrew form. However, mysticism as part of a new model of leadership on a large scale seems to be unique to Hasidism. Although Sufi masters were influential beyond the circle of their close disciples, the establishment of a modus vivendi between extreme mystical ideals—which include, as we have seen, *unio mystica*—and involvement in practical communal and individual affairs are characteristic of Polish Hasidism.

Michael Sells

In reading over the essays in this volume, one is struck by the self-critical nature of much mystical language of union, a language that turns back to challenge and transform its own referential grounds. In that spirit I will use this response to raise questions about some of the vocabulary used in comparative mysticism. Louis Dupré and Daniel Merkur have called attention to the problematic nature of the term *experience*. I will focus upon the very delicate problems involved in using the terms *God* and *union* and will then offer a critique of the term *substantial union*, suggesting that it is based upon a language of substance rejected by the mystical tradition to which it most often applied.

God

Studies in Western mysticism have for the most part assumed the interreligious validity and the philosophical intelligibility of the term *God*. However, the term presents a multilayered set of problems. It is now widely accepted that meaning and reference are generated through language in a manner that goes beyond a simple one-to-one correspondence between a word and an outside entity that is its referent. A particular term *(God, Brahman, al-haqq, Eiyn Sof, YWHW, Son, Logos)* achieves meaning and definition through relationships with other words within the religious language worlds of which it is a part.

Religions often use the English term *God* interconfessionally in such as way as to stress a commonality of purpose and value. In a wide variety of contexts such a use is eminently defensible and at times indispensable. When a Hindu uses the term *God*, we

163

may not know to what extent the reference is to a deity like Vishnu and to what extent it is to Brahman, but an aspect of commonality and mutual understanding of worship and belief is suggested. To translate the Islamic *tahlīl, lā ilāha illa-llāh* in any other way than "There is no god but God" would be very difficult, and a giving up of the term *God* might well lose the immediacy so important to the *tahlīl*. Yet there are also real problems in using the term *God* in other situations. Religions have in part defined their own identity against the identity of the other. It is common to hear that the three Abrahamic religions recognize the "same God," but if that is the case, that "same God" either has a son or does not have a son, and the movement toward commonality ends in a stark contradiction between Christian and Muslim faiths. It seems clear that the issue of when the interlinguistic generic term *God* is applicable and when it is problematic is complex and subtle, particularly, I will suggest, in comparative mysticism.

A cultural-linguistic view of language would not see any necessary contradiction between an Allah that has no son and a God (or "Allah" in Christian Arabic literature) that has a son until and unless the cultural-linguistic systems were examined, the precise meaning of sonship and godship in each was determined, and the contradiction was shown to exist: a large endeavor. The point can be illustrated by an analogy to three snowflake configurations, representing three religious languages, with the central shape in each of the snowflakes representing the divine or transcendent realm. Although all three share some of the same space, each central shape is of a different configuration, relating to the rest of the snowflake through differing angles, lines, curves, and other relationships. To call all three central shapes God may imply, and often does imply for those who hear such terminology, that the three central shapes are or should be the same, or that one of them should be the right one, the valid one, or the only one. To use three original terms, for example, *Deus* (and its vernacular equivalents), *al-ḥaqq*, and *YHWH*, would avoid such an implication, affirming the particular configurations and contours within each religious language system and affirming that the meaning of the central shape is dependent upon the relations it has with the rest of the system of shapes, lines, and angles. This point may seem evident enough that the need for such an admittedly less than perfect analogy might be questioned. Indeed, when other aspects of the religious language worlds are at issue, the premises stated here are almost universally accepted within contemporary scholarship. It is rare to find terms like *shari'a* or *dharma* translated as "law" in comparative discussions. Objections would be made to the reduction of two only partially overlapping notions under a common-denominator English term with its own, only partially overlapping semantic field. It is somewhat puzzling that God language, particularly within the three Abrahamic religions, has often been exempt from such considerations.

The difficulties that can be produced *among* traditions by the translation of several diverse terms by the same word, *God*, also can occur *within* particular traditions. Islamic religious language is intricately pitched and keyed among a rich set of terms: *Allah*, *al-haqq*, *al-rahmān*, other Qur'anic divine names, and other important ways of referring to the divine, such as the circumlocutions *subhānahu* (may he be praised) and *ta'ālā* (may he be affirmed transcendent). *Allah*, a term the exact origin of which is still a matter of controversy, has the closest apparent relationship to the English *God*, especially if we accept the view that *Allah* derives from the fusion of the common noun *ilāh* (god) and the definite article *al*, a fusion that transforms the generic, common noun into a form of proper noun. The proper nominal sense personalizes the term and makes it especially appropriate for a creative deity, object of prayer, and subject of confession. The term *al-haqq* (the real, the truth) has no innate status as a proper noun but can borrow such status from context. It tends to be used more in the sense of the absolute or the unmanifest source of emanation or being. When both terms are translated as "God," Islamic religious language is impoverished through the loss of one of its richest and most semantically dynamic distinctions.

Islamic writers, and particularly the Sufis, play upon both the distinction and the interfusion of these two terms through a parallel play upon the two genders of the Arabic personal pronoun *hu* (his, it). By grounding the term in various contexts, with variously personal or impersonal antecedents, the Sufis develop a rich and nuance-filled dialectic between personal and impersonal, between poetic union and mystical union. They heighten that tension by separating the pronoun further and further from its antecedent. The richness, dynamism, and nuance of Sufi language can be lost in translating both *al-haqq* and *Allah* as God and by reducing the he/it tension in the pronoun to "he."

A similar problem is posed by the practice of translating the Neoplatonic "One" as "God." Plotinus considered Nous as well as the One to be part of the divine realm. When *the One* is translated as "God," the divine is stripped of a major aspect, as well as of the dynamic relation between Nous and the One. Plotinian writing contains a dialectic between personal and impersonal similar to that occurring in Sufism between the impersonal and personal aspects of the pronoun and the impersonal and personal aspects of deity. While the One is usually referred to through neuter nouns *(to on, to agathon)*, Plotinus's most moving passages concerning mystical union often switch to the personal demonstrative *autos*, at which point the language becomes deeply personal, or perhaps all the more personal, insofar as it becomes more deeply interactive with the elements of the One that transcend the personal-impersonal polarity. This dialectic between the One (which transcends the distinction between personal and impersonal) and Nous (which has both personal and impersonal aspects) is lost when the term *God* is imposed upon the One and the delicate balance of relation, dialectic, and deity is dislocated.

A central particuliarity of the locution, or rather the "nonlocution," *YWHW* is that it is not spoken, at least in normal human discourse. To actively refrain from speaking a term, or to indicate a term that is not to be pronounced, is a fundamentally different speech act from the speaking of the word *God* or the writing of the word *God* with the assumption that it can and should be pronounced. Other terms with divine reference, such as *elohim* and *el* and circumlocutions like *ha shem* and *adonai* also have distinctive features that are lost in the generic translation of all of them as "God." This question has of course a long history within Jewish thought, and it would be beyond the bounds of a short response to review its classical context. From the more limited perspective of method we find particularly interesting questions. Take, for example, this statement of Rabbi Pinhas of Koretz: "Man ought to cleave during the whole year, this cleaving being understood as the imperative: to go into God, Blessed be He." (Idel, p. 40) The words here translated as "God, blessed be He" are given by Professor Idel in the note as *ha-shem, itbarakh*. Seeing the term is *ha shem*, we can sense immediately the force of the withholding of writing and speaking the name, a particular compelling aspect of Jewish mystical language. From the semantic perspective, the keeping of the original terminology in the translation or a more direct reflection of it ("the name, blessed be he") would be desirable. In many translations and comparative discussions, the original divine name or divine nonname is not even given in the notes, thereby cutting off from scrutiny its essential and particular semantic field.

To the cultural-linguistic problems with the use of standard

God language in comparative religions are joined equally compelling philosophical problems. God language has become so common in Western academic discourse that articles in the philosophy of religion often begin with the question "Can God . . . ?" The meaning, referential validity, and comprehensibility of the term *God* is often assumed. This usage is often grounded in the assumption that the Abrahamic religions are monotheistic in some categorical sense. However, much mystical writing participates in the tradition of radical apophasis, a tradition as critical of easy reference as some theologians are of easy virtue. Rigorous, as opposed to merely formal, apophasis is not simply the negative theology embodied in statements like "God is ineffable." Rigorous apophasis is compelled to point out the incoherence in even the negative statements: if God is ineffable, then the term *God* cannot denominate what it pretends to denominate, in which case the sentence "God is ineffable" is meaningless. The critique of naming is based on the premise that to name is to *delimit* and that therefore *the infinite* cannot be named. This critique turns back upon itself constantly (against the name "the infinite" in the above formulation, for example) in a spiral of infinite regression that generates an entire new *genre* of mystical language. Divine names, the object of rigorous critique on the level of normal reference, are retrieved only at the point of mystical union when standard polarities (subject-object, divine-human, transcendent-immanent, eternal-temporal) are overcome. The names are retrieved then not as denominations of a referential object but as realizations (simultaneous understandings and self-manifestations). At such moments the correspondence between word and referent often implied in normal usage of the term *God* opens onto a more complex and dynamic mode of signification. The term *God* yields to the new language of the sefirot and their interrelations, to the birth of the Son-life-*logos* in the soul, to the retrieval of the Qur'anic divine names as *realizations* within the self-manifestation that occurs in *fanā'*. For many mystics, the first step toward arriving at these interior and dynamic realms of signification is a critique of conventional understandings of divine names and predication, particularly present in most uses of the term *God*. Although it is common to use the term *God* with the apology that it is somehow inadequate, most religious language is far most comfortable with such reference than the apophatic tradition. For the apophatic mystic, the gravity of language works powerfully and subconsciously to vitiate any simple affirmations that God transcends the deliminating nature of the name God.

Associated with the common generic use of the term *God* is

the practice of capitalizing pronouns thought to refer to God. This practice does not exist in Arabic, Persian, Hebrew, Latin, or Greek texts, and it was rejected by the British Catholic tradition as well.[1] The creators of King James biblical English, themselves so superbly sensitive to questions of translation, might have agreed that such a practice should not be adopted across the board in treating a wide variety of religious traditions and religious discourses. The common practice of capitalizing terms and pronouns thought to refer to the divine is incompatible with the often deliberate fusing of human-human and human-divine paradigms of lover and beloved. It is also incompatible with apophatic language of realization, since in apophatic writing the reference and the antecedence are sometimes deliberately bivalent. At the moment of union both human and divine parties may be antecendent to a given pronoun. A compromise, the dropping of capitalizations in passages concerning mystical union, is unfeasible; once the convention is established, any lack of capitalization will be read as a sign that the referent and antecedent of the pronoun is not divine. This convention is based upon, and locks the interpreter into, the either-or, subject-object relationship between human and divine that is challenged by the language of mystical union.

How might these semantic concerns relate to Professor Merkur's psychological typology? Assuming that terms like *personal* and *impersonal* in a semantic analysis and in a psychological analysis are used similarly enough to allow us to compare the methods, and I assume here that they are or could be made to be, the following criterion might be offered: if the types and subtypes suggested by Professor Merkur are seen as existing together, in complicated interactions, within a given mystical text, then such a psychological typology would be consonant with such semantic analysis. If the types are applied categorically to mystics or texts, such that mystic A is labeled impersonal and mystic B personal, then there may be less compatibility; the results of the above semantic study of mystical union in Islam, and the premise of much of this response, suggest that mystical writings take their literary power from the interaction and creative tensions among the various gender, personality, relational, referential, and antecedental possibilities. While it may be convenient to put a mystical text into one category or another according to the dominant type exhibited, such a convenience may also be costly, leading to a neglect of the dynamic and interactive elements in favor of stable categories.

Union

There is a moment within the mystical literature of the Abrahamic religious traditions that brings the three into a close and resonant conversation. That moment has for some time been labeled *union*. The term is useful insofar as it has helped us to identify this element, but it is not unproblematic. *Webster's Ninth New Collegiate* (1986) gives as the first meaning of *union* "an act or instance of uniting or joining two or more things into one." *The Shorter OED* (1970) gives "the act of uniting one thing with another . . ." On the level of metaphor (streams merging with the sea, wine mingled with water), and in the poetic and erotic language common to the three traditions, this conception is present within the three mystical traditions. However, on the more explicitly theological level, it is doubtful whether union, as commonly defined as a conjunction of two things, can be applied without qualification. Particularly in the apophatic traditions, union takes place not between two entities or substances but within a ground of "nothingness," the self-emptying nothingness of the contemplative soul or the beyond-being nothingness of the unmanifest Godhead. Often the metaphoric and erotic imagery of *union* is in tension with same writer's more theologically detailed language: of *"beyond-ousia"* nothingness, of *fanā'*, or of the Eckhartian ground of being, or of *ayin* (the "nothing" realm usually associated with the first of the sefirot, *Keter*).

When *union* is combined with *with God*, the phrase becomes weighted: two entities, the soul and God, conjoined in union. However, in many of the mystical writings what occurs, occurs both *between* human and divine and *within* the divine itself, and the two unions are one union. In the birth-of-the-son-in-the-soul, in the union of Binah and Tiferet, in the manifestation of the divine to it/self in/itself in *fanā'*, the *between* is always deentified by the *within:* the notion of a union between two entities always in dialectical tension with the already and always being realized union within the already one.

Substantial Union

By grounding it in context, the term *union* can be used in a manner that overcomes some of its problematic implications. However, those problematic implications are locked into the term when it is combined with *substantial. Substantial union* (or *essential union*) is the term traditionally used to distinguish between two large categories of mystical union. In his introduction, for example, Louis Dupré contrasts an "interpersonal relation of love," to the mysticism of "ontological or substantial union" that he associates with Eckhart's *unio indistinctionis*, with Hallaj, and with Rumi. It is true that these writers employ metaphorical statements, such as Rumi's wine and water metaphor cited by Professor Dupré, that imply a union between substances. Bernard McGinn shows that the use of such metaphors within the Christian mystical tradition, particularly within the writings of John of the Cross, does not entail a mystical theology of substantive union.

To point out the lack of substantial union in these mystics is not to imply that their notion of union was any less radical or controversial. Indeed, the most radically unitive understandings of union were often those least compatible with substance language. Following Plotinus, who placed the One beyond "essence" or "substance" *(ousia)* and beyond "being" *(to on)*, the Christian Neoplatonists Pseudo-Dionysius and John the Scot placed the Godhead in the realm of "beyond being" *(superessentia)*. Erigena speaks of divine "nothingness," namely, what we might render as *no-thingness*, in an attempt to free the deity from delimiting notions of being and substance. For all three writers, the realization of oneness does not take place through a fusion of two substances, essences, or entities. The One, or the Godhead, is by definition beyond *ousia*, a proposition emphasized most strongly in the texts most concerned with mystical union. The Sufis never adopted the Plotinian "beyond being" language of Plotinus. Indeed, the Arabic Plotinian texts have omitted all crucial references to this doctrine. However, the Sufis found another way to articulate a nonsubstance-based union. In *fanā'*, union is not a union of two substances, essences, or entities but rather the obliteration of one and the filling of its psychic space with other, a union-in-the-act-of-perception. Meister Eckhart, who is often associated with the term *substantial union*, uses a double paradigm doubly incompatible with it, a paradigm that contains features similar to both the Dionysian and the Sufi traditions. Insofar as the divine is considered as being, the world and soul are nothing; insofar as the world and the soul are considered as being, the divine is beyond such being, is nothing. In neither of Eckhart's paradigms can union occur between two stable, substantive entities. Union occurs dynamically and only insofar as one of the entities is considered to be beyond, emptied of, or transcending its being and substance. In a complex pun, Eckhart suggests that when the soul becomes "equal to nothing," then it becomes equal to the ground of being or to the Father and gives birth to the Son.

Why has the term *substantial union* historically been applied to the very mystics who most radically rejected the substance language upon which it is based? The case of Hallaj may suggest an interesting perspective on the problem. Hallaj was accused of advocating *hulūl* (incarnationism), and of all the statements attributed to Hallaj, it is those formulations advocating *hulūl* that have had the least following within Islam. We have the case of the famous verses "I am whom I love, whom I love is I/two spirits we have alighted (or become incarnate, *hallalna*) in a single body."[2] The first, very strongly unitive hemistich has been deeply influential within Islam and accepted by generations of Sufis. But the doctrine of *hulūl* (whether or not Hallaj actually advocated it) has been dropped from the tradition. The unacceptability of *hulūl* is not based upon the radical nature of the union. The first hemistich ("I am who am love, whom I love is I") expresses a far more radical union than the hemistich that was rejected ("two spirits we have alighted in a single body"): in the second verse there are still *two* spirits. This case highlights a common misconception. In Islam the controversies over Sufism seldom concerned the radical quality of the union. Bistami, Niffari, Junayd, Ibn ʿArabi, Rumi, and their countless contemporaries and successors have advocated the strongest positions on *fanā'*. Their writings on such topics are read with admiration among even the most traditional Muslims. (Ibn ʿArabi is appreciated among the Iranian mullahs, for example, including the Imam Khoumeini). In those rare cases where mystics were martyred, such as the cases of Hallaj, Hamadhani, and Suhrawardi, political factors and issues other than mystical union were involved. Modern reaction against Sufism by groups such as the Wahhabis of Saudi Arabia centers on concrete issues like veneration of shaykhs, saints, and the tombs of saints, not on the subtleties of mystical union.

The mystical union of *fanā'* is robustly grounded in a variety of Islamic language worlds. The doctrine of *hulūl* had a foreign ring. To the Muslims of the third (ninth to tenth centuries C.E.) century, the language must have brought to mind the arguments within Christianity over the nature(s) of Christ, the hypostatic union, and the Trinity. Here, the Islamic tradition may offer an insight into the treatment of mysticism within the Western Christian tradition. Much controversy over substantial union within Christianity, and much of the traditional attribution by Western writers of *substantial* union to Islamic mystics, may be based upon a reading of mystical union language through the lens of the substantive language of the creeds. From Nicaea to Chalcedon, *ousia* language, whether translated as *substantia, natura,* or *physis,* was applied without hesitation to both the Trinity and the natures of Christ. The phenomenon is clear in the Nicene Creed, where the doctrine of *homoousia* is directed against the Arian view of Christ as creature. In the creed, the affirmation that Christ is "from the same *ousia* of the Father" and the anathematization of those who believe that "he came into existence out of nothing" or is "of a different hypostasis or *ousia*" combine a substantive view of the Godhead with a view of creation as being *ex nihilo*.[3] The crucial point here is this: the Neoplatonic Christian tradition completely reformulated the Nicene notions of *ousia* and *creatio ex nihilo*. From Dionysius to John the Scot to Eckhart, the Christian Neoplatonists placed the Godhead beyond *ousia* seen as either essence or substance and reformulated the *ex nihilo* to refer to the emanation from the superessential Godhead. Union for them did not amount to union of one thing or one substance or one entity with another, since the ground of union radically transcended *ousia*. This union in the ground of superessential nothingness, what one might call *unio in nihilo,* is quite the opposite of any union of substance or essence. The fundamental transformation by Neoplatonic mystics of the *ousia* and *creatio ex nihilo* doctrine of the Nicene Creed has not been perceived (or not taken seriously enough) by those accustomed to substantialist language of the creeds and of later theologians. Since at least the time of Eckhart's condemnation there has been a tendency to read the substantive language of the creeds into any mystical language concerning the divine. There is an irony here. While it would be impossible for anyone holding the divine to be beyond *ousia,* or holding the world to be lacking in *ousia,* to advocate a union based upon substance language, it *would* be a temptation for those taking a more substantive view of the divine and the created world to use such language. Yet the term *substantive union* has usually been applied to the former group to distinguish it from the latter.

The traditional attribution of substantial union has been highly misleading. An extreme can be seen in the popularity of Denis de Rougement's passionate polemic against the "Oriental heresy" of mystical union, *Love in the Western World.* Rougement divides mysticism between the *erotic* (i.e. union-based) and the *agapic* (marriage-based). His confusion of the erotic category with "union

in substance" and "essential union" leads him to deny to all believers in mystical union the possibility of love of neighbor on the
grounds that the goal of union is the absorption of all individuals
into an impersonal "substance."[4] Beyond such extreme examples,
the substantial union language has resulted in another, more per-
vasive misconception: the assumption that mystical union in Eckhart or Ibn ᶜArabi must be impersonal, less relational, more static.
Because of the widespread belief that Jewish mysticism was almost
exclusively a mysticism of communion rather than union, Jewish
mystical texts have more often escaped being labeled as advocating
substantial union, or essential union. However, with Moshe Idel's
demonstration that mystical union was an important part of the
Jewish tradition, those texts now become vulnerable to the substantial union label and the preconceptions it entails. In all three
cases the label contradicts, and by contradicting, diverts attention
away from the beyond-*ousia* language of apophatic mysticism in
the three traditions. It obscures the intense dynamic and dialectic
between personal and impersonal, between objective language and
a language of realization, between transcendent and immanent,
between the intentionality of desire and the giving up of such intentionality, that is at the heart of apophatic mystical union. In
many areas of modern discourse it is common to speak of the *on-
tocentric* nature of Western thought. This generalization may be
founded in part upon an ignorance of the critique of *ousia* language
by the apophatic mystics or a reading of that critique through the
language of substantial union that has traditionally been substi-
tuted for it. The result is the obscuring of the radical nature of the
critique of substance language inherent in much of the language
of mystical union, as well as an ignoring of the profound alternative
offered in its place, an alternative that puts into question categorical
generalizations about the nature of Western thought and offers re-
sources from within the Western tradition for the contemporary
effort to find a language that can resist the reification of meaning.

Daniel Merkur

Let me try to bridge at least part of the gap between the psychoanalytic approach of my essay and the orientations of my fellow contributors. To begin, I suggest that mystical experiences and mystical language are properly treated as independent variables of the history of mysticism. The complexity of history is reducible to neither factor alone. Mystics' formulations were sometimes in agreement with reference to the same type of experience, but other doctrines were harmonious precisely because they were designed to apply simultaneously to differing experiences. Again, mystics sometimes dispute single experiences, but some inconsistencies reflect differences among the experiences.

Consider a comparative perspective. Plotinus, the third-century founder of Neoplatonism, was the earliest individual in Western culture who certainly had unitive experiences of the kind that I have described as impersonal.[1] Impersonal mysticism had been practiced in India for over a millennium prior to Plotinus, and Indians are known to have lived in Alexandria when Plotinus resided there. Plotinus was certainly interested in things Indian: he attempted (unsuccessfully) to visit India in his later years. For these and other reasons,[2] it is doubtful that Plotinus independently discovered impersonal mysticism. It is probable—although unproved—that he westernized Indian meditative practices. However, Plotinus was by no means the first Western mystic. Although Neoplatonism was the immediate source of the subsequent practice of impersonal mysticism in the Western religions, Plotinus expressly differentiated his experiences of union with the One from his experiences of union with the Nous, or Active Intellect.[3] In other words, he grafted impersonal mysticism onto an indigenously

175

Western mystical tradition that stemmed, so far as we are able to prove, from Plato and Aristotle.[4]

Philo, an Alexandrian Jew writing circa 50 C.E., was apparently the first philosopher to expand the Greek view of contemplation to include experiences of a type that we may recognize as unitive. Philo's innovations had antecedents in Jewish apocalypticism; I refer in particular to the practice of visionary ascensions through the heavens that climaxed in communion with God.[5] In other words, Philo used middle Platonism to refine his Jewish heritage. Personal mysticism continued to be experienced, but visionary experiences of ascending to heaven were replaced by ideational meditations on the sequence of the heavens. The eschatological concerns of apocalypticism were abandoned in favor of the unitive language of philosophy. Of course, the actual experiences were likely never the pure types that literary remains might seem to suggest. Later mystics attempting to achieve purely ideational personal mysticism sometimes experienced visions inadvertently.[6] In all events, Philo founded a philosophically oriented tradition of personal mysticism that scholars have termed "intellectualist," "rationalist," or "rational."[7]

A similar process occurred in the early history of Christianity, where it was to have considerably greater impact. Paul's ascension to the third heaven belongs to the apocalyptic visionary tradition. However, his unitive language about Christ implies a later shift in his thinking, which may indicate a turn to rational mysticism. The Gospel of John presupposed Middle Platonism in identifying its Logos with God; but we reach firm ground only in observing that Christian rational mysticism had reached maturity by the late second century, when Clement of Alexandria and Origen termed it *gnosis*, "knowledge."[8] Rational mysticism both before and after Plotinus is a considerably neglected aspect of the history of Western mysticism. Although there are several excellent studies of individual instances, there are also large gaps in the historical record, and no overview has yet been developed. My colleagues' essays encourage me to regard the history of Western mysticism as an intertwining of impersonal and personal mysticism. Professor Idel's essay builds on his previous refutation of Gershom Scholem's categorical assertion that Jewish mystical experiences of *devekut*, "cleaving" or "adhesion," consisted of *communion* to the exclusion of *union*.[9] Idel contends that there are "two recurring expressions for the mystical experiences in Jewish mysticism: universalization and integration." In accounting for the differences between the two terms, he advances several explanations but fails to question whether different experiences were reflected by the terms.

Let us consider, for example, the *Tract on Ecstasy* by Rabbi Dov Baer of Lubavitch (1773–1827), the second-generation leader of Ḥabad Hasidism. Dov Baer developed a typology of ten kinds of ecstatic experience. The tenth and most desirable type was *yehidah*, "union" or "unification."

> [It] is the category of the actual essential *yehidah*. This is known as "simple song", that is to say, the category of actual essence ascending in song. . . . As Rabbi Simeon ben Yohai said: "With one knot", that is the "one knot" by which essence is attached to essence in the category of *yehidah*—"to Him attached", actually "burning for Him". As it is written: "My soul shall glory in the Lord". . . . This is also called one simple, essential will, which is not sensed and does not become divided into many contradictory wills . . . his whole being is so absorbed that nothing remains and he has no self-consciousness whatsoever.[10]

The structure of the doctrine is unmistakably Neoplatonic. Because the divine soul was quite literally a fragment of God,[11] the "simple song" was explained as the divine soul experiencing its divine nature. Like all ecstasies of the divine soul, it was "the actual divine light in itself."[12] We need not doubt that Dov Baer referred to experiences of impersonal mysticism. *Yehidah* both involved the mystic's deification and coincided with an "absence of self-awareness that is known as 'self-annihilation'."[13]

Perhaps because Dov Baer wrote in Yiddish for a popular audience, he did not employ the term *integration*, which his father, Rabbi Shneor Zalman of Lyady, had used freely in Hebrew. However, self-oblivion is a psychologically telling detail that allows us to claim that impersonal mysticism, and references to annihilation were made not only by Dov Baer but also by all of the further integrative Hasidim cited by Idel. On the other hand, self-oblivion was mentioned in none of Professor Idel's citations from the older Safed kabbalists who wrote of integration, nor in any citation from writers on universalization. But let us not draw inferences *ex silentio*.

Consider Dov Baer's account of the ninth—and secondmost important—type of ecstasy, the "duplicated song." Here the same basic process occurred. The divine soul experienced its identity with God in complete oblivion to itself: "This concentration contains the essential, simple delight of the essence and simplicity of the divine soul."[14] However, the event was observed by a second soul, the "natural soul," which retained consciousness of its distance from the union of the divine soul and God. "The illumination of the divine soul is still in the mind," and the mind, a faculty of the natural soul, engages in "the worship of the [divine] soul herself as she ascends to the Source whence she was hewn."[15] In this "surrounding of *yehidah*," this witnessing of union at a distance, God "does not shine in unconcealment at all, only from afar with concealment."[16] The mystical experience was evidently personal, but Dov Baer explained it as the natural soul's observation of the divine soul's impersonal union.

The history of Jewish mysticism encompasses both impersonal and personal experiences. Both were sometimes conceptualized as unions. The kabbalistic doctrine of universalization likely had its roots in rational mysticism. After the isolated early instance of Philo, Jewish rational mysticism was imported from Islam in the twelfth century. The Jewish version tended to blend Sufi ethics with Muslim Neoaristotelian mysticism. We find the blend in Moses Maimonides,[17] his grandson Obadyah Maimonides,[18] and an anonymous tract that stemmed from medieval Egyptian pietism.[19] In the thirteenth century Abraham Abulafia developed the Maimonidian tradition into a property of the kabbalah and referred to universalization in its connection. This meditative practice was popularized in the authoritative sixteenth-century codification of Jewish law, Rabbi Joseph Karo's *Shulchan Aruch*.[20] The tradition has since passed into Hasidism, where it survives as a living practice.

With the idea of integration, however, we are on more treacherous ground. Where, among the Hasidim, reference was also made to annihilation, integration clearly pertains to impersonal mysticism. But I suspect that mystics sometimes blurred the linguistic distinctions. When the Active Intellect was regarded not as a process but as a metaphysical being, union with it might be termed universalization, meaning an acquisition of universal knowledge. It might also be regarded as integration, the entrance of the mystic's thought within the consciousness of the cosmic mind. However, these monopsychic notions—that a single intellect is common both to the cosmos and to all humanity—could also be applied to impersonal mysticism. Although there is very little cognitive experience during the climactic moments of deifying union, ideational inspirations are prominent in the waning phases of the ecstasies. The psychological issue cannot be decided on the basis of monopsychic ideology, but we can approach the problem in another manner. Professor Idel suggests that theurgy was logically consistent with integration in the divine but inconsistent with universalization, which affects the mystic but not the divine. Historically, however, theurgy was discussed both by the Safed kabbalists, who wrote of integration, and by Rabbi Abraham Ibn 'Ezra, who advanced the idea of universalization. To resolve the paradox, I suggest that theurgy obtains only when monopsychism extends to God. In personal mysticism, by contrast, monopsychism with the Active Intellect coincides with an experienced distance from God and so precludes theurgic ambition. In all, if we relocate Ibn 'Ezra on the criterion of theurgy, Idel's findings on Jewish mystical doctrines dovetail precisely with the history of the underlying mystical experiences.

Professor McGinn's essay refutes the conventional distinction between affective and intellectualist mysticism with the observation that because Christianity's God is love all Christian mystics are affective. Emphases differ on the relative importance of knowledge, but categorical oppositions of love and knowledge are not to be found. I assume that Professor McGinn has stressed the mutually exclusive doctrines of *unitas spiritus* and *unitas indistinctionis* in order to document Christian concerns that compare with the issues of universalization and integration in Jewish mysticism. Let me again approach the problems in terms of the underlying mystical experiences.

Christian mysticism developed at least three major trends in response to the introduction of impersonal mysticism. The doctrines of Gregory of Nyssa were a qualified defense or updated restatement of the tradition of personal mysticism that stemmed from Clement and Origen. Gregory conceded to Neoplatonism the doctrine of the One beyond Being, but he insisted that God the Father was unknowable. He allowed no more than a loving communion with the Father through the mediation of Jesus.[21]

The monastic tradition, as represented, for example, by Evagrius of Pontus and John Cassian, developed an impersonal mysticism that either ignored or was ignorant of personal mysticism. Augustine contributed seminally to this trend. Where Gregory had allowed the immanence of Jesus and the Holy Spirit, Augustine held that the full Trinity was present in the soul during contemplation.[22] Again, where Gregory had understood contemplative experiences of love as an affective link to God, much as love functions as a bond between persons, Augustine identified the infusion of love as the triune God himself.[23] And so we see that the meaning of the term *love* varied according to its experiential contexts. Because the love that was experienced was impersonal in both cases, Augustine did not indentify it with the personally experienced God of Gregory's experiences but with the love that is God.

A third basic position was developed by Dionysius the Areopagite, who kept still more closely to the Neoplatonic standard. Dionysius's *Mystical Theology* and *Divine Names* introduced the negative theological interpretation of impersonal mysticism that has played an incalculable role in the histories of both Greek and Latin Christianity.[24] His *Celestial Hierarchies* and *Ecclesiastical Hierarchy* are no less explicit a presentation of a rational mysticism that conceived of Jesus as "the transcendentally divine and supra-essential mind, the source and essence of all hierarchy, holiness, and divine operation."[25]

By the twelfth century the Augustinian tradition of exclusively impersonal mysticism had gained wide acceptance among Catholic mystics, but the renewal of Latin mysticism—and the emphasis on the idea of union—was at least quickened by fertilization from the minority traditions. Bernard of Clairvaux rejected both extremes and preached a personal mysticism of loving knowledge or knowledgeable love, the *unitas spiritus* that he ascribed to the seraphim.[26] Although Bernard (and later Henry Suso) privileged personal mysticism, he tolerated impersonal mysticism as long as it was tempered by measured doctrinal interpretations. Importantly, by shifting emphasis from the cognitive to the emotional dimension of personal mysticism, Bernard divorced personal mysticism from the philosophical doctrines to which it had been joined in Dionysian tradition. The new form of Christian personal mysticism—better, the reversion to Gregory of Nyssa's standard—was accessible to nonintellectuals; the seventeenth-century Brother Lawrence of the Resurrection, teacher of *The Practice of the Presence of God*, is a notable example. The history of Christian mysticism between Bernard and Lawrence displays intricate combinations of impersonal, personal, and rational mysticism.

In several respects, the pattern in Christianity resembles that in Judaism. Impersonal mystics developed a language of their own (integration, *unitas indistinctionis*) that was specific to their experiences, but they also appropriated formulations that personal mystics had devised in reflection on their experiences. Whenever formulations were given new experiential contexts, they underwent subtle shifts in meaning. In at least several cases, however, the new contexts were less experiential than doctrinal. Bernard, Suso, and Bonaventure deliberately constructed at least part of their doctrines in manners that applied simultaneously to both personal and impersonal mysticism.

Locating Professor Sell's contributions within this comparative context is rather more complicated. Existing scholarship on Muslim mysticism maintains that the Sufis depended primarily on impersonal mystical experiences, while rational mysticism was pursued by Neoaristotelian philosophers, principally al-Farabi, Ibn Sīna, Ibn Bajjah, and Ibn Rushd.[27] However, Sells's far-reaching survey of Arabic Sufi terminology encourages us to doubt that the historical distinctions were really as neat and tidy as they have been made to seem.

Professor Sells remarks briefly that pre-Islamic love poetry expressed the idea of union through the term *wasl*. Although the Sufis were indebted to poetic ideas of the moments of love-madness and annihilation, they employed the unrelated term *ittihad* (identification) for union. It is surely significant, however, that *'ittisal* (conjunction, contact) was a technical term of Muslim Neoaristotelian mysticism that also derives from *w-s-l*.[28] On terminological grounds, Muslim rational mystics were as much the heirs of pre-Muslim love poetry as were the Sufis. Again, Sells has cited Muslim Neoaristotelian philosophers, together with the pseudonymous *Theology of Aristotle*, as primary sources of negative theology for the Sufis. Here, as in both Judaism and Christianity, rational mystics evidently developed a doctrine that impersonal mystics later endorsed. The alleged separation of rational mysticism and Sufism further dissolves in the passage by al-Ghazali, cited in my essay (p. 142), that briefly mentions discursive reasoning—the meditative technique favored by rational mystics—as having been a Sufi practice.

In discussing the ascension to the throne in Sufism, Sells devotes several pages to Muslim practices of personal mystical vision while noting that the heretical implications of anthropomorphic language tended to be neutralized. Particularly in accounts of Muhammad's Miᶜraj, ascension through the heavens was said to culminate in a formless seeing—an ideational rather than a visual experience. The operative mechanism here would presumably have been the envisioning of one's form in the celestial realm; the implicit realization that one was watching a vision unfold might well have sufficed to divert the further experience from visual to ideational contents. Even so, it was probably easier to present the doctrinally tidy compromise in a legend of the Prophet than to have such an experience. In living practice, the danger of heretical anthropomorphism might be neutralized differently. For several centuries, a night dream or vision of Muhammad—often an experience of personal mysticism in which the Prophet fulfilled the function of the enthroned anthropomorphic being—served as an initiation into the mystic life.[29] Nonetheless, where we find personal mystical visions, we should be alert to the possibility that we may also find personal mysticism that takes abstract ideational form, and vice versa. Within Islam, motifs of the visionary journey and its climactic communion occur in alchemical texts,[30] even though Muslim alchemy was a major locus of Neoaristotelian rational mysticism.

And so I question: does Islam parallel Judaism and Christianity, where rational mysticism originated when the language of Greek philosophy was applied to the personal mystical experiences that had earlier been pursued during visions of ascension? In all cases, philosophical emphases on language presumably influenced shifts from visions to purely ideational experiences.

Some final thoughts. As Hindu, Buddhist, and Taoist instances prove, impersonal mysticism has no necessarily theistic content; when it is theistic, it is as apt to be as pantheistic as monotheistic. Personal mysticism, by contrast, is an inherently monotheistic experience. Although the experiences may be interpreted within a polytheistic framework, they actually consist of verbal inspirations and emotions that derive from a nonmanifest, numinous, and single Thou. Since personal mysticism plays no part in Hindu Yoga, Buddhist meditation, or Taoism, the question arises whether the historical presence of personal mysticism, albeit primarily as a minority trend, did not contribute in fundamental ways to the monotheism of Western mysticism. The practice of personal mysticism was definitely formative of the Western heritage. It was both the original practice and a lasting minority tradition. But the circumstances that governed the development of alternative practices recurred repeatedly in the lives of at least some individual mystics. A sequential use of personal and impersonal mystical experiences was advocated by Plotinus, Psuedo-Dionysius, Bonaventure, Dov Baer, and others. The implications are obvious. When an experience of personal mysticism, which is inherently monotheistic, occurs prior to impersonal mysticism, it unconsciously contributes content and consciously predisposes interpretations that make impersonal mysticism a monotheistic experience. Dogmatic acceptance of monotheism certainly accomplishes equivalent psychological results, but doctrines can be disbelieved as readily as believed. People continue in their beliefs in large numbers over periods of centuries only because they have experiences that corroborate—or seem to corroborate—the received doctrines. Faith otherwise lapses, as the distemper of modern times proves only too clearly.

And if we seriously entertain the hypothesis that the intertwining of personal and impersonal mysticism in the history of Western mysticism has contributed significantly to its monotheistic character, must we not go a step further? Can we reject the teaching of Bernard and Henry Suso that personal mysticism brings us closer to the root of our knowledge of the mystery of God?

Bernard McGinn

One may be inclined to wonder, after reading these essays, whether the term *mystical union (unio mystica)* is really a useful one at all. First of all, it involves difficulties of translation in both Arabic and Hebrew, which have no real equivalent for the adjective *mystical*. Nor is it a classical term throughout much of the history of Christian mysticism. The Greek adjective *mystikos*, bearing the general sense of "hidden, secret," was early taken over by Christian authors. Origen spoke of *mystikē theoria*, which the Latins translated as *mystica contemplatio;* the Pseudo-Dionysius coined the crucial term *mysticē theologia*. The wide-ranging use of the adjective is found in Latin at least from the time of John the Scot, the translator of the Dionysian corpus.[1] From the thirteenth century on it passed into the European vernaculars. It was not until seventeenth-century France, however, that we find *la mystique,* or "mysticism," used as a substantive and its practioners spoken of as "mystics"—a crucial turning point, as Michel de Certeau has argued.[2]

There was also a rich vocabulary, both in Latin and in the European vernaculars, about union with God, and by the late Middle Ages there was extensive and polemical discussion of the kinds of union. But I have never encountered the term *mystical union* in any medieval author, nor even in the classic Spanish mystics of the sixteenth century. The same seventeenth century that witnessed the creation of the term *mysticism* seems also to have been responsible for the coining of the term *unio mystica* among theological commentators on mysticism.[3] The term's popularity from the nineteenth century on seems to have more to do with the academic study of mysticism than with the mystics themselves.

But precisely because it is primarily a "term of art," a modern creation largely popularized by students of religion, it may still have a useful, if limited, function. Daniel Merkur's survey of the development of modern studies of mysticism has shown how problematic the search for a common core of all mystical experience is, while Louis Dupré's insistence on the special intentionality of mystical texts supports Moshe Idel's plea that what we need today is really a phenomenology of mystical expressions, not of mystical experiences. In this search for a new and more adequate approach that begins from the mystical text, we need not only to be true to the particular vocabulary and semantic fields (to use Michael Sells's language) of each of the three traditions but also to be willing to explore language that may be able to serve as a way of framing the larger, if still provisional, questions that can guide us in the construction of a more adequate comparative mystical philosophy. I would argue that *mystical union*, especially because the term is essentially an academic one (albeit the creation of Christian academics), does allow us to locate a key area in the problematics of any such comparative philosophy. Until a more helpful "term of art" comes along, it can serve a propaedeutic and perhaps even a real hermeneutical role in the conversation.

This seems to me to be borne out by the essays contained here. Each has had to develop, to qualify, and to enrich previous understandings of mystical union as applied to the religious traditions under study, but the term, however transposed, has still managed to mark out an area of real discussion, one in which I sense that we are talking to each other about some central issues rather than past each other about trivia.

My own way of illustrating the fruits of this conversation about *unio mystica* will be to dwell on what I believe are the two essential areas of concern that emerge from all the papers: theology and anthropology. Since God and the human in some way become one in mystical union, what does that have to tell us about the doctrine of God from a comparative perspective, and what message does it contain about the nature and destiny of the human person? These are large issues; what follows is only a series of remarks, observations, and queries on these topics inspired by the previous essays and the other responses.

Michael Sells is quite correct in his comments to insist on the important differences in the terms used for *God* in the three Abrahamic faiths. But in every good comparative endeavor there is always another side to the coin. In thinking about the essays of Idel and Sells, as well as some important issues raised toward the end of Louis Dupré's introduction, I have been struck by a series of significant convergencies, or at least of a similarity of dynamics, in what theories and descriptions of *unio mystica* reveal about Jewish, Christian, and Muslim attempts to talk about God.

It could certainly be argued that what is most distinctive about the Christian understanding of God is the doctrine of the Trinity. Surely, Christian understandings of mystical union must be radically different from Jewish and Muslim ones, if only because union, however understood, is with the triune God, Father, Son, and Holy Spirit. My own essay could easily be rewritten from a more Trinitarian perspective—perhaps to find further important reasons for divergences in views of union based on differing theologies of the Trinity. But while there is no Trinity in Judaism and Islam, there are complexities and dynamisms introduced into the divine nature through the pursuit of mystical union that set up revealing comparisons with Christian understandings of the word *God*.

Toward the end of his essay, Moshe Idel notes how the universalizing model of mystical union fits with philosophical theologies that emphasize the simplicity of God, while the integrative model is found in theosophical systems where "the possibility of the integration of the soul is part of a larger scheme of the inclusion of powers and energy in the divine realm" (p. 51). Michael Sells spends time analyzing how Ibn ʿArabi's retrieval of the divine attributes as "realizations (i.e., simultaneously understandings and actualizations) reflected within the mirror of the human/divine union" (p. 121) played an important role in the way in which the Sufi language of mystical union transformed the theological discourse of Islam. A number of the Christian figures I studied, especially Meister Eckhart, bring the mystic directly into the Trinitarian relations, so that he or she is identified with the Father giving birth to the Son, the Son being born, and the Holy Spirit proceeding from both (p. 76). (Among the other profoundly Trinitarian theories of mystical union not developed in my essay are those of William of Saint-Thierry, Richard of Saint Victor, Jan van Ruusbroec, and John of the Cross.) What we are dealing with in these cases is the insistence of at least some mystics in each of the traditions on a radically dynamic view of the God who unites him/herself with the human.

The dynamism of the mystical God in Judaism, Christianity, and Islam raises important and perhaps disturbing theological questions. How much dynamism can be introduced into God as understood in the three monotheistic faiths without endangering the central insistence on what the Muslims call *tawhīd*, the absolute unity of God? The evidence presented in these essays indicates a rather surprising amount of dynamism and even possible "change" in the "God" of the monotheistic mystics of the three traditions. This is true not only in religions where orthopraxy outweighs orthodoxy, such as Judaism and Islam, but also in medieval Christianity, where orthodox repression created difficulties for some mystics, though rarely on this issue.

One of the key tests here involves the daring claim of some mystics that union actually in some way changes, affects, or even integrates and repairs the divine world. The profound thought of the theurgical kabbalists in this area has been noted by Moshe Idel; Louis Dupré, citing Richard of Saint Victor and others, shows that such an understanding is not totally absent from Christianity (pp. 22–23). Even more daring expressions are found in some Christian mystical theologians, such as Meister Eckhart with his powerful teaching on how the perfect detachment of the mystic "forces" God to act.[4] While Michael Sells does not address this issue directly, it seems clear from his essay that Ibn ʿArabi and a number of the mystics he studies could be said to agree that the loving union of the human and God affects "God" in some way as much as it does the human.

This is especially important, as Louis Dupré notes (pp. 17, 20), because some modern students have understood the more extreme mystical statements about union as teaching a mere intellectual realization of the soul's preexistence in God, so that nothing really happens or changes in the state of union. It is true that mystics from all three traditions have stressed the person's virtual preexistence in God as the root for the possibility of what I have called the union of indistinction.[5] But the end is not just the same as the beginning. What Dupré vindicates for Ruusbroec, namely that "the process of loving devotion *realizes* what existed as only potential in the initial stage" (p. 20), could, I believe, also be shown to be the case for many, if not all, Christian mystics. One of the most profound presentations of this meliorative quality of mystical union, especially in its universal dimensions, is to be found in the thought of John the Scot, the first Western representative of the apophatic Neoplatonic mysticism that later flourished in Eckhart, Nicholas of Cusa, and others.

The mention of apophasis brings us to another element in these brief reflections on how the study of *unio mystica* in the three traditions challenges us to rethink easy generalizations about the classical doctrine of God in the monotheistic religions. Mystics have always insisted on the ineffability of their experiences of God, and the speculative mystics of Judaism, Christianity, and Islam have not surprisingly been among the most profound negative theologians of their respective traditions. In seeking to find a language to suggest what they meant by talking of union with "God," mystics in all three traditions have been deeply influenced by the negative dialectic of Neoplatonic philosophy, as Michael Sells points out in his comments. When we deal with what Moshe Idel calls the "extreme" statements of union in each of the three traditions, Plotinus and his followers are almost always implied partners, if not overt participants, in the discussion.

If God is totally beyond being, substance, and essence, as the strong apophatic tradition would claim, then it makes little sense to talk about "substantial," "essential," or even perhaps "ontological" union. This is the reason that I adopted the term *unitas indistinctionis* to describe this form of *unio mystica* among some late medieval theologians, beginning with the Beguines of the thirteenth century. But the reason that modern investigators have adopted the category of substantial union to categorize the ways some classical mystics have spoken of being "oned" with God may rest with the ambivalent language of the mystics as much as it does with the misunderstandings of modern investigators. Highly dialectical Christian mystics, like Meister Eckhart, sometimes made use of metaphors and examples that were at odds with their underlying metaphysics. It is striking to see Rabbi Shneor Zalman, perhaps the most daring proponent of indistinct union in the Jewish tradition, make use of metaphors of eating and ingestion (see Idel, p. 43) that explicitly suggest a substantial union. It would be easy to supply a host of relevant Christian examples of similar analogies, among both the "hard" and the "soft" apophaticists (that is, those who admit that God is unknowable but who continue to talk about him/her largely through positive, if metaphoric, statements).

One of the favored forms of language for mystics has been the language of love, especially of erotic love. Michael Sells shows the centrality of erotic motifs based on the pre-Islamic love ode (Qasida) to the "bewildered speech" of the Sufis. Judaism and Christianity also have a rich history of the use of erotic language in their mystical traditions,[6] but one senses important differences in tonality that can only be suggested here. The theosophical kabbalists are unique in the way in which they introduce sexuality itself into the divine realm though the relations between the various male and female sefirot, as well as the way in which they incorporate the practice of marital sexuality as the greatest of the *misvot* on the mystical path. For such kabbalists, procreative sexuality is not so much a form of language to help describe mystical union as it is a performative act that helps bring about integration itself, both on the divine and on the human level. Perhaps for this very reason Jewish mysticism tends to be more restricted in its use of sexual imagery than Christian and Islamic mysticism, just as Moshe Idel notes its austerity in general with relation to all forms of "bewildered speech" (p. 158). Comparative study of the rich—and richly different—forms of erotic language in Christianity and Islam still remains to be done.

The union between God and the human person, whether erotically described or not, challenges traditional views of anthropology as well as of theology. The basic issue is well framed by the Sufi question "Who sees whom in whom?" (see Sells, pp. 87, 119–20). One important group of mystics (certainly the majority in Judaism and Christianity) insists, along with Bernard of Clairvaux, that "the human substance remains, though in another form" (see p. 63). Notwithstanding the "expressions of inner experience in bold unitive terms" to be found in Judaism, Moshe Idel concludes that "the center or core of the ego is never totally obliterated" (p. 56). In Islam, mystics like al-Ghazali interpreted the "bewildered" statements of al-Hallaj and Bistami not as indicating actual identity with God but only as pointing to a unification of two things resembling identity.[7] For these mystics the understanding of the human as the image of God, found in all three traditions, always needs to remain conscious of the element of distinction, just as the human beloved remains conscious of the self at the moment of the consummation of love.

But a number of Islamic mystics, and at least some Christian mystics, went further. In the tenth of his vernacular sermons Eckhart says, "The eye in which I see God is the same eye in which God sees me. My eye and God's eye are one eye and one seeing, one knowing and one loving."[8] Texts like this, as well as the entire tenor of Eckhart's dialectical thought, form close analogies to the language fusions developed out of the "union hadith" that were so characteristic of Islamic mysticism (Sells, especially pp. 108–110, 119–24).[9] Such strong expressions of mystical union (or rather mystical identity or, better, indistinction) between God and the human seem to lead to the following dilemma—either they are guilty of a form of autotheism by which the human subject divinizes itself in an unwarranted way, or else they imply the complete obliteration, absorption, or annihilation of the human personality. In either case, is there room for anything that can still be called an anthropology, a doctrine of the human as human or a psychology that studies *human* consciousness?

Objections to the fusion formulas on the basis of illegitimate autotheism often fail to do justice to the dialectical nature of such forms of mystical theory. In mystics like Ibn ʿArabi, Meister Eckhart, and Jan van Ruusbroec, where we have developed theories of *unitas indistinctionis*, the precise nature of the claims made cannot really be understood apart from their dialectical basis. Ruusbroec's teaching that three different levels of union are always simultaneously present (see Dupré, p. 20; McGinn, pp. 79–80) and Meister Eckhart's understanding of the dialectical fusion of distinction and indistinction in the mystical ability "to live without a why" (pp. 75–78) find remarkable parallels in Junayd's notion of the "annihilation of annihilation," Niffari's discussion of separation and intimate union, and especially in Ibn ʿArabi's profound teaching on *taqallub*, or perpetual transformation, in which the fusion of union and separation occurs simultaneously in each moment of breath (Sells, pp. 109–110, 112–15, 122–24).

But "who" is it who is related to "whom," to paraphrase the Sufi question? What about the survival of the conscious self? The issue is a much debated one among students of mysticism and comes up in all the papers here, most especially in those of Louis Dupré and Daniel Merkur. Our modern fascination with the ego has led to much discussion of the loss of self-consciousness described by many mystics. Various psychological explanations have been offered for this. Erich Neumann, writing from a Jungian perspective, saw mysticism as the experience of unity in which the numinous and creative "self" reveals itself to transform both the ego and the nonego.[10] Daniel Merkur's psychoanalytic approach sees both extrovertive and introvertive mysticism (the latter of both personal and impersonal varieties) as manifestations of the superego or, better, as an increasing fusion of the ego and the superego in order to defend against the psychological threat of the trance state (Merkur, pp. 148–53). But we must beware, I think, of identifying all forms of *unio mystica* with trance experiences or even experiences that aim at some form of trance. Meister Eckhart's mysticism rests upon a new awareness of our distinct-indistinct relationship to God—not a form of rational or discursive consciousness, to be sure, but ineluctably conscious and even self-conscious. Similar messages *mutatis mutandis* are put forth by many of the mystics discussed in these essays.

What the mystics are really about is the task of extending to their readers the invitation to transform both consciousness and the self, the subject of consciousness. Thus I would agree in general with Louis Dupré's emphasis that in the unitive state "consciousness itself remains on a different level that transforms *all* experience" (p. 10), a being-with reality where the conscious mind becomes a paradoxical center of both presence and absence (see p. 11). Such a general characterization conforms well with what many mystics have claimed in their own times and in their own ways. From this perspective, the mystics offer a challenge to all forms of both ancient and modern anthropology and psychology that reject in a priori fashion the possibility of the transition of the limited, discursive ego to levels of transcendental awareness. Beyond the merely discursive oppositions between the conscious and the unconscious, the personal and the impersonal, the mystics hold out the possibility of the transconscious and the suprapersonal.[11] Many dismiss these claims as nonsense. The premise of our investigations is that this may be too hasty a solution.

If there is such a thing as suprapersonal and transcendent consciousness of union of the human and the divine, the papers here suggest important questions about both its duration and effects. Moshe Idel points out that in Jewish mysticism descriptions tend to limit the unitive experience to brief moments (p. 56). Many Christian ecstatic mystics, such as Bernard of Clairvaux, the Beguines, and the early Teresa would agree. But this is not the case, for instance, with the mature Teresa and the doctrine of spiritual marriage as an habitual state found in her *Interior Castle*. Nor would it be true for such proponents of the *unitas indistinctionis* as Eckhart and Ruusbroec. I am not competent to answer for the Islamic mystics here, but Ibn ʿArabi, at least, would seem to hold to a more permanent (if dialectical) state as well.

Mystics in all three traditions would agree with the Gospel statement "By their fruits shall you know them" (*Mt.* 7:16). Moshe Idel's remarks on how the integrationist model of *unio mystica* fostered a renewed dedication to halakhocentric Judaism and a commitment to "world-transforming mysticism" (pp. 54–57) is echoed by Louis Dupré's comments on the role of the praxis element in mystical union (p. 17), as well as by Daniel Merkur's warning that "the goal of mature religiosity is not religious experiences but the religious life" (pp. 152–53). In conclusion, I would turn once again to Meister Eckhart and Ibn ᶜArabi for confirmation. Both are difficult thinkers; both advance teachings regarding a union of indistinction that could be thought by some to encourage a denial of, even flight from, the world of quotidian multiplicity. But the evidence of their own active involvement in the issues of their day, the depth of their subsequent influence on their traditions, and the inescapable "inner worldly" nature of their mysticism, which sees the essence of *unio mystica* as being achieved in the midst of everyday life, easily demonstrate that true mystical union, even in its most extreme proponents, is not a call to abandon the world but rather to transform it.

Notes

Unio mystica: The State and the Experience

1. Such was, for instance, the case with Diadochus of Photice. Cf. Hans Urs von Balthasar, *The Glory of the Lord*, vol. 1 (San Francisco, 1982), 276.

2. Hans Urs von Balthasar in his masterly study on Christian aesthetics constantly insists on distinguishing what he calls "abstract mysticism" and "radical union" from a genuinely Christian experience. For one passage among many, cf. *op. cit.* 1:378–85.

3. Du'l-Nūn, as quoted by Abu Bakr Kalābādi, *Ketab al-ta' arrof*, ed. A. J. Arberry (Cairo, 1933), 105. On the concept of *fanā'*, cf. Gerhard Böwering, "Baqā' wa *fanā'*" in *Encyclopedia Iranica* (New York, 1988).

4. Cited in Böwering, *art. cit.*

5. In *The Other Dimension* (New York, 1979) and, most recently, in *Light from Light* (New York, 1988), preface.

6. Michel de Certeau, *La fable mystique*, vol. 1 (Paris, 1982).

7. *The Interior Castle*, Mansion VII, 3, trans. Allison Peers (New York, 1962).

8. Joseph Maréchal, *The Psychology of the Mystics*, trans. Algar Thorold (Albany, 1964), 190, 194.

9. *Autobiography*, in *Obras completas* (Madrid, 1952), 50.

10. *Interior Castle*, Mansion VII, 1.

11. Jacques Maritain, *Redeeming the Time* (London, 1946), 240–42.

12. *Showings* (Long Text), trans. Edmund Colledge and James Walsh (New York, 1978), 184.

13. Quoted in Moshe Idel's essay, from *Likkutei Moharan*, I, 52, fol. 60b.

14. Maréchal, 196.

15. *Ascent of Mount Carmel*, Book II, ch. 26, 2, trans. Allison Peers (New York, 1958).

16. *Ascent*, II, 24, 4.

17. *Interior Castle*, VII, 2.

18. *Castle*, VII, 2.

19. *Castle*, VII, 11.

20. *De exterminatione mali*, Part III, translation in Elmer O'Brien, *The Varieties of Mystical Experience* (New York, 1964), 112.

21. Evelyn Underhill, *Mysticism* (New York, 1961), 414.

22. Harvey D. Egan, S.J., *Christian Mysticism: The Future of a Tradition* (New York, 1984), 96.

23. *The Four Degrees of Passionate Love*, in *Richard of St. Victor: Select Writings on Contemplation*, ed. and trans. Clare Kirchberger (London, 1957), 232.

24. Louis Massignon: *La passion d'al Hosayn-ibn-Mansour al Hallaj martyr mystique de l'Islam* (Paris, 1922). 2 volumes.

25. *Reshit Hokhmah, Gate of Love*, ch. 3, fol. 59b.

26. Cf. Idel's essay, p. 39.

27. Idel, p. 45.

28. Trans. James Wiseman, *The Spiritual Espousals* (New York, 1985), 147.

29. The reader interested in this rhythm may be referred to Louis Dupré, *The Common Life* (New York, 1984).

30. Underhill, 425.

31. Trans. William Hastie, *The Festival of Spring* (Glasgow, 1903).

32. Trans. R. A. Nicholson, *Rumi: Poet and Mystic* (New York, 1950), 184.

33. Cf. Idel, p. 43.

34. Cf. the anonymous text on the death of Ben Azzai in Idel, pp. 35–36.

35. Cf. McGinn essay, pp. 62–63.

36. Trans. Allison Peers, *The Living Flame of Love* (New York, 1969), 37.

37. On all three, see the essays of Idel and McGinn.

38. *De gradibus caritatis* in J.-P. Migne, *Patrologia Latina*, vol. 196, col. 1195–1208.

39. Angelus Silesius, *The Cherubinic Wanderer*, trans. Maria Shrady (New York, 1986), 65, 43.

Universalization and Integration: Two Conceptions of Mystical Union in Jewish Mysticism

1. See Moshe Idel, *Kabbalah: New Perspectives* (New Haven, 1988), ch. 3–4.

2. Rabbi Abraham Ibn 'Ezra's *Commentary* on *Numbers* 20:8. See Aviezer Ravitsky, "The Anthropological Theory of Miracles in Medieval Jewish Philosophy," in I. Twersky, ed., *Studies in Medieval Jewish History and Literature*, 2 vols. (Cambridge, Mass., 1984), 2:238.

3. See Rabbi Ibn 'Ezra's *Commentary* on *Genesis* 2:3 and on *Exodus* 23:21.

4. Compare Ibn 'Ezra's short *Commentary* on *Exodus* 33:12 to the long version *ad locum*.

5. See A. Ravitsky, "The Anthropological Theory of Miracles" and Howard Kriesel, "Miracles in Medieval Jewish Literature," *Jewish Quarterly Review* 75 (1984): 99–133.

6. In manuscript the version is *ba'avur*, translated above as "since." In print the version is *be'od*, namely "as long as," which is an equally reasonable possibility.

7. Rabbi Shem Tov ibn Falaquera, *Moreh ha-moreh* (Pressburg, 1837), 134. The printed text is inadequate in several crucial points, which are corrected according to the quotation of this passage in a mid-fifteenth-century treatise, *Toldot Adam;* Oxford MS. 836, fols. 162b–63a. The text was tangentially referred to by Ravitsky, "The Anthropological Theory of Miracles," 251, n. 55. This text seems to have been known by Rabbi Shumuel ibn Zarza, *Mekor Ḥayyim* (Mantua, 1559), fol. 102a, probably from Falaquera's work.

8. See Ibn 'Ezra's long standard *Commentary* on *Exodus* 3:14.

9. Abraham Abulafia, *Sefer Sitrei Torah*, Paris BN MS. 774, fol. 155a.

10. Abraham Abulafia, *Sefer Mafteah ha-ra'yion*, Vatican MS. 291, fol. 31a–b. Compare *Sefer Sha'arei Zedek*, written by a follower of Abulafia, Jerusalem MS. 8° 148, fol. 39a: "Moses became universal after he was a particular point." According to the context, Moses turned from his position as the center of a circle to its circumference, this being but another way to express the process of universalization.

11. Compare the above assessment of Abulafia that Moses comprised in himself all the people of Israel. Turning universal by integrating into the intellect the inferior forms is known also from Abulafia's older contemporary, Rabbi Isaac ibn Latif, *Sefer Ginzei ha-Melekh*, ch. 4, printed by A. Jellinek, *Kokhvei Iẓḥak* 28 (1862), 12. Ibn Latif, like Abulafia, assumes that this universalization invests the mystic with magical powers.

12. Oxford MS. 1950, fol. 163a. For a discussion of the seventh way of interpretation in Abulafia's hermeneutical system see Moshe Idel, *Language, Torah and Hermeneutics in Abraham Abulafia* (Albany, 1988), 101–109.

13. Abraham Abulafia, *Oẓar 'Eden Ganuz*, Oxford MS. 1950, fol. 53a.

14. Ibid., fol. 27a.
15. This issue has not been treated in a detailed way, and it requires an elaborate examination; see, for the time being, Moshe Idel, "Abraham Abulafia's Works and Doctrines," (PhD diss., Hebrew University, 1976), 87–88, and the pertinent notes.
16. Sassoon MS. 290, 235.
17. Oxford MS. 2047, fol. 68b–69a.
18. Rabbi Isaac of Acre, *Oẓar Ḥayyim*, Moscow-Günzburg MS. 775, fol. 112a.
19. *Toldot Adam*, Oxford MS. 836, fol. 163a. See also fol. 163b, where the author describes the link of the human spirit to God in these words: "She cleaves to the Active Intellect and so if the Active Intellect emanates intelligible forms upon the *hyle*, as the First Cause emanates upon the Active Intellect, there is a power in the prophet who cleaves to the Active Intellect to emanate from his soul, who cleaves to the All, so as to cause changes." The combination of Aristotelian and Neoplatonic languages is again obvious.
20. Rabbi Menaḥem Naḥum of Chernobyl, *Me'or 'Einayim* (Jerusalem, 1975), 11. It seems reasonable to assume that the description of the light of the Infinite shining in the part points to the union of the infinite and the finite, namely human, lights. On the unitive experiences as described as a fusion of two lights, see the passage from the Bretheren of Purity translated and analyzed in A. Altmann and S. Stern, *Isaac Israeli* (Oxford, 1958), 186. On the complete union of the part, i.e., the human soul, and her root, see also Rabbi Menaḥem Naḥum's contemporary, Rabbi Levi Isaac of Berditchev, *Shemu'ah Tovah* (Warsaw, 1938), 56.
21. Gershom Scholem, *The Messianic Idea in Judaism* (New York, 1972), 203–27.
22. See Moshe Idel, *Kabbalah: New Perspectives*, ch. 3–4.
23. Theodor-Albeck, *Genesis Rabba* 34: 314.
24. See D. Goldschmidt, ed., *Maḥzor Yamim Noraim* (Jerusalem, 1970), 339: "Moldotav ha-kelulim be-shimkha."
25. Philo of Alexandria, *De Somniis* I:63. See David Winston, trans. *Philo of Alexandria* (New York, 1981), 135. See also Brian P. Copenhaven, "Jewish Theologies of Space in the Scientific Revolution: Henry More, Joseph Raphson, Isaac Newton and Their Predecessors," *Annals of Science* 37 (1980): 489–548, for the later repercussions of the conception of God as space. Compare to Irenaeus's explanation of the divine names Eloeim and Eloeuth as pointing to that which contains all. See *Against Heresies*, II: 53, 3, in *The Ante-Nicene Fathers*, vol. 1 (Grand Rapids, Michigan, 1985), 412.
26. See ed. Isaiah Tishby, *Commentarius in Aggadot auctore R. Azriel Geronesi* (Jerusalem, 1945), 12.

27. Tishby, ibid., 12, n. 9, notes the resemblance of the Geronese text to the view of a contemporary and compatriot of the Geronese kabbalists, Naḥmanides. Indeed, in the latter's *Commentary on the Torah, Exodus* 16:6, the eschatological state of *devekut* is described using the motif of the *'Atarah* as the means of cleaving. However, the similarity of Naḥmanides's view to the Geronese text is limited, since in the *Commentary* on the Torah, the motifs of entering and overall adornment are absent. It is important to remark that Naḥmanides's interpretation of the crowns of the dead righteous as the means of their cleaving to the *Shekhinah* recurs in Rabbi Moses de Leon's mystical eschatology; see Elliot Wolfson, *Sefer ha-Rimmon: Critical Edition and Introductory Study* (Diss. 1986), 149–50. Compare to the description of the angels as connected to the Holy Spirit by their diadems in the *Apocalypse of Zephania;* see R. M. Grant, *Gnosticism and Early Christianity* (New York, 1966), 18.

28. Nevertheless, the ideal of *devekut* in a mystical sense was very important to these Geronese kabbalists, as Rabbi 'Azriel's *Commentary on the Aggadot* demonstrates and as noted by Tishby. At least in one instance *devekut* may indicate a *unio mystica* experience; see I. Tishby, *The Wisdom of the Zohar* 2 vols. (Jerusalem, 1957–61), 2:288–90; and Moshe Idel, *Kabbalah: New Perspectives*, 42–47.

29. On this Tannaitic figure as an individualistic type of mystic, see Yehuda Liebes, *The Sin of Elisha, The Four Who Entered Paradise and the Nature of Talmudic Mysticism* (Jerusalem, 1986), 106–25. [Heb.]

30. *Exodus* 33:20.

31. Vatican MS. 283, fol. 71b. On this collectanaea of early kabbalistic material, see Tishby, *Commentarius*, xix. See also Moshe Idel, *The Mystical Experience in Abraham Abulafia* (Albany, 1988), 207, n. 15.

32. The vision of the divine light as a deadly experience occurs in several medieval Jewish texts. Compare also to a view adduced in the name of the Besht (Rabbi Israel Ba'al Shem Tov), the founder of Hasidism, who describes the mystic as "stored" or "hidden" in the divine light; see Rabbi Yehudah Leib of Anipole, *'Or ha-Ganuz* (Warsaw, 1887), fol. 8c.

33. Oxford MS. 1954, fol. 68a.

34. On the vision of one's true self as a mystical experience, see Moshe Idel, *The Mystical Experience in Abraham Abulafia*, 95–100.

35. See *Ve-Zot li-Yihudah*, printed in Adolph Jellinek, *Auswahl Kabbalistischer Mystik* (Leipzig, 1853), 20. On the context of this passage, see Moshe Idel, *The Mystical Experience in Abraham Abulafia*, 132–33. This epistle has some strong polemical aspects, sometimes attacking the views of the theosophical-theurgical kabbalah, sometimes, as in this instance, only reinterpreting them.

36. See Cordovero's *Commentary to Ra'ya Meheimna*, printed by Berakhah Zak, *Kovez 'Al Yad* (NS) 20 (1982), 264. This view, extant solely in a manuscript, was well known through its quotation in R. Abraham Azulai, a follower of Cordovero, *Ḥesed Le-Avraham* (Lvov, 1863), fol. 10b, and so it came to the knowledge of early Hasidism.

37. The unification of the sefirot *Ḥokhmah* and *Binah* mentioned beforehand.

38. *Raẓo va-shov*, a classical phrase describing the need to return from mystical contemplation because of the danger of a sustained experience.

39. Rabbi Moses Cordovero, *Shi'ur Komah* (Warsaw, 1883), fol. 10d.

40. See Mordechai Pachter, "The Concept of Devekut in the Homiletical Ethical Writings of the 16th Century Safed," in I. Twersky, *Studies in Medieval Jewish History and Literature* (Cambridge, Mass., 1984) 2:171–230.

41. Rabbi Eliah de Vidas, *Reshit Ḥokhmah*, Gate of Love, ch. 3, fol. 59b. The integration of worlds is a reverberation of the description of the relationship between the sefirot as contained in one another, according to the *Zohar*. See Elliot Wolfson, "Left Contained in the Right: A Study in Zoharic Hermeneutics," *Association of Jewish Studies Review* 11 (1986): 27–52.

42. Rabbi Ḥayyim Vital, *Sha'ar ha-Miẓvot* (Jerusalem, 1978), 78; on the context of this passage, see also Moshe Idel, *Kabbalah: New Perspectives*, 57.

43. The myth that the primal man comprised all souls within him is a Midrashic view that was transferred in this Lurianic passage to the supernal *Anthropos*. See the interesting discussion on the reconstruction of the structure in Rabbi Barukh of Medzibush, the son of Israel the Besht, *Boẓina di-Nehora* (Jerusalem, 1985), 91–92.

44. *Ẓaphnat Pa'aneaḥ*, Jerusalem MS. 4° 154, fol. 40b.

45. Rabbi Pinḥas of Koretz, *Likkutei Shoshanim* (Lodge, 1924), 10. See Scholem, *Major Trends*, 378, n. 7.

46. Ibid., 10: "Then God surrounds man and then He is called Place since He is the place of the world." See also n. 25 above.

47. Rabbi Menaḥem Mendel, *Sefer Peri ha-Areẓ* (Jerusalem, 1970), 64.

48. *Bittulam*. Compare with the view of Rabbi Levi Isaac of Berditchev, who connects the shame of the recipient in regard to the donor to the state of annihilation and return to the source; although integration is not explicitly mentioned, it is implicit in the return to the "root." See his *Shemu'ah Tovah* (Warsaw, 1938), 67.

49. *Nikhlalim*. This verb was apparently used already by the Besht in the context of mystical activity. In an important epistle addressed to his brother-in-law, Rabbi Gershon of Kotov, the Besht—or the

early Hasidic author who could plagiarize this epistle, according to some scholars—refers to the letters that ascend to the Divine and recommends that "you should integrate [*tikhlol*] your soul with them in each and every aspect of them." See J. Mondshein, ed., *Migdal 'Oz* (Kefar Habad, 1980), 124.

50. *"Ha-devekut ha-Gamur."*

51. Rabbi Menaḥem Mendel, *Peri ha-Arez*, 64.

52. *"Irat Shamaim."*

53. Cited in Rudolf Otto, *The Idea of the Holy* (New York, 1959), 37.

54. Rabbi Pinḥas of Koretz, *Likkutei Shoshanim*, 4.

55. See the talmudic dictum, adduced in the name of Rabbi Shimeon bar Yohai, the paragon of Jewish mysticism: "The Holy, blessed be His name, has nothing else in the house of his treasures than the hoard of the fear of heaven." *Berakhot*, fol. 33b. On the meaning and background of this assessment, see E. E. Urbach, "Treasures Above," in G. Nahon-Ch. Touati, ed., *Hommage à Georges Vajda* (Louvain, 1980), 117–24.

56. Rabbi Menaḥem Mendel, *Peri ha-Arez*, 64.

57. G. Scholem, "Mysticism and Society," *Diogenes* 58 (1967): 16.

58. Rabbi Shneor Zalman, *Commentary on the Siddur* (Brooklyn, 1980), 164.

59. See, e.g., Rabbi Isaac of Acre's usage of this term in a unitive description in Moshe Idel, *Kabbalah: New Perspectives*, 70–71.

60. Rabbi Shneor Zalman, *Commentary on the Siddur*, 51.

61. Rabbi Shneor Zalman, *Likkutei Amarim*, ch. 5, 17–19.

62. See note 48.

63. Rabbi Shneor Zalman, *Beurei ha-Zohar* (Brooklyn, 1955), 91.

64. Rabbi Shneor Zalman, *Likkutei Amarim*, ch. 19, 48. On *hitkalelut* in later Ḥabad mysticism see Tali Loewenthal, *"Communicating the Infinite"—The Emergence of the Ḥabad School of Hasidism*, ch. 5 (forthcoming).

65. See, e.g., Abraham Abulafia's *Ḥayye ha-'Olam ha-Ba*, Oxford MS. 1582, fols. 76b–77a.

66. Rabbi Naḥman, *Likkutei Moharan*, I, 22, par. 10 (Benei Berak, 1972), fol. 33b. On this passage, see Arthur Green, *Tormented Master: A Life of Rabbi Naḥman of Bratslav* (University of Alabama, 1979), 319–20; and "Hasidism: Discovery and Retreat," in Peter L. Berger, ed., *The Other Side of God* (New York, 1981), 121. I follow Green's translation except the rendering of the verb *hikalel* as "integreted" in lieu of "included." See also Idel, *Kabbalah: New Perspectives*, 244–45, where I point out the parallel of the identification with the Torah in Rabbi Naḥman's uncle's work, *Degel Maḥane Ephraim*.

67. Rabbi Naḥman, *Likkutei Moharan*, I, 52, fol. 60a–b. Thanks are due to my friend Yehudah Liebes, who has kindly drawn this teaching to my attention.

68. Ibid., I, 22, par. 10, fol. 33c.

69. On the sources of this dictum, see Green, *Tormented Master*, 336, n. 59.

70. *Likkutei Moharan*, I, 21, par. 11, fol. 31a. See Green, 320.

71. Ibid., 320.

72. Ibid., 318–23 and 335, n. 53.

73. Joseph Weiss, "Contemplative Mysticism and 'Faith' in Hasidic Piety," *Journal of Jewish Studies* 4 (1952): 19ff.

74. I.e., the act of self-sacrifice for the sake of God.

75. The nature of the two types of unifications was discussed at length in the preceding pages; see 64–67.

76. Rabbi Alexander Safrin of Komarno, *Zikhron Devarim* (Jerusalem, 1967), 68–69.

77. Rabbi Isaac Jehudah Safrin of Komarno, *Netiv Miẓvotekha* (Jerusalem, 1983), 19.

78. Paris BN MS. 774, fol. 2b. It is important to emphasize that the experience of entering the sphere is rather different from some other visions of circles or spheres in ecstatic kabbalah, which recall the mandala visions but do not stress the element of entering; see Idel, *The Mystical Experience in Abraham Abulafia*, 109–116.

79. See Paris BN MS. 774, fol. 4a: "this great degree to cleave to the '*Illat ha-'Illot.*"

80. Rabbi Isaac of Acre, *Sefer Oẓar Ḥayyim*, Moscow-Günzburg MS. 775, fol. 222a. The term translated here as *Universal* is *Kelal.* Compare also to ibid., fol. 162b, where the hand of God is counted among the terms that designate various kinds of mystical experiences as visions, sights, etc. On the context of this discussion, see Idel, *The Mystical Experience in Abraham Abulafia*, 218–19.

81. Rabbi Isaac of Acre, ibid., fol. 112a. On this passage see Idel, *Kabbalah: New Perspectives*, 47–48.

82. Ibid., fol. 161b. For more on this passage see Idel, ibid., ch. 4, sec. 4. Here as in the previous texts of Rabbi Isaac the term *Mekif* occurs and is translated by "encompasses."

83. See Gershom Scholem, *Sabbatai Ṣevi* (Princeton, N.J., 1973), 242–44, 669–72, 807–20.

84. See Rabbi Eliezer Ze'ev of Kretchinev, *Raza de-'Uvda* (Brooklyn, 1976), part two, *Sha'ar ha-Otiot*, fol. 20b.

85. Ibid., fol. 20a–b.

86. See Moshe Idel, *Kabbalah: New Perspectives*, 96–103.

87. See Moshe Idel, *Studies in Ecstatic Kabbalah* (Albany, 1988), 136–140.
88. See note 77.
89. Compare R. Schatz Uffenheimer, *Quietistic Elements in 18th Century Hasidic Thought* (Jerusalem, 1986) [Heb.]. See also the dichotomy between the atemporal experience of *hitlahavut*, or ecstacy, and *'avodah*, or worship, as described by Martin Buber, *The Legend of the Ba'al-Shem*, trans. M. Friedman (London, 1978), 23. Buber, like Scholem afterward, was not so eager to attribute to Hasidism extreme mystical experiences with unitive implications, but he recognized the possible tensions between an otherwordly oriented mysticism and one rooted in the divine service taking place in time and place. Compare also Green, "Hasidism: Discovery and Retreat" and his interesting analysis of Rabbi Naḥman's problematics in *Tormented Master*, 326–30.
90. "The Mystical Man," in J. Campbell, ed., *The Mystic Vision* (Princeton, N.J., 1968), 397. See also his *The Origin and History of Consciousness* (New York, 1962), 360.
91. For a similar approach see Mordechai Rotenberg, *Dialogue with Deviance: The Hasidic Ethic and the Theory of Social Contraction* (Philadelphia, 1983), passim, esp. 71–75.
92. See also Gustav Dreifus, "Erich Neumanns Jüdisches Bewusstsein," *Analytische Psychologie* 11 (1980): 239–47.

Love, Knowledge, and *Unio mystica* in the Western Christian Tradition

1. The question of the nature of mystical experience and the way in which it might be characterized as in some way "immediate" is not an issue that can be pursued here. In another context I hope to argue that Bernard Lonergan's understanding of "mediated immediacy" can provide a useful tool for approaching this complex question. See B. Lonergan, *Method in Theology* (New York, 1972), 77, 273, 340–42.
2. See A. J. Festugière, *Contemplation et vie contemplative selon Platon* (Paris, 1936), e.g., 164, 286, 288–89.
3. Philip Merlan, *Monopsychism. Mysticism. Metaconsciousness. Problems of the Soul in the Neoaristotelian and Neoplatonic Tradition* (The Hague, 1963), especially 17–25.
4. The best introduction to the mysticism of Plotinus is Pierre Hadot, "Neoplatonist Spirituality. I. Plotinus and Porphyry," in *Classical Mediterranean Spirituality. Egyptian, Greek, Roman*, ed. A. H. Armstrong (New York, 1986), 230–49.

5. For Plotinus's notion of union on the level of Nous, see, e.g., *Enneads* III.8.8, IV.3.5, IV.4.2., VI.9.8 and 10.

6. On loving Intellect *(nous eron)*, see *Enn.* VI.7.35. For some other texts on union with the One, see , e.g., VI.7.31–34, VI.9.8–11. A basic book on the role of love in Plotinus's thought is René Arnou, *Le désir de Dieu dans la philosophie de Plotin* (Rome, 1967).

7. This is clearly the case, despite the efforts of Abbot Cuthbert Butler, who claims that "St. Augustine does not employ this term [union]; yet there are passages in which he equivalently expresses the same idea." Cf. Butler's *Western Mysticism* (New York, 1923), 62. Augustine does, however, speak of being "one" with God in heaven, e.g., *Ennarratio in Psalmos* 36.I.2.

8. *Confessions* 9.25: "attingimus aeternam sapientiam"; *Contra Faustum* 12.42: "aeternam lucem sapientiae contueri" (cf. 22.56); *De vera religione* 55.113: "et pacem qua unitati adhaeremus."

9. *De vera rel.* 31–58: "Omnia ergo judicat, quia super omnia est, quando cum Deo est. Cum illo autem est, quando purissime intelligit, et tota charitate, quod intelligit, diligit." Cited from J.-P. Migne, *Patrologia Latina* (hereafter abbreviated as *P.L.*) 34: 148. Cf. also *Conf.* 9.10.2–3, where the mystical "touching" of God that Augustine and Monica enjoyed at Ostia is described as taking place both "toto ictu *cordis*" and "rapida *cogitatione*." On this issue see Rowan Williams, *Christian Spirituality* (Atlanta, 1980), 74, and Fulbert Cayre, *La contemplation augustinienne* (Paris, 1954), 236–37, 244.

10. *Collationes* 9–10.

11. Gregory speaks of a "momentary glimpse" of the divine light at the summit of contemplation (e.g., *Moralia in Job* 8.50), as well as of the "chink of contemplation" (e.g., *Moralia* 5.52; *Homiliae in Ezechielem* 2.5, 16.18). His account of Benedict's vision in *Dialogi* 2.35 speaks of the saint as "rapt in God" ("in Deo raptus; . . . in Dei lumine rapitur super se"), but not of union. For Gregory's teaching on this question, see Butler, *op. cit.*, 101–33.

12. Some key texts on union from the *De mystica theologia*, as found in the translation of John the Scot are: a. "et ad *unitatem*, ut possibile inscius restituere ipsius qui est super omnem essentiam et scientiam." *De mystica theologia* 1, as found in *Dionysiaca*, ed. P. Chevallier, vol. 1 (Paris, 1937), 568. b. "et totus *adunabitur* voce carenti. . . ." *De mystica theologia* 3, in *Dionysiaca*, vol. 1, 591.

   For other texts on union, consult *De divinis nominibus* 7, and *De ecclesiastica hierarchia* 1.

   In the first book of his *Periphyseon*, or *De divisione naturae*, John the Scot twice cites Maximus the Confessor's *Ambigua* on the nature of the union between God and the soul, making use of the images of air illuminated by the sun and iron glowing in fire to describe this transformation; see *Johannes Scottus Periphyseon Liber*

I, ed. I. P. Sheldon-Williams (Dublin, 1968), 54, 56–58. These analogies appear in John's translation of the *Ambigua* found in J.-P. Migne, *Patrologia Graeca* 91, 1076a and 1088d, but they are not in the Greek texts currently available.

13. Augustine had cited this text in his *De trinitate* 14.14.20 to refer to the perfect cleaving to God to be enjoyed in heaven. In *Epistola* 147.13 (*P.L.* 33, 613) he even uses it to describe adhering in this life.

14. Etienne Gilson was the first to demonstrate the source of these metaphors in his article "Maxime, Érigène, S. Bernard," *Aus der Geisteswelt des Mittelalters (Mélanges M. Grabmann)*, vol. 1, (Münster, 1935), 188–92. The most complete study of the history of these comparisons is to be found in Jean Pepin, " 'Stilla aquae modica multo infusa vino, ferrum ignitum, luce perfusus aer.' L'origine de trois comparisons familières à la théologie mystique médiévale," *Miscellanea André Combes (Divinitas 11)*, vol. 1 (Rome, 1967), 331–75. For a treatment of one of the metaphors in some late medieval authors, see Robert E. Lerner, "The Image of Mixed Liquids in Late Medieval Mystical Thought," *Church History* 40 (1971): 397–411.

15. *De diligendo Deo* 10.28, eds. Jean Leclercq et al. *Sancti Bernardi Opera*, vol. 3, (Rome, 1957–77), 143. In 10.29 Bernard expresses doubts that this kind of union can be achieved prior to heaven (*except* for the martyrs). Later texts on union, such as those cited from the *Sermones super Cantica* below, seem to qualify these early hesitations. Even in his earliest treatise, the *De gradibus humilitatis et superbiae* 7.21 (*Opera*, vol. 3, 32–33), he speaks of the Word cleansing human reason and of the Holy Spirit perfecting the will so that the soul can be briefly joined to the Father in marital union.

16. *Sermones in Cantica* 71.6–10 (*Opera*, vol. 2, 217–22). See also *In Cant.* 2.2, 67.8, 83.3; *De diligendo Deo* 15.39, and *Ep.* 11.8. Bernard discusses nine kinds of union in his treatise *De consideratione* 5.8 and the sermon *De diversis* 80.1. These texts on union should be compared with the passages in which the abbot speaks of the transient nature of the divine visits to the soul, e.g., *In Cant.* 31.4–8.

17. See especially *In Cant.* 83.4–6 (*Opera*, vol. 2, 300–302), which should be compared with *In Cant.* 45.1 and 6, 52.2–6, 59.2, and 69.7. In 82.8 Bernard identifies *caritas* with the *visio Dei* and the *similitudo Dei*.

18. Beside the ascent outlined in the *De diligendo Deo* and in *Ep.* 11.8, see, e.g., *De diversis* 101 (*Opera*, vol. 6, 368).

19. Gregory the Great, *Homilia in Evangelia* 27: "Dum enim audita supercaelestia amamus, amata iam novimus, quia amor ipse notitia est" (*P.L.* 76, 1207). Bernard cites this text in his *De diversis* 29.1 (*Opera*, vol. 6, 210). *In Cant.* 49.4 also speaks of an ecstacy that in-

volves both intellect and will. On the use of the Gregorian theme in the twelfth century, see Robert Javelet, "Intelligence et amour chez les auteurs spirituels du XIIe siècle," *Revue d'ascetique et de mystique* 37 (1961): 273–90, 429–50; and his *Image et ressemblance au douzième siècle*, vol. 1 (Paris, 1967), 427–35.

20. The *unus spiritus* formula is frequently found in William's *Epistola aurea*, e.g., II.257, 262–63, 275, 286, 288; see the edition of Jean Déchanet, *Lettre aux frères du Mont-Dieu (Lettre d'or)* (Paris, 1975. Sources chrétiennes 223), 348, 352–54, 364, 374. For a translation of this central work, see *The Golden Epistle* (Spencer, 1971). The *unitas spiritus* theme appears throughout William's works, e.g., *Speculum fidei* #65, 71–72, in the edition of M.-M. Davy, *Deux traités sur la foi* (Paris, 1959), 78, 82–84; *Super Cantica Canticorum* #78, 80, in the edition of M.-M Davy, *Commentaire sur le Cantique des Cantiques* (Paris, 1958), 106, 108; *De natura corporis et animae* (*P.L.* 180, 725b); *Meditativae orationes* (*P.L.* 189, 224ab). William sometimes speaks of an *unitas similitudinis* with God, e.g., *In Epistola ad Romanos* 5 (*P.L.* 180, 638cd).

21. *Speculum fidei* #66 (ed. Davy, 78).

22. *Super Cant. Cant.* #109 (ed. Davy, 138).

23. Odo Brooke, "William of St. Thierry's Doctrine of the Ascent to God by Faith," *Studies in Monastic Theology* (Kalamazoo, 1983), 134–207.

24. E.g., *Super Cant. Cant.* #46, 52, 64 (ed. Davy, 74, 80, 92). There is a translation of this important text (with different chapter numeration) in *William of St. Thierry. Exposition on the Song of Songs* (Spencer, 1970), 46, 52, 64. For other appearances in William, see, e.g., *De contemplando Deo* 11, *De natura et dignitate amoris* 6, and *Speculum fidei* #64 (ed. Davy, 76).

25. See especially Jean Déchanet, "*Amor ipse intellectus est:* La doctrine de l'amour-intellection chez Guillaume de Saint-Thierry," *Revue du moyen âge latin* 1 (1945): 349–74. Déchanet makes use of the earlier study of Jean Malévez, "La doctrine de l'image et la connaissance mystique chez Guillaume de St.-Thierry," *Recherches des sciences religeuses* 22 (1932): 178–205, 257–79.

26. Déchanet, *art. cit.*, 368–70. See also the same author's "Introduction" in *The Golden Epistle*, xxvii–xxx. Gilson's view may be found in his *The Mystical Theology of Saint Bernard* (New York, 1940), 209–210.

27. Déchanet, *art. cit.*, 360–62 and 368. See also Javelet, "Intelligence et amour," 287. Pierre Rousellot discussed William in his *Pour l'historie du problème de l'amour au moyen âge* in *Beiträge zur Geschichte der Philosophie des Mittelalters* 6.6 (Münster, 1908), 97.

28. For the third, highest level of *intelligentia*, see especially *Aenigma*

fidei #40–41 (ed. Davy, 126–28). Cf. *Super Cant. Cant.* #126 (ed. Davy, 158).

29. *Super Cant. Cant.* #76 (ed. Davy, 104): "cum in contemplatione Dei, in qua maxime amor operatur, ratio transit in amorem et in quemdam spiritualem vel divinum formatur intellectum, qui omnem superat et absorbet rationem."

30. *Epistola de anima* #8 (*P.L.* 194, 1880b).

31. *Epistola de anima* #9–19 (*P.L.* 194, 1880–86). On the relation between love and knowledge in Isaac, see Bernard McGinn, *The Golden Chain* (Washington, 1972), 149–53.

32. E.g., *P.L.* 180, 51b.

33. *In Hierarchiam caelestem S. Dionysii* 6 (*P.L.* 175, 1038–42).

34. These two treatises can be found respectively in *P.L.* 176, 987–94 and 951–70.

35. *Benjamin minor* 85 (*P.L.* 196, 60–61).

36. *Benjamin minor* 13 (*P.L.* 196, 10). The translation is from *Richard of St. Victor. The Twelve Patriarchs, etc.*, trans. and intro. Grover Zinn (New York, 1979), 66.

37. *Benjamin minor* 73–74 (*P.L.* 196, 52).

38. E.g., *Benjamin major* 4.13 and 15; 5.16 and 18 (*P.L.* 196, 149–50, 152–54, 188–89, 190–91).

39. E.g., *Benjamin major* 4.10, 5.5 (*P.L.* 196, 145, 174).

40. *Benjamin major* 4.15, 5.12 (*P.L.* 196, 153, 182).

41. *De quatuor gradibus violentae caritatis* 29, as found in the critical edition of G. Dumeige, *Ives. Epitre à Severin sur la charité. Richard de Saint-Victor. Les quatre degrés de la violent charité* (Paris, 1955), 157: "In tertio gradu animus elevatus ad Deum totus transit in ipsum."

42. *De quatuor gradibus* 39 (ed. Dumeige, 167). In both sacred and profane love the third stage is where the *copula* occurs; cf. n. 26 (ed. Dumeige, 153).

43. *De quatuor gradibus* 40 (ed. Dumeige, 169).

44. Especially *De gradibus caritatis* 4 (*P.L.* 196, 1204–08).

45. 1 *Cor.* 6:17 is cited in 1205a. Richard also makes use of Johannine texts on union in 1208a. On Richard's concept of love, see G. Dumeige, *Richard de Saint-Victor et l'idée chrétienne de l'amour* (Paris, 1952), especially 122–33; and J. Chatillon, "Les quatres degrès de la charité d'après Richard de S. Victor," *Revue d'ascetique et de mystique* 20 (1939): 237–66.

46. See 1205d.

47. See 1205d–1207a.

48. *De gradibus caritatis* 3 (*P.L.* 196, 1203b).

49. *De exterminatione mali* 2.9 (*P.L.* 196, 1096b): "Sane perfectionis gratiam quanto melius agnoscimus, tanto ardentius et concupiscimus, et quo amplius accendimus ad amorem, eo perfectius illuminamur ad agnitionem." Cf. *Explicatio in Cant. Cant.* (*P.L.* 196, 438a).

50. The influential views of Thomas Aquinas on this issue will not be discussed here for two reasons: first, the explicit limitation of this paper to writers who can be described as primarily mystical theologians and, second, my intention to take up the role of Thomas's influence on medieval mystical theories at length in another context.

51. See B. McGinn, "Ascension and Introversion in the *Itinerarium mentis in Deum*," in *San Bonaventura 1274–1974*, vol. 3, (Grottaferrata, 1974), 535–52, for Bonaventure's debt to twelfth-century mystical theology.

52. On *beatitudo*, see, e.g., *Itinerarium mentis in Deum* 1.1 in *Sanctae Bonaventurae Opera Omnia*, vol. 5, (Quarrachi, 1882–1902), 296.

53. The most detailed treatment occurs in the *Collationes in Hexaëmeron* 2.28–34 (*Opera*, vol. 5, 341–42). Other important texts are *Itin.* 7.5 (*Opera*, vol. 5, 312–13), and *De triplici via* 1.4.18 (*Opera*, 8, 7).

54. See *In III Sententiarum* d.6, a.2, qq. 1–2 (*Opera*, vol. 3, 157–62).

55. Cf. *In III Sent.* d.6, a.2, q. 3, dub. 2; d.10, a.1, q.2; d.26, a.2, q.1; d.31, a.3, q.1 (*Opera*, vol. 3, 165, 228–29, 570, 689).

56. *In I Sententiarum* d.31, p.2, a.2, q.1 (*Opera*, vol. 1, 546).

57. *Itin.* 7.4 (*Opera*, vol. 5, 312), as translated in *Bonaventure. The Soul's Journey into God, etc.*, trans. and intro. Ewert Cousins (New York, 1978), 113. Similar stress on the "suprema unitio per amorem" is found in *Coll. in Hex.* 2.30 (*Opera*, vol. 5, 341) and in *De triplici via* 1.3, 16–17 (*Opera*, vol. 8, 7).

58. On the predominantly affective nature of Bonaventure's mysticism, see Karl Rahner, "Die Begriff der ecstasis bei Bonaventura," *Zeitschrift für Askese und Mystik* 9 (1934): 2–15.

59. E. Gilson, *The Philosophy of St. Bonaventure* (Paterson, 1965), 420.

60. *In III Sent.* d.24, a.3, q.2, dub.4 (*Opera*, vol. 3, 531): "haec est cognitio excellentissima, quam docet Dionysius, quae quidem est in ecstatico amore et elevat supra cognitionem fidei secundum statum communem." The passage is immediately preceded by a citation of 1 *Cor.* 6:17. *Coll. in Hex.* 2.29 speaks of the "sleep" of the intellect as resulting from its inability to conceptualize or to express what it experiences in loving union, but 2.31 goes on to insist that the darkness of the union floods the soul with light, thus implying a supraconceptual form of knowing (*Opera*, vol. 5, 341–42).

61. E.g., Endre von Ivánka, *Plato Christianus* (Einsiedeln, 1964), 325–73, 379–82. For a related view, at least in terms of its stress on the

importance of Thomas Gallus, see David Knowles, "The Influence of Pseudo-Dionysius on Western Mysticism," *Christian Spirituality. Essays in Honour of Gordon Rupp* (London, 1975), 79–94.

62. On Thomas Gallus, see Robert Javelet, "Thomas Gallus ou les écritures dans une dialectique mystique," *L'Homme devant Dieu. Mélanges offerts à Henri de Lubac*, vol. 2, (Paris, 1964), 99–110; and "Thomas Gallus et Richard de Saint-Victor mystiques," *Recherches de théologie ancienne et médiévale* 29 (1963): 206–233, and 30 (1964), 88–121. More recently, see F. Ruello, "La mystique de l'Exode," *Dieu et l'être. Éxegèses d'Exode 3, 14 et de Coran 20, 11–24* (Paris, 1978), 214–43.

63. Gallus's paraphrase of this text can be found in *Dionysiaca*, vol. 1, 696.

64. See *Prohemium super Cantica Canticorum hierarchiche exposita*, ed. J. Barbet, *Thomas Gallus. Commentaires du Cantique des Cantiques* (Paris, 1967), 65.

65. A survey of some texts from the two surviving commentaries on the *Song of Songs* makes this evident, e.g., *Comment.* 2 (ed. Barbet, 68–69, 102); *Comment.* 3 (ed. Barbet, 110–13, 120, 155, 173). (Gallus wrote an early commentary that has been lost.) Crucial to this new accent is the following kind of language:

   a. "Scintilla siquidem apicis affectualis, que est principalis et pura participatio divine bonitatis que fluit de veritate in imaginem, *ab omni inferioritate ineffabiliter separata* et quasi in vitam divinam transiens quodam modo ineffabili deificatur" (111).

   b. "Mens autem sponse *secans suas intellectuales operationes* per suum seraphim ad supersubstantialem radium secundum quod fas est se immittit . . ." (173).

66. On love as *superintellectualis cognitio*, see the texts from the *Explanatio super Mysticam Theologiam* given in R. Javelet, "Thomas Gallus ou les écritures," 108–10.

67. For some illustrative texts from the commentaries on the *Song of Songs*, see ed. Barbet, 68–70, 204–205. Gallus insists that the union is transient, or *separabilis* (e.g., ed. Barbet, 110, 118, 223–24). On the experiential character of the union, see ed. Barbet, 181, 206.

68. It would be rewarding to pursue this issue in relation to other major proponents of the "affective" Dionysianism of the late Middle Ages, such as the Carthusian Hugh of Balma (d. 1340) and the Franciscan Hendrik Herp (d. 1477), who was a bridge between this tradition and the Spanish mystics. On Hugh of Balma, see von Ivánka, *op. cit.*, 343–51, 379–83; Anselme Stoelen, "Hugues de Balma," in the *Dictionnaire de spiritualité*, vol. 7.1, cc. 859–73; and Jean Krynen, "La pratique et la théorie de l'amour sans connaissance dans le *Viae Sion Lugent* d'Hugues de Balma," *Revue d'asce-*

tique et de mystique 40 (1964): 162–83. On Herp or Harphius, see "Herp, Henri de," *Dictionnaire de spiritualité* 7.1; cc. 346–66.

69. *The Cloud of Unknowing*, ed. and intro. James Walsh (New York, 1981). ch. 8 (139). See also chs. 4 and 34 (123, 186) where Gallus's notion of the "cutting off" of knowing is cited. The critical edition of the works of the Cloud author is that of Phyllis Hodgson, *The Cloud of Unknowing and related treatises* (Exeter, 1982. Analecta Carthusiana 3).

70. E.g., ch. 8 (135–36).

71. The anonymous author's other works include *The Book of Privy Counselling, The Epistle of Prayer, The Epistle of Discretion, Hid Divinity* (a translation of the Pseudo-Dionysius's *De mystica theologia*), *Benjamin Minor, or The Study of Wisdom* (a translation of Richard's work), and *Of Discerning Spirits*.

72. William Johnston, *The Mysticism of the Cloud of Unknowing*, 2d ed. (Wheathampstead, 1978), 34–36, 89–91, 119–33, 136–38, 208–10, 257–58, 271).

73. The fifth chapter of *The Book of Privy Counselling* (ed. Hodgson, 81–84) places strong emphasis on the intellectual aspects of the work of love in the soul. For a translation, see ed., Abbot Justin McCann, *The Cloud of Unknowing and Other Treatises* (London, 1960), 112–15.

74. Johnston, *op. cit.*, 91.

75. Johnston attempts to mitigate this by suggesting that the *Cloud* author's higher dimension of knowing can be understood through contrasting existential or vertical knowing with the horizontal or essential knowing of everyday life (e.g., 45–46, 269–74). For such a contemporary reading to have historical validity, it would need to be supplemented by the recognition that such "vertical" thinking in the Middle Ages was expressed through Platonic language regarding the soul's higher dimension (e.g., *mens, apex mentis, intelligentia,* and the like).

76. E.g., *Cloud*, ch. 21 (163–65). Johnston also criticizes the author here, *op. cit.*, 262–64.

77. Ibid., ch. 67 (249–50) on being made "god by grace" and not by nature.

78. Ibid., ch. 68 (251–52).

79. See the fourth part of Johnston's book (189–256) for a detailed study of the *Cloud* author's teaching on union.

80. *Cloud*, ch. 71 (257–59).

81. "Dicere quod anima sit sumpta de substantia Dei . . .," as found in the *Compilatio de novo spiritu* in Ignaz von Döllinger, *Sektengeschichte des Mittelalters*, reprint, vol. 2 (New York, 1970), 395. On

this and related texts, see Robert E. Lerner, *The Heresy of the Free Spirit in the Later Middle Ages* (Berkeley, 1972), 14–18.

82. Jean Gerson, *De mystica theologia speculativa* #43, ed. Steven E. Ozment, *Jean Gerson. Selections* . . . (Leiden, 1969), 50. For remarks on the history of essential union in Christian and Islamic mysticism, see David N. Bell, "A Doctrine of Ignorance: The Annihilation of Individuality in Christian and Muslim Mysticism," in *Benedictus. Studies in Honor of St. Benedict of Nursia,* ed. E. Rozanne Elder (Kalamazoo, 1981), 30–52.

83. For an introduction to these three major Beguine writers, see Kurt Ruh, "Beginenmystik. Hadewijch, Mechthild von Madgeburg, Marguerite Porete," *Kleine Schriften,* vol. 2, (Berlin, 1984), 237–49. The more general context of female mysticism in the later Middle Ages is presented by Valerie Lagorio, "The Medieval Continental Women Mystics: An Introduction," in *An Introduction to the Medieval Mystics of Europe,* ed. Paul Szarmach (Albany, 1984), 161–93.

84. *Hadewijch. The Complete Works,* trans. and intro. Mother Columba Hart (New York, 1980), letter 9 (66). (This translation allows easy reference to the critical edition of the Middle Dutch Letters and Visions by Jozef van Mierlo.)

85. Letter 16 (80).

86. E.g., Letter 22 (95 and 97) makes use of 1 *Cor.* 6:17. Cf. Visions 3 (272), 4 (274), 7 (280), as well as Poem 3, lines 110–114 (324). A similar kind of understanding seems at work in the unusual union with Augustine that Hadewijch experienced in Vision 11 (290–91).

87. E.g., Letter 2 (50), Letter 14 (76), Vision 1 (263), Vision 5 (277).

88. E.g., Letter 17 (84). Cf. Letter 19 (90), and Letter 30 (118), which says of the unity of love between God and the soul, "In this state one *is* the Father."

89. E.g., Vision 7 (281–82), Vision 12 (296), and Poem 12, ll. 85–96 (342).

90. This occurs in Vision 14 (303), where Hadewijch describes the appearance of the transfigured Christ as follows: "The Countenance, which he had at that moment, was invisible and inaccessible to the sight for all creatures who never lived human and divine love in one single Being, and who could not grasp or cherish the notion of attaining union with the Divinity, so as to have been flowed through by the whole Godhead, and to have become *totally* one, flowing back through the Godhead itself."

91. For an introduction to Mechthild, see Margot Schmidt, "Mechtilde de Magdebourg," *Dictionnaire de spiritualité,* vol. 10, cc. 877–85. Other helpful works are Grete Lüers, *Die Sprache der deutschen Mystik im Werke Mechthild von Magdeburg* (Munich, 1926); Jeanne Ancelet-Hustache, *Mechtilde de Magdebourg. Étude de psychologie*

religieuse (Paris, 1926); and Alois Haas, "Mechthild von Magdeburg," *Sermo mysticus. Studien zu Theologie und Sprache der deutschen Mystik* (Freiburg, 1979), 67–135.

92. *Das fliessende Licht der Gottheit,* which Mechthild wrote down in brief sections in her native low German survives in two translations, an edited Latin version of about 1285 and a later but more authentic Middle High German one of about 1345. Gall Morel edited the latter as *Offenbarungen der Schwester Mechthild von Magdeburg oder Das fliessende Licht der Gottheit* (1869; Darmstadt, 1969). There is a partial and not always accurate English translation by Lucy Menzies, *The Flowing Light of Godhead* (London, 1953).

93. See Kurt Berger, *Die Ausdrucke der Unio mystica im Mittelhochdeutschen* (Berlin, 1935), especially under Abschnitt IV and V.

94. *Das fliessende Licht* 4.19:

> O gebenedeite miñe, de was sunder begiñe
> Din ambaht und ist noch,
> De du got und des menschen sele zesamene bindest,
> De sol din ambaht sunder ende sin.

(Morel ed., 114; trans. of Menzies, 114). Cf. 2.1, 6.30, 7.17, etc., on the same theme.

95. *Das fliessende Licht* 2.26 claims: "Wan dù vrie miñe mùs je das hòhste an dem menschen wesen" (ed. Morel, 53). Cf. 2.23, 3.9, 7.43, etc.

96. E.g., 1.2, 1.21, 2.11, 2.19, 2.25, 3.24, 4.2, 5.29, 6.31, 7.8, 7.48. Ancelet-Hustache, *op. cit.*, 115, also insists that Mechthild's notion of mystical ecstasy includes both love and knowledge. Ulrike Wiethaus has brought to my attention the use of the term "bekantù miñe" ("discerning love") in passages such as 5.33 (ed. Morel, 165).

97. For an overview of her teaching on union, see Haas, *op. cit.*, 108–13, and Ancelet-Hustache, *op. cit.*, 106–38. A recent article by Pascal Baumstein, "Mechtild von Magdeburg's Imagery of Union," *Cistercian Studies* 21 (1986): 43–50, is less helpful. For more on Mechthilde's imagery, see James C. Franklin, *Mystical Transformations: The Imagery of Mixed Liquids in Mechthilde of Magdeburg* (Washington, 1978).

98. E.g., 1.5, 2.22, 4.16, 5.6, 5.25, 6.1, 7.37.

99. E.g., 1.4 (using the traditional water and wine analogy), 2.6, 3.1, 4.8, 4.12, 5.4, etc.

100. 1.44: "Frow sele, ir sint so sere genaturt in mich, de zwischent ùch und mir nihtes nit mag sin" (ed. Morel, 22; my trans.). On this text, see Kurt Ruh, "Beginenmystik," 245.

101. 6.31 (ed. Morel, 205–06). The key passage reads: "Er hat si [the

soul] in sich beschlossen und hat siner gótlichen nature so vil gegos-
sen, de si anders nit gesprechen mag, deñe de er mit aller einunge
me deñe ir vatter ist."

102. E.g., 3.5 (ed. Morel, 66).

103. Mechthild, like Hadewijch, has some interesting passages on union
with Christ in the Eucharist (e.g., 3.15). She also speaks in several
places about a "constant union" with God (stetú einunge) of a non-
ecstatic sort (e.g., 4.15, 7.7).

104. The fundamental work on Marguerite Porete remains that of Ro-
mana Guarnieri, "Il movimento del libero spirito dalle origini ai
secoli XVI," *Archivio italiano per la storia della pietà* 4 (1964): 353–
708, with an edition of one ms. of the Old French version of the
text on 513–635. Considerable debate about Marguerite's orthodoxy has developed in recent years. See, e.g., Edmund Colledge,
"Liberty of Spirit: 'The Mirror of Simple Souls,'" *Theology of Renewal*, vol. 2, (Montreal, 1968), 100–17, which takes a negative
view, as compared with J. Orcibal, "Le 'Miroir des simples ames'
et le 'secte' du Libre Esprit," *Revue de l'histoire des religions* 88
(1969): 35–60, which gives a more positive judgment. Two recent
considerations are Kurt Ruh, " 'Le miroir des simples ames' der
Marguerite Porete," *Kleine Schriften*, vol. 2 (1975; Berlin, 1984),
214–36, and Peter Dronke, *Women Writers of the Middle Ages* (Cambridge, 1984), 217–28.

105. On leaving the virtues behind, see, e.g., chs. 6, 8, and 21 (ed. Guarnieri, 524–25, 526–27, and 540–41); but see the qualifications introduced in ch. 105 (600). Mechthild insists that the virtues serve
the Lover and not vice versa (e.g., 3.10, 4.19), though the Lover
must always practice them (6.30).

106. E.g., chs. 19, 43, 51, 66, 134 (539, 555, 561, 571, 632).

107. Ch. 87 (588).

108. See the references to "l'Entendement d'Amour" in chs. 2 and 12
(522, 532).

109. Ch. 118 (609–13). Cf. ch. 61 (568).

110. E.g., 49 (560).

111. Ch. 118 (613): "Or est toute, et si est nulle, car son Amy la fait
une." (My thanks to Ellen Babinsky for allowing me to consult and
make use of her unpublished translation of *Le Mirouer* for some of
these translations.)

112. Ibid.: "Mais Dieu se voit en elle de sa majeste divine, qui clarifie
de luy ceste Ame, si que elle ne voit que nul soit, fors Dieu memes,
qui est, dont toute chose est . . . "

113. Cf. ch. 21 (541).

114. The connection has been recently studied in an article by Edmund

Colledge and J. C. Marler, " 'Poverty of Will': Ruusbroec, Eckhart and 'The Mirror of Simple Souls'," in *Jan van Ruusbroec. The Sources, Content and Sequels of his Mysticism*, eds. P. Mommaers and N. de Paepe (Leuven, 1984), 14–47. See also Kurt Ruh, "Meister Eckhart und die Spiritualität der Beginen," *Kleine Schriften*, vol. 2, 327–36, and the summary remarks in his *Meister Eckhart. Theologe. Prediger. Mystiker* (Munich, 1985), 95–114.

115. Ch. 91 (592): "Or l'a maintenant, sans nul pourquoy, en tel point comme il l'avoit, ains que telle en fust dame. Ce n'est nul fors qu'il; nul n'ayme fors qu'il, car nul n'est fors que luy, et pource ayme tout seul et se voit tout seul, et loe tout seul de son etre mesmes." For some comparable texts, see chs. 11, 27, 45, 51, 64, 70, 82, 89, 104, 110, 111, and 133 (531, 544, 558, 561, 570, 574, 584, 590, 600, 604, 605, 631–32).

116. On this point, see Alois Haas, "Meister Eckhart im Spiegel der marxistischen Ideologie," *Sermo mysticus*, 246–49; K. Ruh, "Meister Eckhart und die Spiritualität der Beginen," 329–30; and B. McGinn, "Meister Eckhart: An Introduction," *An Introduction to the Medieval Mystics of Europe*, 241–43, 248.

117. E.g., ch. 23 (542) insists there is no difference of natures, while ch. 39 (553) stresses the absence of distinction in Love. Other texts that suggest essential union may be found in chs. 68, 71, 80, 101, 116, 135, and 138 (572, 574, 582, 597, 607, 633, and 634).

118. E.g., ch. 21 (541) uses the traditional formula of becoming a god by grace and not by nature, and ch. 77 (578) speaks of love helping two things to be one.

119. On the importance of "principial" existence in Eckhart, see C. F. Kelley, *Meister Eckhart on Divine Knowledge* (New Haven, 1977).

120. On the unity of God's ground and the soul's ground, see, for instance, German Sermon (abbreviated Pr.) 5b and 15, as translated in *Meister Eckhart. The Essential Sermons, Commentaries, Treatises and Defense*, trans. and intro. Edmund Colledge and Bernard McGinn (New York, 1981), 183, 192 (hereafter abbreviated as *Essential Eckhart*). The critical edition of Eckhart's works may be found in *Meister Eckhart. Die deutschen und lateinischen Werke* (Stuttgart and Berlin, 1936–). The Latin works will be cited as LW, the German works as DW.

121. For a study of these terms, see B. Schmoldt, *Die deutsche Begriffssprache Meister Eckhart* (Heidelberg, 1954), and the "Theological Summary" in *Essential Eckhart*, 42–44.

122. See Latin Sermon (abbreviated Serm.) IV.1, n. 28, as translated in *Meister Eckhart. Teacher and Preacher*, trans. and intro. Bernard McGinn in collaboration with Frank Tobin and Elvira Borgstadt (New York, 1986), 209–10 (hereafter *Teacher and Preacher*).

123. Jean Gerson, as we shall see below, attacked essentialistic understandings of virtual existence in his sermon "A Deo Exivit" (ed. Ozment, 12–20).

124. On union without a medium, see, e.g., Pr. 62, 76, 81 (DW, vol. 3, 64, 323–24, 400–01); *Liber Parabolorum Genesis*, n. 146 (LW, vol. 1, 615); *Expositio in Sapientiam*, nn. 282–84 (LW, vol. 2, 614–16); Serm. VI.1 (LW, vol. 4, 53).

125. Hugo Rahner, "Die Gottesgeburt. Die Lehre der Kirchenväter von der Geburt Christi aus dem Herzen der Kirche und der Gläubigen," *Symbole der Kirche* (Salzburg, 1964), 13–87.

126. See "Historical Data," in *Essential Eckhart*, 7–9.

127. Pr. 6, as translated in *Essential Eckhart*, 188.

128. Ibid., 187.

129. On the "just man insofar as he is just" see especially the commentary on John's Prologue, nn. 14–22, as translated in *Essential Eckhart*, 126–29, and *The Book "Benedictus": The Book of Divine Consolation* 1 (ibid., 209–13).

130. E.g., Pr. 22 in *Essential Eckhart*, 194.

131. E.g., Pr. 6, and *The Book of Divine Consolation* 2 (*Essential Eckhart*, 187, 227).

132. Pr. 48 in *Essential Eckhart*, 198.

133. *The Book of Divine Consolation* 2 (*Essential Eckhart*, 247).

134. Pr. 40 in *Teacher and Preacher*, 301. For some other representative passages, cf. Pr. 12, 39 and 76 (*Teacher and Preacher*, 269, 298, 329). An important text in Serm. XXX.1 states, "Unum autem, non unus, omnes sancti in Deo" (LW, vol. 4, 276). Also see Pr. 16a (DW, vol. 1, 267).

135. A useful account is Richard Kieckhefer, "Meister Eckhart's Conception of Union with God," *Harvard Theological Review* 71 (1978): 203–35.

136. E.g., *Quaestiones Parisienses* 1 (LW, vol. 5, 37–48).

137. Cf. *Expositio Sancti Evangelii secundum Iohannem*, nn. 673, 697 (LW, vol. 3, 587–88, 612), and Serm. XI.2 (LW, vol. 4, 114–15).

138. E.g., Pr. 7 and 21 (*Teacher and Preacher*, 254, 281).

139. Serm. XXIX n. 304 in *Teacher and Preacher*, 226. The Latin is "Ascendere igitur ad intellectum, subdi ipsi, est uniri deo" (LW, vol. 4, 270).

140. E.g., Serm. VI.1–4, XXX.1–2, XL.1–3, XLVII.2–3; Pr. 5a, 5b, 27, 28, 41, 48, 63, 65, 67, 75, and 82. See the entry under *caritas* in the Glossary in *Teacher and Preacher*, 390–91; and B. McGinn, "St. Bernard and Meister Eckhart," *Cîteaux* 31 (1980): 380–86.

141. Pr. 70 in *Teacher and Preacher*, 317.

142. *In Sap.* n. 282, in *Teacher and Preacher*, 172.

143. Pr. 39: "The Holy Spirit's being lies in my catching fire in him and becoming totally melted and becoming simply love" (*Teacher and Preacher*, 298).

144. Pr. 28 (DW, vol. 2, 5).

145. Pr. 39 (*Teacher and Preacher*, 298). Cf. Pr. 7 (*Teacher and Preacher*, 254), and Pr. 52 (*Essential Eckhart*, 201).

146. *Essential Eckhart*, 292.

147. See B. McGinn, "Meister Eckhart's Condemnation Reconsidered," *The Thomist* 44 (1980): 390–414.

148. On God as distinct and indistinct, see, e.g., *In Sap.* 7.27 in *Teacher and Preacher*, 166–70; and B. McGinn, "Meister Eckhart on God as Absolute Unity," ed. D. J. O'Meara, *Neoplatonism and Christian Thought* (Albany, 1982), 128–39.

149. See "Documents Relating to Eckhart's Condemnation," in *Essential Eckhart*, 72.

150. For a discussion of this, see "Meister Eckhart's Condemnation Reconsidered," 408–09 (see note 147).

151. The Bull is translated in *Essential Eckhart*, 77–81.

152. Sermon XI for the Monday of Passion Week, as translated by E. Colledge and M. Jane, *Spiritual Conferences by Johann Tauler* (Rockford, 1961), 177. This solution is not unlike that found in some Sufis for the interpretation of radical statements of unity with God. See, e.g., *Al-Ghazzali's Mishkat Al-Anwar ("The Niche of Lights")*, trans. and intro. W. H. T. Gardner (Lahore, 1925), 106–08. On Tauler's understanding of union, see Gösta Wrede, *Unio mystica. Probleme der Erfahrung bei Johannes Tauler* (Stockholm, 1974).

153. The critical edition of Suso's works is by Karl Bihlmeyer, *Heinrich Seuse. Deutsche Schriften* (Stuttgart, 1907). There is an English translation of the *Little Book of Truth* by J. M. Clark, *Henry Suso. Little Book of Eternal Wisdom and Little Book of Truth* (New York, n.d.). See especially ch. 3, on the distinction of virtual from created existence; ch. 4, based in part on Bernard, which distinguishes two forms of union; ch. 5, which is close to Tauler; and ch. 6, where Suso refutes the misunderstandings of a false mystic labeled the "namelose wilde."

154. Suso, *Leben* 32 (Bihlmeyer, 93, ll. 18–20): "ich wil sú als inneklich durkússen und als minneklich umbrahen, daz ich sú und sú ich, und wir zwei ein einiges ein iemer me eweklich súlin bliben."

155. E.g., *Leben* 48 (Bihlmeyer, 162–63).

156. E.g., *Büchlein der Wahrheit* 5 (Bihlmeyer, 343).

157. E.g., *Leben* (Bihlmeyer, 188); *Büchlein der ewigen Weisheit* 12 (Bihlmeyer, 245).

158. John of Ruysbroeck, *The Adornment of the Spiritual Marriage. The Sparkling Stone. The Book of Supreme Truth*, trans. C. A. Wynschenk Dom (London, 1951). See *The Adornment* 3.3–4 (17–78).

159. E.g., *The Sparkling Stone* 9–10 and 12 (201–12, 216–18).

160. Ibid., 9 (203).

161. Ibid., 10 (208–12).

162. *Jan van Ruusbroec. Opera omnia 1. Boecksken der verclaringhe* (Leiden, 1981), 110.

163. Ibid., 110–20.

164. Ibid., 122–40 (the quotation is on 122). In discussing this level of union Ruusbroec uses the traditional metaphors of iron in fire and light in the air, but he insists ". . . though this union between the loving spirit and God is without intermediary, there is nevertheless a great distinction, for the creature does not become God nor God creature. . . ." (130).

165. E.g., 132.

166. See 136–40.

167. See 146–48.

168. Insisted upon on 152.

169. See P. Mommaers, "Introduction," *Boecksken der verclaringhe*, 29–31.

170. For the debate on the Free Spirit heresy, see the revisionist views of Robert E. Lerner, *The Heresy of the Free Spirit in the Later Middle Ages* (Berkeley, 1972), as compared with the more traditional account in Gordon Leff, *Heresy in the Later Middle Ages*, vol. 1, (New York, 1967), 308–407.

171. See Robert Lerner, "The Image of Mixed Liquids in Late Medieval Mystical Thought," 403–06.

172. See the text in ed. S. Ozment, *Jean Gerson*, 48–58. For a complete edition of the treatise, see *Ioannis Carlerii de Gerson De Mystica Theologia*, ed. André Combes (Lugano, 1958).

173. Ed. Ozment, 50 (cf. the mention in "A Deo Exivit," 18). On the quarrel between Gerson and Ruusbroec, see the exhaustive study of André Combes, *Essai sur la critique de Ruysbroeck par Gerson*, 4 vols. (Paris, 1945–72). For another detailed fifteenth-century discussion of the kinds of union, see Nicholas Kempf, *Tractatus de mystica theologia*, ed. K. Jellowschek (Salzburg, 1973), II.7 and III.3–4.

174. "licet in aliis scriptis eius hunc errorem correxisse videatur" (ed. Ozment, 50). Was he referring to the *Book of Enlightenment?*

175. See the references to Tauler noted by Ozment, *op. cit.*, 86, n. 8.

176. Ed. Ozment, 52–56.

177. Eckhart used the analogy of transsubstantiation in his Pr. 6 (*Essential Eckhart*, 188), tried to modify it in his "Defense," but still had it condemned as heretical in article 10 of the Bull (ibid., 78).

178. The union of form and matter as an analogy for the union of God and the soul might be extrapolated from what Eckhart says about the *sine medio* character of the two, e.g., *In Io.* nn. 31–32, 100 (*Essential Eckhart*, 104–05, 160).

179. Ed. Ozment, 64: "mystica theologia est cognitio experimentalis habita de Deo per coniunctionem affectus spiritualis cum eodem."

180. Ibid.

181. See especially 64–66, where *mystica theologia* is described not only as *cognitio experimentalis* but also as a *sapida scientia* congruent with *mentalis intelligentia*. This agrees with the position taken in the sermon "A Deo Exivit," which describes the return to God thus: "Sic soli tibi ad Deum regredi concessum est *per cognitionem et amorem*" (ed. Ozment, 18).

182. For a brief account, see Alois M. Haas, "Schools of Late Medieval Mysticism," *Christian Spirituality. High Middle Ages and Reformation*, ed. Jill Raitt in collaboration with Bernard McGinn and John Meyendorff (New York, 1987), 171–73.

183. E. van Steenberghe, *Autour de la docte ignorance. Une controverse sur la théologie mystique au XVe siècle* (Münster, 1915. *Beiträge zur Geschichte der Philosophie des Mittelalters* 14), 112: "Inest igitur in omni tali dilectione qua quis vehitur in Deum, cognicio, licet quid sit id quod diligit ignoret. Est igitur coincidencia sciencie et ignorancie, seu docta ignorantia."

184. See, e.g., *Mediaeval Mystical Tradition and Saint John of the Cross*, by A Benedictine of Stanbrook Abbey (London, 1954).

185. *The Life of Teresa of Jesus*, trans. and ed. E. Allison Peers (Garden City, 1960), ch. 20 (197).

186. *Teresa of Ávila. The Interior Castle*, trans. Kieran Kavanaugh and Otilo Rodriguez (New York, 1979), 5.1.4 (87–88).

187. Ibid., 7.2.3 (178).

188. Ibid., 7.2.5 (179).

189. The most profound study of the mysticism of John of the Cross is to be found in Jacques Maritain, *The Degrees of Knowledge* (New York, 1959), chs. VIII–IX (see especially 368–72 on the *unitas spiritus*). Helpful for comparing Teresa and John is E. W. Trueman Dicken, *The Crucible of Love* (New York, 1963).

190. E.g., Saint John of the Cross, *Living Flame of Love*, trans. and ed. with intro. E. Allison Peers (Garden City, 1962), Second Redaction, I.35 (178). See also Saint John of the Cross, *Spiritual Canticle*, trans. and ed. with intro. E. Allison Peers (Garden City, 1961), Second Redaction, XII.7, XXXII.6, and XXXIX.3–6 (304, 439, 475–77) for passages comparable to some in Eckhart. (Despite doubts ex-

pressed by some scholars, the second, more complete redaction of the *Spiritual Canticle* is now generally recognized as authentic, and I shall quote from it throughout.) John sometimes even speaks of "substantial union or transformation," e.g., *Canticle* XXXIX.6 (477), *Living Flame* III.78 (257).

191. *Canticle* XII.7 (304).

192. *Canticle* XXXI.1 (430). For some key texts on union, see *Canticle* XII.7–8, XXII.3–4, XXVII.6–8, XXXVIII.3, XXXIX.3–6; *Living Flame* I.3–4, 16 and 35, II.1 and 34, III.24–26.

193. *Canticle* XXII. 3.

194. For some of these images, see *Canticle* XIV–XV.2, XXVI.4, XXXI.1; *Living Flame* I.3–4.

195. See especially *Canticle* XXII.4, XXXIX.3–6; *Living Flame* II.1.

196. *Canticle* XIII.11 (313).

197. See especially *Living Flame* II.1 (180) and II.34, where we read: ". . . the understanding of this soul is now the understanding of God; and its will is the will of God; and its memory is the memory of God; and its delight is the delight of God" (202).

198. See, e.g., *Canticle* XIV–XV.12–20 (322–28), XXVI.5–9 (399–400), XXXV.5 (452–53), XXXVII.2–6 (462–65), XXXIX.12 (481).

199. *Canticle* XXVI.16–17 (403).

200. See especially *Canticle* XXXVIII.5 (470–71).

201. Inadequate typologies of late medieval mysticism based on such a contrast can be found in older works, such as J. Bernhart, *Bernhardische und Eckhartische Mystik in ihren Beziehungen und Gegensätzen* (Kempten, 1912), as well as newer ones, e.g., S. Ozment, *The Age of Reform 1250–1550* (New Haven, 1980), 115–24. More nuanced reflections on the problems of the affective-intellectual typology can be found in Francis Oakley, *The Western Church in the Later Middle Ages* (Ithaca, 1979), 94–97.

202. This tradition has found powerful proponents in twentieth-century theories of mysticism, especially in J. Maritain, *The Degrees of Knowledge*, e.g., 258–63, 283–88, 338, 349–51.

203. In the translation of Roy Campbell, *Poems of St. John of the Cross* (New York, 1956), 21.

Bewildered Tongue: The Semantics of Mystical Union in Islam

1. The famous *ḥadīth al-nawāfil* (ḥadith of superogatory devotions) *Ṣaḥīḥ al-Bukhārī* 81:38. Translations are my own unless otherwise noted. For the ḥadith in full and a discussion of it, see William

Graham, *Divine Word and Prophetic Word in Early Islam* (The Hague, 1977), 173.

2. The translation, slightly emended, is from A. J. Arberry, *Mystical Poems of Rumi, First Selection*, Poems 1–200 (Chicago, 1968), 79, no. 92. Jalal al-Din Rumi died in 672/1273.

3. Ibn al-Farid [d. 632/1235], *Diwān* (Beirut, 1962), 140.

4. For two examples from Abu Nuwas bearing directly upon the Sufi verses cited above:

> Give me a cup of distraction
> from the prayer caller's call.
>
> *   *   *
>
> Give me to drink a choice wine
> which preceded the creation of Adam.

The translation, slightly emended, is from T. Emil Homerin, "Filled with a Burning Desire: Ibn al-Farid—Poet, Mystic, and Saint" (PhD diss., University of Chicago, 1987), 329, 331. Homerin cites these verses in the course of his critical reevaluation of the relation between Ibn al-Farid's poetry and the Arabic poetic tradition.

5. For the phrase "Arabic Qur'an," see Qur'an 12:2; 13:37; 20:13; 39:28; 41:3; 32:7; 43:3; 27:190 (*shuᶜarā'*); 16:103. Early Islam was comfortable affirming that the Qur'an is embedded in its Arabic sociolinguistic context. No less an authority than Al-Ashᶜari himself appealed to the expression *Qur'añan ᶜArabiyyan* in arguing against Muᶜtazila allegorical interpretation of the Qur'anic "hands" of Allah, pointing out the lack of such allegorical use of the word *hand* in the pre-Islamic sources. The example is cited by Goldziher (Ignaz Goldziher, *Introduction to Islamic Theology and Law*, trans. Andras and Ruth Hamori [Princeton, 1981], 105), who ridicules Al-Ashᶜari's argument. Though Ashᶜari's appeal to pre-Islamic philology may or may not have been convincing in this particular case, his unembarrassed acknowledgement of the inseparability of Qur'anic discourse from its Arabic sociolinguistic context contrasts with the hesitancy sometimes found in more modern treatments of this issue.

6. The extent to which ᶜUdhri and Sufi literature is intertwined is highlighted by Asᶜad E. Khairallah, *Love, Madness, and Poetry: Interpretation of the Majnun Legend* (Beirut, 1980). This study puts into question the standard chronological divisions and the genre boundaries between the ᶜUdhri and the Sufi traditions.

7.   Hal ma ᶜalimta wa ma-stūdiᶜta maktūmū,
      am habluhā idh na'atka-l-yawma masrūmū

See the Diwan of ʿAlqama, ed. W. Ahlwardt, *The Diwans of the Six Ancient Arabian Poets* (Osnabrück, 1972 [reprint of 1870]), 111. This ode is also included in the famous collection ed. Charles Lyall, *Al-Mufaḍḍaliyāt* (Leiden, 1924), no. 120, 396–404.

8. This presentation of the Qasida is condensed from detailed work that can be found in other essays. A more extended presentation of my view of the Qasida will appear in M. Sells, *Desert Tracings: Six Classic Arabian Odes* (Wesleyan University Press, forthcoming, 1989). A brief summary of the argument for the nondescriptive and nonpredicative aspects of Arabic poetry can be found in Sells, "The Muʿallaqa of Ṭarafa," *Journal of Arabic Literature* 17 (1986): 21–33. For a major study of *cortezia* in Islam, see J. Vadet, *L'esprit courtois en Orient dans les cinq premiers siècles de l'Hégire* (Paris, 1968). For the current understanding of early Arabic poetry as an oral-performative tradition see J. T. Monroe, "Oral Composition in Pre-Islamic Poetry," *Journal of Arabic Literature* 3 (1972): 1–53; and Michael Zwettler, *The Oral Tradition of Classical Arabic Poetry: Its Character and Implications* (Columbus, Ohio, 1978). Examples of the profound recent change in our understanding of the Qasida can be found in Suzanne Stetkevych, "Structuralist Interpretations of Pre-Islamic Poetry: Critique and New Directions," *Journal of Near Eastern Studies* (hereafter *JNES*) 42:2 (1983): 85–107; idem, "The Suʿlūk and His Poem: A Paradigm of Passage *Manqué*," *Journal of the American Oriental Society* 104:4 (1984): 661–678; Jaroslav Stetkevych, "Name and Epithet: The Philology and Semiotics of Animal Nomenclature in Early Arabic Poetry," *JNES* 45:2 (1986): 89–125; and T. Emil Homerin, "Echoes of a Thirsty Owl," *JNES* 44:3 (1985): 165–185.

9. Parallels between the Qasida journey and the Sufi journey can be seen in Ibn Abi-l-Khayr's life story: R. A. Nicholson, *Studies in Islamic Mysticism* (Cambridge, 1921), 1–76.

10. This parallel was brought out by Carl W. Ernst, *Words of Ecstasy in Sufism* (Albany, 1985), 36–40.

11. A good example can be seen in Lois Anita Giffen, *Theory of Profane Love Among the Arabs: The Development of the Genre* (New York, 1971), 19–20. The passage is found in ʿAla' al-Din Mughultai, *al-Wāḍiḥ al-Mubīn fi Man Ustushhida min al-Muḥibbīn* (The Elucidation concerning the Martyred Lover), ed. O. Spies, vol. 1 (Stuttgart, 1936). Giffen suggests it is part of a lost treatise on love, the *Kitāb al-Riyāḍ* or *Kitāb al-Mutayyamīn* by al-Marzubani.

12. Ibn ʿArabi, *Dhakhā'ir al-Aʿlāq*, ed. M. al-Kurdi (Cairo, 1968), 50.

13. Trans. from Persian by Elizabeth Gray, *Plowshares* II, 4 (1985): 255.

14. Trans. from Persian by Abdul Jabbar in "Reflections on the Real: Omar Khayyam," presented to the California Humanities Associa-

tion, May 1984, at the Vallombrosa Center, Menlo Park, Calif. For the Persian text, transliteration, the Fitzgerald translation, and a more literal poetic and prose version, see Eben Francis Thompson, *Edward Fitzgerald's Rubáiyát of Omar Khayyám* (Privately Printed, 1907), 60–61.

15. Qur'an 82:1–6.

16. Qur'an 7:172.

17. A few examples: Qur'an 2:7; 6:125; 7:178; 10:100; 42:44–46.

18. These ḥadith are discussed and translated by Graham, *Divine Word*, 212–214, who lists three major formulations and numerous variants: *yu'dhīnī ibn Ādam yasubbu ad-dahr wa-anā ad-dahr . . .* ("The son of Adam vexes Me when he curses Time for I am Time . . ."; *lā yaqul ibn Ādam yā khaybat ad-dahr fa-innī anā ad-dahr . . .* ("The son of Adam should not say, 'Curse Time!' For I am Time . . ."); *yashtimunī ʿabdī wa huwā la yadrī yaqūlu wā dahrāh wā dahrāh wa anā ad-dahr* ("My servant curses Me, and he is not aware. He says, 'O Time! O Time!' and I am Time"). Western treatments have often called pre-Islamic or Islamic notions of *dahr* fatalistic, but the term *fatalism* does little to illuminate the specific articulations in pre-Islam and Islam of this central human and religious dilemma.

19. The discussion of Goldziher, *Introduction*, 76–115, is valuable. While dismissing on one level the significance of the texts he studied, Goldziher nevertheless offers central and illustrative passages. For a recent study see Eric Ormsby, *Theodicy in Islamic Thought: The Dispute over Al-Ghazali's "Best of All Possible Worlds"* (Princeton, 1985).

20. See Al-Farabi, *Mabādiʿ Arā' Ahl al-Madīna al-Fāḍila* [On the Perfect State], *Revised Text with Introduction, Translation, and Commentary by Richard Walzer* (Oxford, 1985), ch. 1, 57–87.

21. *Averroes' Tahāfut al-Tahāfut* [The Incoherence of the Incoherence], trans. Simon Van Den Bergh, vol. 1 (Oxford, 1954), 87–88. "Ghazali's words 'The agent must be willing, choosing, and knowing what he wills to be the agent of what he wills' are by no means self-evident . . . He who chooses and wills lacks the things he wills, and God cannot lack anything He wills. And he who chooses makes a choice for himself of the better of two things, but God is in no need of a better condition. Further, when the willer has reached his object, his will ceases and, generally speaking, will is a passive quality and a change, but God is exempt from passivity and change."

22. My summary is based upon the version of the Greek *shaykh* writings found in Al-Shahrastani, *Kitāb al-Milal wa al-Niḥal*, 2 vols., ed.

Ahmad Sayyid Kilani (Cairo, 1396/1976) 2: 144–147. The difference in emphasis between the *Theology of Aristotle*, which evades the Plotinian passages emphasizing the absolute unity-beyond-being of the One, and the Greek *shaykh* writings, which concentrate solely on that aspect of Plotinian thought, suggests some interesting divergences in Plotinian Arabic thought. The history of the Arabic Plotinus question in the West and the state of research on this complex and compelling problem can be found in Paul Fenton, "Pseudo-Aristotle in the Middle Ages: The Theology and Other Texts" (offprint, The Warburg Institute, 1986), 241–64.

23. Goldziher, *Introduction*, 96–97, cites this passage as an example of the absurd lengths to which the dialectician will go. For a contemporary emphasis upon the primacy of such metaphorical force within even the most unassuming prepositions, see George Lakoff and Mark Johnson, *Metaphors We Live By* (Chicago, 1980).

24. This issue is discussed by Goldziher, *Introduction*, 108, who bases some of his comments upon al-Batalawsi, *Al-Inṣāf fī al-Tanbīh*, ed. A. ʿUmar al-Mahmasani (Cairo, A.H. 1319), 120f. Goldziher dismisses the Ashʿarite interpretation as a "grammatical trick," whereas this essay suggests that in fact the Ashʿarites made an important discovery concerning the problem of reference at this point of tension, a discovery that later Sufis would build upon in their dual-reference language.

25. Qur'an 2:30–34.

26. Al-Hallaj, *Kitāb al-Ṭawāsīn*, ed. Louis Massignon (Paris, 1913), 43, no. 10. The passage is found only in the Baqli manuscript, not in the Arabic manuscript, even though Baqli tends to be wary of this aspect of Hallaj's thought. The ambiguous last line is *wa man fi l-bayni iblīs*. For an excellent discussion of the Iblis theme in Hallaj and the Islamic tradition, see Peter Awn, *Satan's Tragedy and Redemption: Iblis in Sufi Psychology* (Leiden, 1985), 124. The translation of the second alternative for the ambiguous verse is based on the translation given by Awn, though I have changed the syntax slightly.

27. Al-Hallāj, *Kitāb*, 45, no. 12.

28. Ibn ʿArabi, *Fuṣūṣ al-Ḥikam* [Ring Settings of Wisdom], ed. A. A. Afifi, 2 vols. (Cairo, 1946), *passim*.

29. The first two warnings are discussed by Ormsby, *Theodicy in Islamic Thought*, 72–73. Ibn Majah, *Sunan*, 2 vols. (Cairo, 1952), 37. Al-Ghazali, *Kitāb al-Arabaʿīn fī Uṣūl al-Dīn* (Cairo, 1344 A.H.), 245. The second saying is by Abu Hamid al-Ghazali, who was himself accused by traditionalist opponents of theology of revealing the secret. The third warning is a Sufi saying that is the subject of an essay by Ibn Sina. For the Arabic text and translation see George F.

Hourani, "Ibn Sina's Essay on the Secret of Destiny," *Bulletin of the School of Oriental and African Studies* 29 (1966): 25–48. The fourth saying is quoted by Ibn Sina at the beginning of the above mentioned treatise as a saying of ʿAli.

30. Qur'an 10:3.

31. The Qur'an speaks of Joseph as having been given the gift of *ta'wīl* (12:6,21,44,100,101), or symbolic interpretation, of seeing events as signs or symbols (*āyāt*). The philosophers used an allegorical *ta'wīl* along with a critique from the standpoint of *tawḥīd* of a literal interpretation of divine attributes. A symbolic "hermeneutic" was developed, appropriately, by the "Hermetics" (i.e., those inheriting the esoteric sciences and the mythology associated with Hermes-Idris-Enoch). The intimate relationship between hermeneutics in Islam and the affirmation of unity can be glimpsed in the formation of the two Arabic words: *tawḥīd* being the causative gerund form of the Arabic cardinal number *wāḥid* (one), meaning to make or assert oneness, and *ta'wīl* being the causative gerund form of the Arabic ordinal number *awwal* (first). Cardinals present number, ordinals present numerical relation. The relational activity of interpretation reflects on the ordinal sphere its cardinal counterpart. That a pure affirmation of unity is beyond the ability of normal language reference endows the cosmos with symbolic intensity even as it places language within an open-ended process of interpretation.

32. The night journey is mentioned briefly in Qur'an 17:1: "Praise to the one who took his servant by night from the sacred mosque to the furthest mosque."

33. How this universe functions as a symbolic system can best be seen in Shahrastani's account (*Kitāb, op. cit.*, note 22, 2:5–51) of the dispute between the Sabaean gnostics and a group calling themselves *al-ḥunafā'* (after Abraham, who is called in the Qur'an *ḥanīf*, a term interpreted by many as meaning the first pure monotheist, the first to break with polytheistic star worship (Qur'an 2:135, 3:67,90, 4:125, 6:79,161, 10:105, 16:120–3, 30:30). The Sabaeans defended a worldview in which the ten spheres served as temples (*hayākīl*) for purely spiritual entities (*rūḥāniyyāt*). The object of religious life was to rise from the material and impure world through successive stages of purification and spiritualization. The Sabaeans denied that prophets, mere humans, could be mediators between this world and the divine, preferring the pure world of angelic mediation. The *ḥunafā'* counter with the Qur'anic story of the angels being forced to prostrate themselves before Adam because of his knowledge of the names, a position that will be increasingly important as the tension develops within Sufism between humanistic trends that emphasize becoming more fully

human as a goal of the ascent and spiritualist trends that emphasize the progressive shedding of one's humanity.

34. The text was first discussed by Franz Rosenthal, "A Judaeo-Arabic
Work under Sufi Influence," *Hebrew Union College Annual*, vol. 15
(Cincinnati, 1940): 433–485. A new study has identified this text,
al-Murshid ilā al-Tafarrud wa al-Murfid ilā al-Tajarrud (The Guide to
Solitude and the Director to Detachment) as the work of David b.
Josua Maimonides (born 1355 c.e. in Egypt). See Paul Fenton,
*Deux traités de mystique juive: ʿObadyāh b. Abraham b. Moïse Maï-
monide, le traité du puits; David b. Josué, dernier des Maïmonide, le
guide du détachement* (Lagrasse, 1987). For a translation of the section discussed here, see 287, and for a juxtaposition of that passage
with the al-Ghazali passage from the *Ihyāʾ ʿUlūm al-Dīn* (Revivica-
tion of the Spiritual Sciences) see 222–23. For the text of the first
treatise, see Paul Fenton, *The Treatise of the Pool, Al-Maqāla al-Ḥ
awḍiyya by ʿObadyah Maimonides* (London, 1981). Fenton's edition
of the second treatise, *al-Murshid*, with a Hebrew translation, is
forthcoming.

35. Qur'an: 42:11, *laysa ka mithlihi shay'un wa huwa al-samīʿu l-baṣīr.*

36. Qur'an 10:3, *Istawā ʿalā al-ʿarsh yudabbiru al-amr.*

37. 3 Enoch, ed. H. Odeberg (Cambridge, 1928; reprint KTAV: New
York, 1973). For a recent translation and appraisal see P. Alex-
ander, "3 (Hebrew Apocalypse of) Enoch," ed. James Charlesworth,
The Old Testament Pseudepigrapha (New York, 1983), 223–315.

38. Qur'an 27: 15–44, especially verses 42–44. For a Sufi treatment of
the theme see Ibn ʿArabi, *Fuṣūṣ*, 151–60.

39. For a discussion of Hekhalot interpretations of the Talmudic story
(*Hagigah* 14b) see Gershom Scholem, *Major Trends in Jewish Mysticism* (New York, 1946), 52.

40. Ibn Ishaq (via Ibn Hisham), *Sīrat Rasūl Allāh* [The Life of the Messenger of Allah], trans. A. Guillaume as *The Life of Muhammad*
(Karachi, 1955), 184–86.

41. Qur'an 11:7.

42. Reynold Nicholson, "An Early Arabic Version of the Miʿraj of Abu
Yazid al-Bistami," *Islamica* 2 (1926): 402–15. Also see Nazeer Al-
Azma, "Some Notes on the Impact of the Story of the Miʿraj on
Sufi Literature," *The Muslim World* 63 (April 1973): 93–104.

43. From Helmut Ritter's edition of ʿAttar's *Ilahi-name* (Istanbul,
1940), 16–17. Also see Annemarie Schimmel, *And Muhammad is
His Messenger: The Veneration of the Prophet in Islamic Piety* (Chap-
el Hill, 1985), 167, upon whose translation my version is based.

44. Ibn ʿArabi, *al-Futūḥāt al-Makkiyya* [Meccan Openings] (Cairo,
1876–77), vol. 2, 273 ff. Henry Corbin's subsuming of all hermetic
worldviews, including that of Ibn ʿArabi, under the term *angelic*

pedagogy may underestimate the depth of disagreement within the hermetic world over just what kind of pedagogy is involved. See Henry Corbin, *Avicenna and the Visionary Recital*, trans. Willard Trask (Irving, Texas, 1980), 120, 169, where Ibn ʿArabi's discussions of angels and this particular passage are put into the general context of Gnostic and Ishraqi views, with no mention of his very different attitudes on the relation between the angelic and human.

45. Ibn ʿArabi, "Risālat al-anwār [Treatise on the Lights]," in *Rasā'il Ibn ʿArabi* (Cairo, 1968). The italics are mine. I have slightly modified the translations of Rabia Terri Harris, *Journey to the Lord of Power* (New York, 1981). For a more detailed discussion of the treatise and Harris's translation, see M. Sells, "Ibn ʿArabi's *Journey to the Lord of Power*, trans. Terri Rabia Harris," *JNES* 45:2 (April 1986): 167–69. For the primordial covenant in early Sufism associated with Sahl al-Tustari, and for the important theme of the Muhammadian light, a theme related to the issues discussed here, which the limitations of space do not allow us to discuss, see G. Böwering, *The Mystical Vision of Existence in Classical Islam* (Berlin, 1980).

46. See William Chittick, "Death and the World of Imagination: Ibn al-ʿArabī's Eschatology," *Muslim World* 78:1 (1988): 51–82.

47. Trans. Scholem, *Major Trends*, 154–55. The range and the duration of such meditative practices can be seen by comparing this passage to the Nag Hammadi text, *Marsanes*, as discussed by Birger Pearson: "Gnosticism as Platonism: with Special Reference to Marsanes (NHC 10kl)," *Harvard Theological Review* 77, 1 (1984): 69; and with Martin Lings's *A Sufi Saint of the Twentieth Century*, (Los Angeles, 1971). A study of the symbiotic world of medieval Islamic and Jewish Jafr/Gematria has been made by Steven Wasserstrom, "Sefer Yetzirah and Early Islam," a paper presented at the 1985 meeting of the American Academy of Religion, Anaheim, Calif.

48. Ithamar Gruenwald, *Apocalyptic and Merkavah Mysticism* (Leiden, 1980), 3–27.

49. Ibn ʿArabi, *Rasā'il, Kitāb al-Isrā'* (Book of the Night Journey), 32.

50. I have translated this passage from the text given by Rosenthal, "A Judaeo-Arabic Work," 444, n. 41. See also Paul Fenton, *Deux Traités*, 288–89 (both cited above, note 34). The more famous formulation, "I am whom I love, whom I love is I" *(anā man ahwā wa man ahwā anā)*, is usually attributed to Hallaj. See Al-Hallaj, *Dīwān*, ed. L. Massignon (Paris, 1955), 92–93. Cf. ed. Mustafa al-Shaybi, *Sharḥ Dīwān al-Ḥallāj* (Beirut, 1974), 279; Abu Nasr al-Sarraj cites it, but under indefinite attribution: ed. R. A. Nicholson, *Kitāb al-Lumaʿ fī al-Taṣawwuf* (London, 1914), 361, 384. Cf. Al-Hallaj, *Kitāb al-Ṭawāsīn (op. cit., note 26), 134. A second hemistiche, or verse, depending upon the version, refers to two spirits *(rūḥanay)*

in a single body and was never fully accepted within the Sufi tradition. It implied a union in incarnation *(hulūl),* an understanding that, although it was a less radical form of union (there are still two spirits), was less acceptable to Islam than many more radically unitative formulations.

51. Abu Talib al-Makki, *Qūt al-Qulūb* (Cairo, 1306 A.H.).

52. Trans. A. J. Arberry, *A Sufi Martyr: The Apologia of ᶜAin al-Qudat al-Hamadhani* (London, 1969), 53: "Such terms are *baqā'* (remaining), *fanā'* (passing away), *ᶜadam* (not-being), *talāshi* (annihilation), *qabḍ* (contraction), *basṭ* (expansion), *sukr* (intoxication), *saḥw* (sobriety), *ithbāt* (affirmation), *maḥw* (effacement), *ḥuḍūr* (presence), *ghayba* (absence), *ᶜilm* (knowledge), *maᶜrifa* (gnosis), *wajd* (ecstasy), *kashf* (unveiling), *maqām* (station), *ḥāl* (condition), *firāq* (separation), *wiṣāl* (love union), *isqāṭ* (rejection), *ittiṣāl* (conjunction), *jamᶜ* (union), *tafriqa* (parting), *dhawq* (mystical taste), *fahm* (understanding), *wuṣūl* (attainment), *suluk* (path), *shawq* (yearning), *uns* (intimacy), *qurb* (nearness), *tajallī* (revelation), *ru'ya* (vision), *mushāhada* (contemplation), and such expressions as "So-and-so continued *bi-lā huwā* (without personal identity), and 'He sloughed off his skin.' " (I have modified Arberry's translation for the sake of terminological consistency with the rest of this essay.)

53. Discussed by Ernst, *Words of Ecstasy, op. cit.,* note 10. Trans. Paul Nwyia, *Exégèse coranique et langage mystique, Nouvel essai sur le lexique technique des mystiques musulmans* (Beirut, 1970), 179–80. I have revised the translation here and eliminated, for reasons explained in my "Comments," the capitalizations used by Nwyia to indicate divine referents.

54. See Junayd's *Kitāb al-Mithāq* (Book of the Covenant) and *Kitāb al-Fanā'* (Book of Annihilation) in trans. and ed. Ali Hassan Abdel-Kader, *Personality and Writings of Junayd* (E. J. W. Gibb Memorial, 1976), 31–43 (Arabic text), and 152–64 (translation). In the case of Junayd, I have used "annihilation" as a translation for *fanā',* rather than "passing away," since the more violent connotations of annihilation fit the tone and tenor of Junayd's language. This and other important texts were discussed by David Martin in his paper "Al-Junayd's Conception of the Divine Comprehension of Time and Place Compared with the Views of Plotinus and His Arabic Translators," delivered at the "Plato and Islamic Philosophy" conference sponsored by the Society for the Study of Islamic Philosophy and Science, New York, 1983. Also, Muhammad Abdul Haq Ansari, "The Doctrine of One Actor: Junayd's View of *Tawḥīd," Muslim World* 73, 1 (1983): 33–56.

55. Cited by Ernst, *Words of Ecstasy,* 12, from Abu Nasr al-Sarraj, *Kitāb al-Lumaᶜ fī al-Taṣawwuf,* ed. Reynold A. Nicholson (London: E. J. W. Gibb Memorial Series), 31–32. Ernst also provides (25–28) a

discussion of the doctrine of *ana'iyya*, or "I-ness," the doctrine, based on the union ḥadith, that there is only one "I," only one real actor.

56. While the poetic language world can serve as a subtext for Sufi language, the reverse is also true. An example can be found in the opening verses of Ibn Zaydun's "Nūniyya," in which the Qur'anic *yawm al-dīn* and the Sufi stages of *balā'* and *fanā'* add a powerful resonance to the poetic topos of the morning of separation *(ghadāt al-bayn). Dīwān* (Beirut, 1975), 9.

57. I have translated this passage from the Arabic text found in ed. and trans. A. J. Arberry, *The Mawāqif and Mukhātabāt of Muḥammad Ibn ʿAbdi'l-Jabbār Al-Niffarī with Other Fragments* (Cambridge, 1935), Arabic Text, 73.

58. This passage offers interesting similarities to the poetry of John of the Cross. Luce López Baralt offers a full discussion of John of the Cross and Islam in *San Juan de la Cruz y el Islam: Estudio sobre las filiaciones semíticas de su literatura mística* (Mexico City, 1985).

59. *Man ʿarafa nafsahu faqad ʿarafa rabbahu.* More literally: "Whoever has known his self (or himself) has known his lord." This ḥadith is central to many Sufi texts, but it rests upon an *isnad* or chain of transmission that is considered by some to be weak. A book on weak ḥadith gives a fascinating entry for this particular statement, relating that its authenticity was considered by Ibn Taymiyya to be dubious and that Ibn ʿArabi stated that even if its *isnād* is not strong, it can be validated through *kashf.* See Ismaʿil al-ʿAjluni, *Kashf al-Khifā' wa Muzīl al-Ilbās ʿammā Ashtahara min al-Aḥādīth ʿalā Alsina al-Nās*, 2 vols. (Cairo, n.d., the author died in 1162 H.), vol. 2, 361. (I am indebted to Alan Godlass for guiding me to this volume.) The ḥadith also has a counterecho. Although its primary meaning seems to be "whoever knows his true self or inner self" (the inner self revealed in mystical union), "knows his lord" (the divine as revealed to the mystic in mystical union and as encountered by the precreated self in the primordial convenant), it can also be a more cautionary warning: "whoever knows his ego-self" (the dominating self or *al-nafs al-ʿammāra*) "knows his lord" (i.e., that lord of the world or *al-dunyā*, who controls any human being outside of divine guidance).

60. Hallaj, *Kitāb (op. cit.,* note 26), 42, no. 7 (reading *sirr* for *sayr* in the Arabic text, as is suggested in the Persian text).

61. Awn, *Satan's Tragedy and Redemption*, 146.

62. Al-Sarraj, *Kitāb al-Lumaʿ (op. cit.,* note 50), 340, 369. See also Rosenthal, "A Judaeo-Arabic Work," 452; Paul Fenton, *Deux Traités*, 233 (both cited above, note 23). In these witnesses this verse is preceded by the verse "If he is distant he torments me, if near he fills me with fear." For the question of the complex attribution of the verse, see Rosenthal, 452, n. 66.

63. Ibn ʿArabi, *Fuṣūṣ*, 48. The following discussion of mystical dialectic is based in part upon more detailed treatment, translations, and selected Arabic texts in Michael Sells, "Ibn ʿArabi's Garden Among the Flames: A Reevaluation," *History of Religions* 23 (May 1984): 287–315; "Ibn ʿArabi's Polished Mirror: Perspective Shift and Meaning Event," *Studia Islamica* 68 (1988): 121–49. For a similar analysis of Plotinian texts see M. Sells, "Apophasis in Plotinus: A Critical Approach," *Harvard Theological Review* 78 (1985): 47–65.

64. See Eric Ormsby, 148, for a discussion of the seven existential attributes in Islamic thought, a discussion of relevance here, though Ibn ʿArabi's seven *sadana* do not correspond exactly to the seven existential attributes.

65. This redefinition anticipates Carl Jung's preference of completion over perfection as a religious idea. Carl Jung, *Aion: Researches into the Phenomenology of the Self* (Princeton, 1959).

66. *Corpus Hermeticum*, ed. and trans. Walter Scott (Oxford, 1924), Libellus I, 122.

67. Ibn ʿArabī, *Fuṣūṣ*, 48.

68. Al-Hallaj, *Sharḥ (op. cit.*, note 50), 142–43.

69. Al-Sarraj, *Kitāb al-Lumaʿ (op. cit.*, note 50). The close connection between the *badīʿ* school and the Sufi poets and the criticism of poets like the famous Mutanabbi for sounding like Sufis have been discussed by Homerin, "Filled with a Burning Desire" (*op. cit.*, note 4), ch. 2. The relationship between the *badīʿ* poetry and the Muʿtazila school of *kalam* has been demonstrated by Suzanne Stetkevych, "Toward a Redefinition of *'Badīʿ'* Poetry," *Journal of Arabic Literature* 12 (1981): 1–29. These two studies contribute to a view of Arabic and Islamic literature in which poets, scholastics, and Sufis are understood as interacting and influencing one another in creating a common cultural history, rather than, as is more commonly assumed, working in isolation or at cross-purposes.

70. Qur'an 55:29.

71. Ibn ʿArabi, *Tarjumān al-Ashwāq* [Interpreter of Desires] (Beirut, 1966), 43–44.

72. Ibn ʿArabi, *Risālat al-anwār (op. cit.*, note 45), 17. For a discussion of a similar passage (He/he gives him/Him of Himself/himself // in accordance with the image in which He/he appears to him/Him, *Fuṣūṣ*, 121) see M. Sells, "Ibn ʿArabi's Garden Among the Flames," 298–99.

73. A particularly interesting example is the manner in which such reference fusion transforms the patriarchal structures of language and tradition in the *Ring Settings* chapter on Muhammad. A similar referential analysis and split-reference translation has recently been applied to the Muhammad chapter of *Fuṣūṣ* by Seemi Ghazi, "The Symbolism of the Feminine in Ibn al-ʿArabi and Issues Ad-

dressed by Three Contemporary Feminists," (Haverford: Haverford College, B.A. thesis, 1987).

74. Sections of this essay were presented at the November 1985 meeting of the American Academy of Religion ("Towards a Poetics of Sufi Literature"); at the Oriental Club, University of Pennsylvania, January 1987, ("Remembrance, Secret, and Mystical Union in Arabic Literature"); and at the Institute for Contemporary Arab and Islamic Studies, Villanova University, 2/11/87 ("The Semantics of Mystical Union in Islam"). I owe special thanks to Anne McGuire, Bill Werpehowski, Richard Luman, John Seybold, and Emil Homerin for their careful readings and comments.

Unitive Experiences and the State of Trance

1. Cuthbert Butler, *Western Mysticism: The Teaching of Augustine, Gregory and Bernard on Contemplation and the Contemplative Life,* 2d ed., with *Afterthoughts* (1926; New York, 1966), xiii–xiv; David Knowles, *What Is Mysticism?* (1967; London, 1979), 9–10.

2. Ernst Arbman, *Ecstasy or Religious Trance: In the Experience of the Ecstatics and from the Psychological Point of View,* 3 vols. (Stockholm, 1963–70), vol. 1, 418–515.

3. Augustine, *The Literal Meaning of Genesis,* trans. John Hammond Taylor (New York, 1982), vol. 2, book 12.

4. William Ralph Inge, *Christian Mysticism* (1899; New York, 1956), 15–19; Augustin François Poulain, *The Graces of Interior Prayer: A Treatise on Mystical Theology,* trans. Leonora L. Yorke Smith (London, 1910), 299, 320–48; Joseph Maréchal, *Studies in the Psychology of the Mystics,* trans. Algar Thorold (London, 1927), 111.

5. Evelyn Underhill, *Mysticism: A Study in the Nature and Development of Man's Spiritual Consciousness* (London, [1911], 1930), 72.

6. Gershom G. Scholem, *Major Trends in Jewish Mysticism,* (New York, 1961), 4–7, 40–118.

7. Åke Hultkrantz, "The Relation between the Shaman's Experiences and Specific Shamanic Goals," in Louise Backman and Åke Hultkrantz, *Studies in Lapp Shamanism* (Stockholm, 1978); Daniel Merkur, *Becoming Half Hidden: Shamanism and Initiation Among the Inuit* (Stockholm, 1985), 70–117.

8. Jordan Paper, "From Shaman to Mystic in Ojibwa Religion," *Studies in Religion/Sciences Religieuses* 9 (1980): 185–99; Jordan Paper, "From Shamanism to Mysticism in the Chuang-tzu," *Scottish Journal of Religious Studies* 3 (1982): 27–45.

9. Daniel Merkur, "Breath-Soul and Wind Owner: The Many and the One in Inuit Religion," *American Indian Quarterly* 7 (1983): 23–39.

10. William James, *The Varieties of Religious Experience: A Study in Human Nature* (1902; New York, 1958), 321.

11. Ibid., 313, n. 28.

12. Ibid., 292–94.

13. Robert M. Gimello, "Mysticism and Meditation," in ed. Steven T. Katz, *Mysticism and Philosophical Analysis* (London, 1978), 170–99.

14. Brother Lawrence of the Resurrection, *The Practice of the Presence of God*, trans. John J. Delaney (Garden City, 1977), 56.

15. James, 387–88.

16. Ibid., 326.

17. Ibid., 316–17.

18. George Albert Coe, *The Psychology of Religion* (Chicago, 1925); James Bissett Pratt, *The Religious Consciousness: A Psychological Study* (New York, 1921); Robert H. Thouless, *An Introduction to the Psychology of Religion* (Cambridge, 1924); J. Cyril Flower, *An Approach to the Psychology of Religion* (New York, 1927).

19. The extensive literature includes Anton T. Boisen, *The Exploration of the Inner World: A Study of Mental Disorder and Religious Experience* (1936; Philadelphia, 1971); C. Marshall Lowe and Roger O. Braaten, "Differences in Religious Attitudes in Mental Illness," *Journal for the Scientific Study of Religion* 5 (1966), 435–45; David Terry Bradford, *The Experience of God: Portraits in the Phenomenological Psychopathology of Schizophrenia*, American University Series VIII, 4 (New York, 1984).

20. Authors for whom *hypnosis* refers to the use of suggestion, rather than the state of trance, have regarded mystic union and self-hypnosis as different uses of trance states, but the issue is then nominalistic. For my position on the state/nonstate controversy, see Daniel Merkur, "The Nature of the Hypnotic State: A Psychoanalytic Approach," *International Review of Psycho-Analysis* 11 (1984): 345–54.

21. Coe, 274; Pratt, 449–51; Francis L. Strickland, *Psychology of Religious Experience: Studies in the Psychological Interpretation of Religious Faith* (New York and Cincinnati, 1924), 249; James H. Leuba, *The Psychology of Religious Mysticism* (1925; London, 1972), 171–72.

22. Ernest Jones, "The Nature of Auto-Suggestion," *International Journal of Psycho-Analysis* 4 (1923): 293–312; Merton M. Gill and Margaret Brenman, *Hypnosis and Related States: Psychoanalytic Studies in Regression* (New York, 1961), 294–318; George Devereux, "Cultural Factors in Hypnosis and Suggestion: An Examination of Some Primitive Data," *International Journal of Clinical and Experimental Hypnosis* 14 (1966): 273–91; Silvano Arieti, *Creativity: The Magic Synthesis* (New York, 1976), 253.

23. Bernard C. Gindes, *New Concepts of Hypnosis: As an Adjunct to Psychotherapy and Medicine* (North Hollywood, 1979), 11–12; Griffith W. Williams, "Hypnosis in Perspective," in Leslie M. LeCron, ed., *Experimental Hypnosis* (New York, 1952); G. H. Estabrooks, *Hypnotism* (New York, n.d.), 97–123; Simeon Edmunds, *Hypnotism and Psychic Phenomena* (North Hollywood, 1977); Charles T. Tart, "Transpersonal Potentialities of Deep Hypnosis," *Journal of Transpersonal Psychology* 2 (1970), 27–40; H. B. Gibson, *Hypnosis: Its Nature and Therapeutic Uses* (New York, 1980), 95–118; George Matheson, "Hypnotic Aspects of Religious Experiences," *Journal of Psychology and Theology* 7 (1979): 17.

24. Charles T. Tart, "Transpersonal Potentialities of Deep Hypnosis"; and Spencer Sherman, "Brief Report: Very Deep Hypnosis," *Journal of Transpersonal Psychology* 4 (1972): 87–91.

25. Cited by James (*op. cit.*, note 10), 295, n. 3.

26. Richard Alpert and Sidney Cohen, *LSD* (New York, 1966), 58.

27. George Albert Coe, "The Sources of the Mystical Revelation," *Hibbert Journal* 6 (1908): 362–63; Arbman, vol. 2, 336; Merkur, "Nature of the Hypnotic State," 349, 352.

28. Ferdinand Morel, *Essai sur l'introversion mystique, études psychologique de Pseudo-Denys l'Aréopagite et de quelques autres cas de mysticisme* (Geneve, 1918); Cavendish Moxon, "Mystical Ecstasy and Hysterical Dream-States," *Journal of Abnormal Psychology* 15 (1920): 330; Theodore Schroeder, "Prenatal Psychisms and Mystical Pantheism," *International Journal of Psycho-Analysis* 3 (1922): 448, 452, 454; Alfred Carver, "Primary Identification and Mysticism," *British Journal of Medical Psychology* 4 (1924): 108, 113; Franz Alexander, "Buddhistic Training as an Artificial Catatonia (The Biological Meaning of Psychic Occurrences)," *Psychoanalytic Review* 18 (1931): 136.

29. James, 310, n. 12.

30. Sigmund Freud, *Civilization and Its Discontents* (1930), in *Standard Edition of the Complete Psychological Works of Sigmund Freud*, vol. 21 (London, 1961), 67. Later writers who subscribed uncritically to the common-core hypothesis generalized that all mystical experiences were regressions to early postnatal experience: e.g., Mortimer Ostow and Ben-Ami Scharfstein, *The Need to Believe: The Psychology of Religion* (New York, 1954), 117–18; Richard Sterba, "Remarks on Mystic States," *American Imago* 25 (1968): 77–85; Committee on Psychiatry and Religion (Sidney S. Furst, Stanley A. Leavy, Richard C. Lewis, Albert J. Lubin, Mortimer Ostow, and Michael R. Zales), *Mysticism: Spiritual Quest or Psychic Disorder?*, Group for the Advancement of Psychiatry, 9 (1976): 780. A further theory, which was originally based on the evidence of manic psychosis, referred to still later developmental stages in early infancy in order to account for representations of loved objects other than

self: Bertram D. Lewin, *The Psychoanalysis of Elation* (London, 1951); Louis Linn and Leo W. Schwarz, *Psychiatry and Religious Experience* (New York, 1958), 200–205; Herbert Moller, "Affective Mysticism in Western Mysticism," *Psychoanalytic Review* 52 (1965): 258–74; Jeffrey Moussaieff Masson and T. C. Masson, "Buried Memories on the Acropolis: Freud's Response to Mysticism and Anti-Semitism," *International Journal of Psycho-Analysis* 59 (1978): 199–208.

31. Harold G. Coward, "Jung's Encounter With Yoga," *Journal of Analytic Psychology* 23 (1978): 339–57.

32. Paul Tillich, "The Relation of Religion and Health: Religious, Magic, and Natural Healing Distinguished," *Pastoral Psychology* 5 (1954): 48.

33. Underhill, *Mysticism*, 63–69.

34. A typological approach had earlier been proposed by George Albert Coe, "Recent Publications on Mysticism," *Psychological Bulletin* 12 (1915): 459–62.

35. Friedrich Heiler, *Prayer: A Study in the History and Psychology of Religion*, trans. Samuel McComb with J. Edgar Park (London, 1932), 140.

36. Ibid., 139.

37. Ibid., 136.

38. Ibid., 140.

39. Agehananda Bharati, *The Light at the Center: Context and Pretext of Modern Mysticism* (Santa Barbara, 1976), 39.

40. Bharati, personal communication, 1986.

41. Bharati, *The Light at the Center*, 40–41.

42. Henry Suso, *The Life of the Servant*, trans. James M. Clark (London, 1952), 19–20.

43. Rudolf Otto, *The Idea of the Holy: An Inquiry into the Nonrational Factor in the Idea of the Divine and Its Relation to the Rational*, trans. J. W. Harvey (London, 1950), 39.

44. Rudolf Otto, *Mysticism East and West: A Comparative Analysis of the Nature of Mysticism*, trans. Bertha L. Bracey and Richenda C. Payne (New York, 1932), 57–88.

45. W. T. Stace, *Mysticism and Philosophy* (Philadelphia, 1960), 61, 110.

46. Gershom G. Scholem, "*Devekut*, or Communion with God," in *The Messianic Idea in Judaism and Other Essays on Jewish Spirituality* (New York, 1971), 203–27.

47. Johannes Lindblom, *Prophecy in Ancient Israel* (Philadelphia, 1962), 302.

48. Ibid.

49. Martin Buber, *I and Thou*, trans. Ronald Gregor Smith (New York, 1958).

50. Hugh L'Anson Faussett, *A Modern Prelude* (London, 1933), 144–55, as cited by Michael Paffard, *The Unattended Moment: Excerpts from Autobiographies with Hints and Guesses* (London, 1976), 91.

51. B. H. Streeter and A. J. Appasamy, *The Sadhu: A Study in Mysticism and Practical Religion* (London, 1922), 117–18, 120, 155.

52. Stace (*op. cit.*, note 45), 110; Bharati (*op. cit.*, note 39), 32–61; Ninian Smart, *The Yogi and the Devotee* (London, 1968), 42; Ninian Smart, "The Purification of Consciousness and the Negative Path," in *Mysticism and Religious Traditions*, ed. Steven T. Katz (Oxford, 1983), 117–29; Thomas Merton, "The Inner Experience: Infused Contemplation (V)," ed. Patrick Hart, *Cistercian Studies* 19 (1984): 62–78.

53. Aldous Huxley, *The Doors of Perception* and *Heaven and Hell* (1954 and 1956; London, 1977).

54. The claim was presented in three major studies: Robert Charles Zaehner, *Mysticism Sacred and Profane: An Inquiry into some Varieties of Praeternatural Experience* (Oxford, 1957); *Concordant Discord: The Interdependence of Faiths* (Oxford, 1970); *Zen, Drugs and Mysticism* (New York, 1974).

55. Zaehner, *Mysticism Sacred and Profane*, 28, 168.

56. Ibid., 128, 168, 29.

57. Ibid., 29, 168.

58. Angela of Foligno, *The Book of Divine Consolation of the Blessed Angela of Foligno*, trans. Mary G. Steegmann (New York, 1966), 171–72.

59. Ninian Smart, "Interpretation and Mystical Experience," *Religious Studies* 1 (1965): 75–87.

60. Cf. Edward Conze, *Buddhist Thought In India: Three Phases of Buddhist Philosophy* (London, 1962). Perhaps because Conze understood Nirvana as a conscious state lacking both cognitions and affects, he documented the history as a dispute over doctrinal formulations and never recognized—or conceded—that the term *Nirvana* had historically also been applied to experiences lacking cognitions but containing affects.

61. Arbman, (*op. cit.*, note 2), vol. 2, 339.

62. Ibid., 310, 334.

63. Ibid., 319.

64. Mechthild of Magdeburg, *The Revelations of Mechthild of Magdeburg (1210–1297), or, The Flowing Light of the Godhead*, trans. Lucy Menzies (New York, 1953), 9.

65. Richard of Saint Victor, *The Twelve Patriarchs. The Mystical Ark.*

Book Three of the Trinity, trans. Grover A. Zinn (New York, 1979), 285–86, citing *The Mystical Ark*, book IV, ch. XV.

66. Saint Teresa of Ávila, *The Complete Works of St. Teresa of Jesus*, 3 vols., trans. E. Allison Peers (London, 1946), vol. 2, 334–35 (*Interior Castle*, Seventh Mansion, ch. II).

67. Arbman, (*op. cit.*, note 2), vol. 2, 371–73.

68. Ibid., 384–85, 390–92.

69. Ibid., 359–62, 370.

70. Butler (*op. cit.*, note 1), 151.

71. Saint John of the Cross, *The Living Flame of Love*, I, 35; in *The Collected Works of St. John of the Cross*, trans. Kieran Kavanaugh and Otilio Rodriguez (Washington, D.C., 1979), 594.

72. Arbman, vol. 2, 357–59.

73. Louis Bouyer, *The Spirituality of the New Testament and the Fathers* (New York, 1963), 417–21.

74. Martin Buber, *Ecstatic Confessions*, ed. Paul Mendes-Flohr, trans. Esther Cameron (San Francisco, 1985), 41, 109, 110, 121.

75. Robert E. Lerner, *The Heresy of the Free Spirit in the Later Middle Ages* (Berkeley, 1972), 16, 18, 126, 144, 240, 241.

76. Dobh Baer of Lubavitch, *Tract on Ecstasy*, trans. Louis Jacobs (London, 1963), 62–64, 94–97, 128, 130, 135–39.

77. Teresa, vol. 1, 158 (*Life*, ch. XXV).

78. Arbman, vol. 2, 133–44, 371–73.

79. Henry Suso, *Little Book of Eternal Wisdom* and *Little Book of Truth*, trans. James M. Clark (New York, 1953), 184.

80. Ibid., 192.

81. Ibid., 194.

82. Ibid., 192.

83. Ibid., 191–92.

84. Ibid., 195–96. The utterly indescribable is the "Something More" of the *fascinosum* as distinct from the "Wholly Other" of the *mysterium tremendum*; cf. Otto, *Idea of the Holy*, 26, 28–29, 35.

85. Suso, *Little Book of Eternal Wisdom*, 194.

86. Ibid., 193–94.

87. Al-Ghazzali, *Mishkat al-Anwar*, ed. Sabri (Cairo, 1353/1935), text 121–23; translation, 103–108; as cited by Zaehner, *Mysticism Sacred and Profane*, 157–58.

88. Martin Buber, *Between Man and Man* (New York, 1965), 24.

89. Arbman, vol. 2, 373–75.

90. Ibid., 376.

91. Ibid., 377.

92. Teresa, vol. 1, 158 (*Life*, ch. XXV).

93. Ibid.

94. Arbman, vol. 2, 372–73.

95. Angela of Foligno, (*op. cit.*, note 58), 129.

96. Arbman, vol. 2, 381–84.

97. Hadewijch, *The Complete Works*, trans. Columba Hart (New York, 1980), 296.

98. Angela of Foligno, 220–21.

99. Smart, "Interpretation and Mystical Experience."

100. H. P. Owen, "Christian Mysticism: A Study in Walter Hilton's *The Ladder of Perfection*," *Religious Studies* 7 (1971): 31–42.

101. Nelson Pike, "Comments," in eds. W. H. Capitan and D. D. Merill, *Art, Mind and Religion* (Pennsylvania, 1965), 147–48; Bruce Garside, "Language and the Interpretation of Mystical Experience," *International Journal for Philosophy of Religion* 3 (1972): 101–02; Philip C. Almond, *Mystical Experience and Religious Doctrine: An Investigation of the Study of Mysticism in World Religions* (Berlin, 1982), 162, 173–74.

102. Almond, 174–79.

103. Ibid., 128.

104. Steven T. Katz, "Language, Epistemology, and Mysticism," in ed. Steven T. Katz, *Mysticism and Philosophical Analysis* (London, 1978), 56; cf. "Models, Modeling, and Mystical Training," *Religion* 12 (1982): 247–75; "The Conservative Character of Mystical Experience," in ed. Steven T. Katz, *Mysticism and Religious Traditions* (Oxford, 1983), 3–60.

105. Arbman, vol. 1, 347.

106. Streeter and Appasamy, (*op. cit.*, note 51), 135–36.

107. Albert J. Deikman, "Experimental Meditation," *Journal of Nervous and Mental Disease* 136 (1963): 330.

108. Ibid., 331.

109. Ibid., 334.

110. Ibid., 337.

111. Albert J. Deikman, "Implications of Experimentally Induced Contemplative Meditation," *Journal of Nervous and Mental Disease* 142 (1966): 105; cf. Albert J. Deikman, "De-automatization and the Mystic Experience," *Psychiatry* 29 (1966): 324–38.

112. Nathaniel Ross, "Affect as Cognition: With Observations on the Meanings of Mystical States," *International Review of Psycho-Analysis* 2 (1975): 91.

113. Paul C. Horton, "The Mystical Experience: Substance of an Illu-

sion," *Journal of the American Psychoanalytic Association* 22 (1974): 379.

114. Merkur, "Nature of the Hypnotic State," 351–52.

115. Sigmund Freud, *New Introductory Lectures on Psycho-Analysis* (1933), in *Standard Edition of the Complete Psychological Works of Sigmund Freud*, vol. 22, (London, 1964), 66.

116. Merkur, "Nature of the Hypnotic State," 347–48.

117. P. Hopkins, "Analytic Observations on the *Scala Perfectionis* of the Mystics," *British Journal of Medical Psychology* 18 (1940): 217; Sidney Barza, "The Mystical Experience: A Psychoanalytic View," *R. M. Bucke Memorial Society Newsletter-Review* 2, 1 (1967): 8–9.

118. Ross, "Affect as Cognition," 90; Ralph W. Hood, Jr., "Conceptual Criticisms of Regressive Explanations of Mysticism," *Review of Religious Research* 17 (1976): 182–83.

119. Much less is impersonal mysticism a "regression in the service of the ego," as was suggested by Raymond Prince and Charles Savage, "Mystical States and the Concept of Regression," *Psychedelic Review* 8 (1966): 59–81. The phrase refers, not to a temporal or developmental regression, but to a "topographic" regression from consciousness to unconsciousness—or, as current theory holds, from the ego to the id. Both impersonal and extrovertive mysticism are presumably temporal regressions of the superego, but the evidence reviewed in the present essay does not suffice to establish the point.

120. Albert J. Deikman, *The Observing Self: Mysticism and Psychotherapy* (Boston, 1982), 10–11, 94–96.

121. Observed differences among mystical experiences have led several theorists to abandon the common-core hypothesis and to refer to a plurality of discrete regressions: Prince and Savage, "Mystical States and the Concept of Regression"; Arnold M. Ludwig, "Altered States of Consciousness," *Archives of General Psychiatry* 15 (1966): 225–34; David S. Werman, "The Oceanic Experience and States of Consciousness," *Journal of Psychoanalytic Anthropology* 9 (1986): 348.

122. Hans H. Penner, "The Mystical Illusion," in ed. Steven T. Katz, *Mysticism and Religious Traditions* (Oxford, 1983), 89.

Comments: Moshe Idel

1. On this point see Gershom Scholem's important essay, "Religious Authority and Mysticism," in his *On the Kabbalah and Its Symbolism* (New York, 1969), 5–31. However, given the basic denial of the

existence of *unio mystica* in Jewish mysticism by this scholar, the specific problematic of the creativity of mystics like Abraham Abulafia or Isaac of Acre is not even hinted in this essay.

2. This fact seems to complicate the scheme proposed by Gershom Scholem, *Major Trends in Jewish Mysticism* (New York, 1967), 7–8, who envisions the emergence of mysticism as the third stage in the development of all religion.

3. See ibid., 55, 123, 226.

4. See Moshe Idel, "*Unio Mystica* in Abraham Abulafia," in *Studies in Ecstatic Kabbalah* (Albany, 1988), 1–31.

5. Gershom Scholem, *Major Trends*, 37–38.

6. See Moshe Idel, "*Hitbodedut* as Concentration in Ecstatic Kabbalah," in A. Green, ed., *Jewish Spirituality* (New York, 1986), 413 ff., and Paul Fenton, *Deux Traités de mystique juive* (Lagrasse, 1987), 22–111.

7. See Georges Vajda in "En marge du commentaire sur le Cantique des Cantiques," *Revue des études juives* 124 (1968): 187, n. 1; idem, "Comment le philosophe juif Moise de Narbonne comprenait-il les paroles extatiques des soufies?" *Actas del primer congreso de estudios arabes islamicos* (Madrid, 1964), 129–35. See also above in my paper, note 20. It seems that we may supply a further possible use of Sufic language by an ecstatic kabbalist, probably Abraham Abulafia himself, or someone from his circle, who uses the phrase "I am I, the Lord" in order to hint at the unitive experience. See Sells, p. 106, and Idel, note 4.

8. On the influence of this term on Jewish philosophy, see Shelomo Pines, "Shi'ite Terms and Conceptions in Judah Halevi's *Kuzari*," *Jerusalem Studies in Arabic and Islam* 2 (1980): 196ff.

9. See Moshe Idel, *Kabbalah: New Perspectives*, 40–41; idem, "Perceptions of Kabbalah in the Second Half of the 18th Century," a paper submitted at a symposium on *Jewish Thought in the 18th Century* (Harvard University, 1984); idem, "Judaism and Hermeticism," in a volume dedicated to Hermeticism, eds. I. Merckel and A. Debus, 1988, etc.

Comments: Michael Sells

1. I am grateful to Dom Sylvester Houédard for pointing this out to me.

2. I have used here the version that appears in the Diwan. The version that appears in al-Sarraj with indefinite attribution leaves out the term *hallalna*, but the theological implications are equally

problematical. For the full citations see note 50, above, in the essay "Bewildered Tongue."

3. See Jaroslav Pelikan, *The Christian Tradition, vol. 1, The Emergence of the Catholic Tradition (100–600)* (Chicago, 1971), 201.

4. Denis de Rougement, *Love in the Western World*, trans. Montgomery Belgion (New York, 1956). In contrasting the erotic paradigm of mystical union to the agapic paradigm of marriage, Rougement states on p. 70 that Eros "requires union—that is, the complete absorption of the essence of individuals into the god," and thus, "there is no such thing as our neighbor."

Comments: Daniel Merkur

1. A. H. Armstrong, personal communication, 1987.

2. Jean W. Sedlar, *India and the Greek World: A Study in the Transmission of Culture* (Totowa, N.J., 1980), 199–207.

3. Richard T. Wallis, "NOYS as Experience," in ed. R. Baine Harris, *The Significance of Neoplatonism* (Albany, 1976), 121–53.

4. Philip Merlan, *Monopsychism. Mysticism. Metaconsciousness. Problems of the Soul in the Neoaristotelian and Neoplatonic Tradition* (The Hague, 1963); Andrew Louth, *The Origins of the Christian Mystical Tradition: From Plato to Denys* (Oxford, 1981).

5. Christopher Rowland, "The Visions of God in Apocalyptic Literature," *Journal for the Study of Judaism* 10 (1979): 137–54; Ithamar Gruenwald, *Apocalyptic and Merkavah Mysticism* (Leiden, 1980).

6. E.g., Bernard of Clairvaux, *On the Song of Songs*, 4 vols., trans. Kilian Walsh and Irene M. Edmonds (Kalamazoo, Mich., 1971, 1976, 1979, 1980), Sermons 2:2, 31:4–5, 41:3–5, 45:5; ʿObadyah b. Abraham b. Moses Maimonides, *The Treatise of the Pool: Al-Maqala al-Hawdiyya*, ed. and trans. Paul Fenton (London, 1981), 76, 79, 82, 96; Brother Lawrence of the Resurrection, *The Practice of the Presence of God*, trans. John J. Delany (Garden City, 1977), 40.

7. Philo of Alexandria, *The Contemplative Life, The Giants, and Selections*, trans. David Winston (New York, 1981), 21–22.

8. Jean Daniélou, *Gospel Message and Hellenistic Culture (A History of Early Christian Doctrine Before the Council of Nicaea)*, trans. John Austin Baker, vol. 2 (London, 1973), 445–500.

9. Gershom G. Scholem, "*Devekut*, or Communion with God," in *The Messianic Idea in Judaism: And Other Essays on Jewish Spirituality* (New York, 1971), 203–27.

10. Dobh Baer of Lubavitch, *Tract on Ecstasy*, trans. Louis Jacobs (London, 1963), 136–39.

11. Ibid., 62–63.
12. Ibid., 132–33.
13. Ibid., 160.
14. Ibid., 133.
15. Ibid., 134.
16. Ibid., 136.
17. David R. Blumenthal, "Maimonides' Intellectualist Mysticism and the Superiority of the Prophecy of Moses," *Studies in Medieval Culture* 10 (1977): 51–68; reprinted in David R. Blumenthal, ed., *Approaches to Judaism in Medieval Times* (Chico, Calif., 1984), 27–51.
18. ʿObadyah Maimonides, *The Treatise of the Pool.*
19. Franz Rosenthal, "A Judaeo-Arabic Work Under Sufic Influence," *Hebrew Union College Annual* 15 (1940): 433–84.
20. *Shulchan Aruch, Orah Hayyim* 231:1.
21. Louth, *The Origins of the Christian Mystical Tradition*, 80–97.
22. Ibid., 146–58.
23. Ibid., 157–58.
24. David Knowles, "The Influence of Pseudo-Dionysius on Western Mysticism," in ed. Peter Brooks, *Christian Spirituality: Essays in Honour of Gordon Rupp* (London, 1975), 79–94.
25. Dionysius the Pseudo-Areopagite, *The Ecclesiastical Hierarchy*, trans. Thomas L. Campbell (Lanham, 1981), 17.
26. Bernard of Clairvaux, *On the Song of Songs I*, trans. Kilian Walsh (Kalamazoo, Mich., 1971), Sermon 19:3, 5–6.
27. Majid Fakhry, "Three Varieties of Mysticism in Islam," *International Journal for Philosophy of Religion* 2 (1971): 193–207.
28. Blumenthal, "Maimonides' Intellectualist Mysticism," 28.
29. Geo Widengren, *Literary and Psychological Aspects of the Hebrew Prophets*, Uppsala Universitets Arsskrift 1948: 10 (Uppsala, 1948), 101–11.
30. Geo Widengren, *The Ascension of the Apostle and the Heavenly Book*, Uppsala Universitets Arsskrift 1950:7 (Uppsala, 1950), 77–85.

Comments: Bernard McGinn

1. On the history of the term, see Louis Bouyer, "Mysticism/An Essay on the History of a Word," in Richard Woods, O.P., *Understanding Mysticism* (Garden City, 1980), 42–55.
2. Michel de Certeau, S.J., " 'Mystique' au XVIIe siècle. Le problème du langage 'mystique,' " in *L'Homme devant Dieu. Mélanges offerts au Père Henri du Lubac*, vol. 2 (Paris, 1964), 267–91.

3. See, for example, the discussion in Maximilian Sandaeus, *Pro theologia mystica clavis* (Cologne, 1640), 365–66, who refers to his *Theologia mystica* of 1627. His definition: "Unio mystica est terminus hujus unitionis, per quem mens contemplatrix manet Deo coniuncta" (366).

4. See especially Eckhart's "Book of Divine Consolation" in *Essential Eckhart*, 209–39.

5. See, for example, the anonymous kabbalistic text cited by Idel on p. 36, as well as some of the passages from Rabbi Shneor Zalman. In Christianity, we have the examples of Mechthild, Eckhart, Suso, and Ruusbroec among those mentioned in my essay. For Islam, see Farid al-Din 'Attar, Junayd and, of course, Ibn ʿArabi.

6. For remarks on erotic language in Jewish and Christian mysticism, see Moshe Idel, "Métaphores et pratiques sexuelles dans la Cabale," in *Lettre sur la Sainteté*, Etude préliminaire, traduction de l'hébreu et commentaires par Charles Mopsik (Paris, 1986), 327–58; and Bernard McGinn, "The Language of Love in Jewish and Christian Mysticism," in ed. Steven Katz, *Mysticism and Language* (forthcoming).

7. Al-Gazali, *The Niche for Lights*, ch. 6, in *Four Sufi Classics*, intro. Idries Shah (London, 1984), 122–23.

8. See trans. Bernard McGinn et al., *Teacher and Preacher* (New York, 1986), 270.

9. The wide use of the mirror image in all three religions (and also in the pagan mysticism of the Poimandres and the Neoplatonists) as a way to present various forms of union, especially in contexts of extreme formulas, would be worth a detailed study.

10. Erich Neumann, "Mystical Man," in ed. Joseph Campbell, *The Mystic Vision. Papers from the Eranos Yearbooks* (Princeton, 1970), 375–415.

11. Because of the insistent claims of the mystical texts for the perdurance and transpositions of personal consciousness even in the higher levels of union, I find Daniel Merkur's Buberian analysis of "personal" and "impersonal" forms of introvertive mysticism not sufficiently nuanced to do full justice to the evidence.

Name Index

Abraham, 90, 104
Abraham of Kalinsk, 33
Abulafia, Abraham, 30–32, 37, 55, 106, 159, 178
Adam, 35, 96, 98–100, 102–103, 104, 106, 107, 113, 117–18, 119, 123
Akiva, 47, 103–104
Alashkar, Joseph, 40
ʿAlgama, 91
Amalric of Bène, 71, 80
Angela of Foligno, 136–37, 139, 143–44
Angelus Silesius, 23
Arbman, Ernst, 137, 139–140, 143–44, 145
Aristotle, 176
ʿAttar, Farid al-Din, 104–105
Augustine of Hippo, 13, 61–62, 63, 83, 126, 179–80
ʾAzriel of Gerona, 35

Ben Azzai, 35–36
Bernard of Clairvaux, 19, 20, 22, 62–63, 70, 71, 78, 80–81, 83, 84, 180, 181, 183, 190, 192
Bharati, Agehananda, 131–32, 133, 137

Bistami, Abu Yazid al-, 5, 104, 105, 110, 115, 116, 171, 190
Boehme, Jacob, 22
Bonaventure, 66–67, 78, 181, 182
Bourguignon, Antoinette, 140
Brother Lawrence of the Resurrection, 180
Buber, Martin, 133–34, 142–43

Cassian, John, 62, 179
Catherine of Genoa, 140
Catherine of Siena, 14
Clement of Alexandria, 176, 179
Coe, G. A., 128
Cordovero, Moses, 37–38, 47, 48, 55

de Certeau, Michel, 185
de Rougemont, Denis, 172–73
de Vidas, Eliah, 13, 15, 38
Déchanet, Jean, 64
Deikman, Albert J., 147–49, 151
Dov Baer of Mezhrich (the Great Maggid), 34, 47

Dov Baer of Lubavitch, 177–78, 182
Dupré, Louis, 157, 170, 186, 188, 191, 192

Eckhart, Meister, 17, 67, 71, 72, 73, 74, 75–79, 80, 81, 84, 85, 159, 161, 170–71, 172, 173, 187, 188, 189, 190–91, 193
Enoch (Idris), 102, 114
Evagrius Ponticus, 62, 179

Farabi, al-, 97
Fénelon, François de Salignac de la Mothe, 23
Ficino, Marsilio, 81
Flower, J. C., 128
Francis of Assisi, 14
Freud, Sigmund, 130, 133, 150

Gallus, Thomas, 68–69, 70, 80, 85
Gaon of Vilna, 54
Gerson, Jean, 71, 79, 80–81
Ghazali, Abu Hamid al-, 102–103, 115, 142, 181, 190
Gilbert of Hoyland, 64
Gilson, Etienne, 64, 67
"Greek Master," 97, 103, 110
Green, Arthur, 47
Gregory I the Great, 13, 22, 62, 63, 81, 85
Gregory of Nyssa, 179–80
Gruenwald, Ithamar, 107
Guyon, Madame, 23, 139

Hadewijch of Brabant, 18, 71–72, 75, 144
Hafiz, 94, 122

Hallaj, Husayn ibn Mansur al-, 6, 13, 15, 18–19, 98–99, 110, 113, 115, 116, 118, 120, 159, 170, 171, 190
Hamadhani, ʿAyn al-Qudat, 108, 113, 171
Heiler, Friedrich, 131, 132, 133, 145
Henry of Friemar, 75
Hugh of Saint Victor, 64
Huxley, Aldous, 135

Iblis, 98–99, 113, 114, 118
Ibn ʿArabi, 17, 22, 93, 99–100, 105–107, 113, 115–24, 171, 173, 187, 188, 191, 192, 193
Ibn ʾEzra, Abraham, 28–30, 50–51, 179
Ibn Falaquera, Shem Tov, 29, 32
Ibn Ishaq, 104
Ibn Rushd (Averroes), 97
Ibn Zaydun, 91
Idel, Moshe, 15, 166, 176–77, 179, 186, 187, 189, 190, 192
Idris; see Enoch
Ignatius Loyola, 10, 14, 16, 17
Isaac of Acre, 32, 49–50
Isaac of Stella, 64
Isaac Luria, 15, 39, 47

Ja ʿfar al-Sadiq, 108, 109, 110
James, William, 7, 127–28, 130, 131, 145
Janet, Pierre, 139
Jesus Christ, 4, 59, 72, 76, 134–35, 138–39, 144, 171–72, 179, 180

Jilani, ʿAbd al-Qadir al-, 115
John (and Johannine writ-
    ings), 4, 59, 75, 84
John of the Cross, 10, 11–12,
    18, 19–20, 82–86, 139,
    170, 187
John the Scot (Erigena), 170,
    172, 185, 188
Johnston, William, 69–70
Jordan of Quedlinburg, 80
Julian of Norwich, 14
Junayd, Abu'l-Qasim Muham-
    mad, 109–110, 112–13,
    115, 118, 171, 191
Jung, Carl Gustav, 130–31

Karo, Joseph, 54, 178
Katz, Steven, 145–46
Khayyam, Omar, 94

Lindblom, Johannes, 133
Lombard, Peter, 80

Maimonides, David ben Jo-
    sue, 102
Maimonides, Moses, 31, 178
Maimonides, Obadyah, 178
Makki, Abu Talib al-, 108
Maréchal, Joseph, 9, 11
Marguerite Porete, 71, 73–75,
    159
Maria Maddalena de'Pazzi,
    140
Marie of the Incarnation, 10,
    14–15, 23
Maritain, Jacques, 11
Maximus the Confessor, 16,
    62
McGinn, Bernard, 17, 159,
    179
Mechthild of Magdeburg, 71,
    72–73, 75, 137–38

Menahem Mendel of Vitebsk,
    33, 34, 40, 41, 43
Menahem Nahum of Cherno-
    byl, 33
Merkur, Daniel, 157, 186, 191,
    192–93
Metatron, 49, 103, 114
Molinos, Miguel, 23
Mommaers, Paul, 80
Mordekhai of Nadworna, 54
Moses, 6, 29, 30, 50, 70, 104,
    108–109
Muhammad, 102, 104–105,
    181–182

Nahman of Braslav, 11, 15–
    16, 21, 45–47
Nahmanides, 54
Neumann, Erich, 56–57, 191
Nicholas of Cusa, 81, 188
Niffari, 'Abdu'l-Jabbar an-,
    11–12, 114–15, 171, 191

Origen of Alexandria, 13, 176,
    179, 185
Otto, Rudolph, 40, 133
Owen, H. P., 145

Parmenides, 21
Paul (and Pauline writings),
    4, 61, 62–63, 65, 70, 75,
    82, 83, 176
Philo of Alexandria, 34–35,
    176, 178
Pinhas of Koretz, 33, 34, 35,
    40, 41, 166
Plato, 5, 61, 176
Plotinus, 5, 22, 61, 64, 70,
    165–66, 170, 175–76, 182,
    189
Pratt, J. B., 128
Proclus, 70

Pseudo-Dionysius, 62, 66, 67, 68, 69, 80, 170, 172, 180, 182, 185

Qays, 91

Rabiah, 17
Rahner, Hugo, 75
Récéjac, J., 40–41
Richard of Saint Victor, 13, 14, 20, 23, 65–66, 138, 187, 188
Rousselot, Pierre, 64
Rumi, Jalaluddin, 17, 18–19, 170, 171
Ruusbroec, Jan van, 16–17, 20, 73, 79–80, 187, 188, 191, 192

Sabbatai Sevi, 54
Safrin, Alexander, of Komarno, 47–48, 49
Safrin, Isaac Jehudah, of Komarno, 48–49, 55
Sarraj, Abu Nasr al-, 110, 120
Scholem, Gershom, 6–7, 33, 42, 126, 133, 160, 176
Sells, Michael, 22, 158, 159, 160, 161, 181, 186, 187, 188, 189, 190, 191
Shelomo ben Abraham ibn Adret, 54, 159
Shneor Zalman of Lyady, 19, 20, 33, 41–42, 43–45, 177, 189

Simeon ben Yohai, 177
Singh Sundar, 134–35, 146–47
Smart, Ninian, 137, 145
Spinoza, Baruch, 21
Stace, W. T., 133
Suhrawardi, 'Abdu'l-Qahir, 159, 171
Suso, Henry, 79, 132–33, 137, 140–42, 180, 181, 183
Symeon the New Theologian, 140

Tauler, John, 78–79, 80
Teilhard de Chardin, Pierre, 16
Tennyson, Alfred Lord, 128–29, 137
Teresa of Ávila, 8, 9, 10, 12, 17, 18, 23, 82, 138–39, 140, 143, 192
Thérèse of Lisieux, 23
Thomas Aquinas, 70, 76, 83
Thouless, R. H., 128

Underhill, Evelyn, 14, 18, 126, 131

William of Occam, 80
William of Saint-Thierry, 22, 63–64, 187

Zaehner, R. C., 135–37, 145

Subject Index

Active and contemplative
lives, 13–16, 17, 21, 55–
56, 70, 152–53; *see also*
Contemplation
Active intellect, 30, 31, 49,
175, 178, 179; *see also* Intellect
Affection; *see* Love
Annihilation of self, 11, 19,
33, 34, 40, 41–44, 44–46,
47, 48, 49–50, 52, 55, 56–
57, 73–74, 89, 104, 105,
106, 109, 110, 112–13,
136, 139, 173, 177, 178,
181, 191; *see also* Identity, *Unio mystica*
Anthropology; *see* Humanity,
nature of
Anthropomorphism (*tajsīm*),
97, 98, 100, 103, 116, 117,
118, 120–21, 181–82
Antinomianism, 53–54, 80
Apophasis; *see* Negative theology
Aristotelianism, 4, 19, 32, 43,
51, 52, 61, 70, 80, 97, 158,
178, 181, 182
Ascent, mystical, 15, 37, 44–
45, 49, 62, 63–64, 66–67,
73–74, 90, 92, 101–108,
119, 121, 176, 181

Baqā' (remaining), 87, 109,
112, 113, 123
Beatific vision, 60, 66, 76–77,
84
Beguines, 22, 71–75, 78, 189,
192
Being, 9, 10, 21, 32, 61, 80,
129, 130, 137, 150, 165,
169, 170, 172, 189
of God, 16, 18, 23, 45–46,
67, 74, 76, 78, 94, 97, 103,
110, 142–43
Bewilderment, mystical, 88,
96, 101, 103–105, 108–
109, 111, 114, 115, 158–
59, 189–90
Breaking-through (to God-
head), 75, 76, 79
Buddhism, 42, 126, 127, 131,
133, 135, 137, 182

Charity; *see* Love
Cistercians, 13, 63–64, 72,
85
Cleaving; *see* Devekut
Cloud of Unknowing, 14, 69–
70, 84, 85
Cognition; *see* Intellect
Coincidentia oppositorum (co-
incidence of opposites),
81, 99–100, 113

Commandments, 40, 43, 51–
52, 53–55, 56, 192; *see
also Halakhah*
Consciousness, 9–11, 21, 53,
76, 89, 108, 109, 113, 114,
117, 127, 128–29, 137,
139, 141, 144, 146, 147,
148, 149, 150, 151, 178,
190, 191–92; *see also* Intellect
Contemplation, 14, 47, 50, 55,
59, 61, 64, 65, 102, 128,
137, 138, 176, 179; *see
also* Active and contem-
plative lives

Dark Night (of the Soul), 11,
29, 84, 108
Deification, 10, 18–19, 59, 83,
139–40, 143, 146, 150–51,
159–60, 177; *see also*
Transformation, and
Unio mystica
Devekut (cleaving), 19, 28–29,
31, 33–43 *passim*, 45, 47–
50, 53–56, 176
Dhikr (remembrance), 90, 95,
101, 123
Dialectic, mystical, 77, 116–
24, 165–66, 169, 173, 189,
190–91, 192
Doctrine, 3–4, 6, 7, 100, 122,
135, 136, 145, 146–47,
171–72, 180, 182–83
as overbeliefs, 127, 150–51
Drunkenness, mystical, 89–
90, 92, 105, 110, 140, 142

Ecstasy, 5, 7–8, 9–10, 35, 49,
50, 54, 59, 62, 65, 66, 67,
70, 82, 105, 108, 110, 112,
113, 131, 132–33, 134,
140, 141, 146, 148, 177–
78, 192; *see also Unio
mystica*
Eiyn Sof (Hidden God), 32,
33, 37, 40, 45, 47, 48, 50,
140, 163
Eroticism, 5, 13, 17–19, 22,
63, 64, 65–66, 71–74, 79,
88, 89–95, 110, 124, 169,
172, 189–90; *see also* Love
Experience, mystical, 6, 7, 8,
27–28, 35, 39, 40, 49, 50,
55–57, 60, 82, 116, 124,
125, 131, 135, 139, 140–
46, 150–52, 157, 158, 163,
175, 176–77, 179–80,
182–83, 191–93; *see also*
Mysticism, nature of
common-core hypothesis,
125–31, 135, 186
mediate or immediate, 3–4,
8–9, 59–60
oceanic feeling, 130, 133
zero experience, 132, 135,
145, 151, 152

Fanā' (passing away), 6, 87,
89, 93, 99, 101, 107, 109,
110, 112, 113, 119, 121,
123, 167, 169, 170–71; *see
also* Annihilation of self,
Identity
Free Spirit movement, 71, 80,
140
Free will, 74, 96–98, 102, 121

God-language, 97–98, 163–69,
186–90; *see also* Mystical
theology, Negative theology
Gnosticism, 4, 19, 22, 51, 101,
102
Grace, 4, 6, 9, 68, 79, 92, 140

Halakhah (Jewish religious law), 53–56, 192; *see also* Commandments

Hasidism, 11, 15–16, 19–20, 21, 30, 32–34, 38, 39, 40–47, 54–57, 140, 160–61, 178
  Habad Hasidism, 42, 44, 45, 56, 177–78
  Komarno Hasidism, 47–49

Hekhalot texts, 101, 103–104

Hermetism, 101, 102, 114, 115, 117, 118, 119

Hinduism, 7, 42, 126, 131–32, 134, 135, 137, 146, 163–64, 182

Hitkalelut (comprehension, or inclusion), 35, 42–44, 47, 50

Humanity, nature of, 36–37, 44, 52–53, 75–78, 83–84, 117–19, 122, 186, 190–93; *see also* Intellect, and Soul
  biblical doctrine of, 5, 62
  human as image of God, 14, 98–100, 102–03, 107, 119–22, 190

Hypnosis, 128, 129, 130, 149

Identity or fusion (with God), 11, 28, 31, 36, 41, 45–46, 52, 56–57, 61, 71, 75–77, 87, 89, 100, 104–05, 106, 109–110, 120–24, 139, 142, 150, 177, 181, 190; *see also* Annihilation of self, *Unio mystica*

Image of God; *see* Humanity, nature of

Indistinction, 70–80 *passim*, 82–83, 85, 142, 188, 190, 191, 193; *see also* Identity, *Unio mystica*

Influx (from God), 29–30, 38, 40, 51, 160

Integration, 28, 31, 33–50, 51–53, 176–79, 190
  cosmic, 15–16, 21
  of the self, 10, 13, 14, 39, 41–42
  of God, 15, 23, 39, 52, 188

Intellect (human), 31–32, 37, 43, 46, 49, 50–51, 52–53, 60–61, 63, 66–67, 69–70, 75, 76–78, 85, 95, 97, 104, 110, 122; *see also* Active Intellect, Soul

Intention (*kavvanah*), 44, 51

Intuition; *see* Intellect, Vision

Journey, mystical; *see* Ascent, mystical

Kabbalah, 15, 19, 23, 28, 35, 36–37, 42, 51, 53, 54–55, 140, 158, 160, 178
  ecstatic kabbalah, 30–32, 33, 37–38, 49–50, 55
  Lurianic kabbalah, 38, 39–40, 47–49
  Safedian kabbalah, 38, 48, 177, 179
  theosophical or theurgical kabbalah, 33, 37–38, 39, 55, 188, 189–90

Kalam (disputational theology), 96, 98

Knowledge; *see* Intellect

Language, mystical, 8–9, 76, 78, 80–81, 87–89, 94–95, 99–101, 103, 110–11, 114–15, 116–24, 158, 163–73, 175, 185–86, 190;

Language, mystical, *(cont.)*
see also Mysticism, na-
ture of
Logos or Word, 17, 20, 59,
75–76, 163, 164, 167, 169,
176; *see also* Trinity
Love, 60–61, 63, 88, 99, 120,
122, 123, 135, 136, 137–
39, 143, 150, 168, 171,
172–73, 179–80; *see also*
Eroticism
  love and knowledge, 21–24,
  60–61, 62–70, 72, 76–78,
  81, 82–85, 110–11
  love and union, 17–20, 63,
  71–74
  love madness, 91–94, 95,
  99, 108, 111, 114, 122, 181

Magic, 29, 41, 101
Maqamāt (mystical stations),
90, 92, 108, 124
Marriage, mystical (also spiritual marriage), 9, 12, 14,
18, 63, 82–83, 86, 134,
138–39, 144, 192; *see also*
Eroticism Mind; *see* Consciousness
Mind; *see* Consciousness
Mir'aj (journey of Muham-
mad), 101–102, 103–104,
181
Mirror, 87, 99, 106–107, 116,
117, 119, 120, 121, 123–
24, 187
Monism, 136–37, 150–51
Monotheism, vii–viii, 3, 7,
20–21, 22, 96, 136–37,
140, 158–59, 164–65, 167,
169, 182–83, 187–88
Mystical theology, 5, 62, 66,
67–68, 80–81, 82

Mysticism, nature of, 7, 59–
60, 126–31; *see also* Experience, Language, *Unio
mystica*
  identical or non-identical,
  7–8
  introvertive and extrovertive, 131, 133–37, 151–52,
  191
  personal and impersonal,
  133–34, 138–39, 141,
  150–52, 168, 175–83, 191
  rational or intellectualist,
  176, 180, 181–82

Nafs (animal soul), 13, 92, 93,
118, 120
Negative theology, 5, 16, 46,
67–68, 70, 77–78, 94, 109,
125, 127, 141, 167–68,
169, 173, 180, 181, 188–
89
Neoplatonism, 4, 5, 13, 14,
19, 22, 28, 32, 33, 51, 71,
72, 97, 158, 165–66, 170,
172, 175, 177, 180, 188–
89
Nothing (Divine Nothing-
ness), 42, 46, 48, 70, 94,
140–41, 169, 170, 172

One (as God, or First Principle), 5, 6, 46, 61, 76, 79,
132, 133, 142, 143, 165–
66, 170, 175, 179
  tawḥīd (divine unity), 96–
  98, 100–101, 102, 107,
  116, 187–88

Phenomenology, 28, 95, 131–
35, 145, 157, 186
Platonism, 5, 52, 70, 176

Poimandres, 119

Presence of God, 4, 7, 8, 11, 12, 15, 59, 70, 107, 109, 137, 139

Psychoanalysis, 125, 128, 129–30, 145, 148–53, 175, 191

Psychology, 94, 127–28, 131, 145, 150, 157, 168, 178–79, 191, 192

Qasida (Arabian ode), 90–93, 114, 189

Quietism, 23

Qur'an, 6, 88, 90, 95–96, 98, 100, 102–103, 104, 106, 108, 111, 113, 114, 116, 117, 121, 122, 165, 167

Rapture; *see* Ecstasy

Reason; *see* Intellect

Sefirot (divine emanations), 15, 23, 33, 35, 37, 38, 47, 51, 52, 140, 167, 169, 189

Self-annihilation; *see* Annihilation

Senses, spiritual, 4, 6, 13, 108

Shekhinah (divine presence), 15, 35, 36; *see also* Presence

Soul, 12, 16–17, 32, 36, 44, 49, 50, 52, 56, 71, 73–74, 133, 138–39, 140, 141, 142–43, 170–71; *see also* Humanity, Intellect, *Nafs*

    faculties and powers, 13, 15, 38, 44, 47, 60, 65–67, 68, 83–84, 109

    substance or center, 10, 12

    as universal, 28–33

    virtual existence in God, 17, 20, 22, 28–29, 36, 52–

53, 73, 74, 75–79, 80, 104, 106, 109, 121, 136, 177, 188

State of Union; *see Unio mystica*

Sufism, 6, 8, 13, 18, 23, 87–124 *passim*, 158–59, 160–61, 165, 166, 170–71, 178, 181–82, 187, 189, 191

Tetragrammaton (YWHW), 29, 166

Theology of Aristotle, 97, 181

Theurgy, 38, 39, 40, 47, 48–49, 51, 179

Tikkun (restoration), 15, 39

Torah, 30, 38, 43, 45, 47, 54, 122

Trance, 128, 129, 130, 137, 145–51, 153, 191

Transformation, 10, 13, 18, 20–21, 36, 37, 43–44, 49, 51–52, 56–57, 63, 64, 65, 67, 68, 74, 81, 83, 102, 118, 121–22, 129, 140, 143, 160, 191–93; *see also* Deification, Integration

Trinity, 4, 16–17, 63, 67, 72, 76, 79–80, 83, 84, 137, 171, 172, 179–80, 187–88

Unconscious, 129–30, 131, 146–53

Unio mystica, vii–viii, 3–7, 14, 16–17, 17–20, 33, 36, 42, 60, 64, 69, 70–73, 75, 78, 80, 125, 126, 136, 152, 157–59, 160–61, 185–89, 193; *see also* Annihilation, Bewilderment, Deification, Ecstasy, Experience, Identity, Mysticism,

Unio mystica (cont.)
  Transformation
  cognitive and affective, 21–
    22
  mediated and unmediated,
    5. 16–17, 20, 75, 79–80
  personal and impersonal,
    133–34, 138–39, 141–45,
    147, 150–51, 175–83
  as psychic reversal, 105–
    107
  unitas spiritus and *unitas
    indistinctionis*, 17–18, 62–
    85 *passim*, 179–80
  substantial-essential-onto-
    logical, 17–20, 22–24, 43,
    45, 63, 69, 70–81 *passim*,
    159, 163, 169–73, 189
  union of wills, 62–70, 71,
    75, 79, 81, 82–84, 143,
    180, 188

  universalization and inte-
    gration, 28–50 *passim*,
    176–79, 187
Universalization, 28–33, 46,
    50–53, 176–79

Victorines, 13, 62, 64–66, 68–
    69, 72, 85
Vision, 61, 105, 106–107, 109,
    126, 129, 130, 133, 134–
    35, 143, 144–45, 150, 152,
    176, 181–82; *see also* Con-
    templation
  imaginative and corporeal,
    126
  intellectual and unitive, 10,
    12, 15, 49, 126, 138

Word; *see* Logos

Zohar, 38, 44, 177